Donald Horne is Australia's leading cultural commen-
tator. He is the author of *The Great Museum* (Pluto), *The
Lucky Country*, and an autobiography, *The Education of
Young Donald*. Currently, he chairs the Australia Council.

Donald Horne

The Public Culture

The Triumph of Industrialism

Pluto  Press

London · Sydney · Dover New Hampshire

First published in 1986 by Pluto Press Limited,
The Works, 105a Torriano Avenue, London NW5 2RX
and Pluto Press Australia Limited, PO Box 199, Leichhardt,
New South Wales 2040, Australia. Also Pluto Press,
51 Washington Street, Dover, New Hampshire 03820 USA

7 6 5 4 3 2 1

90 89 88 87 86

Phototypeset by AKM Associates (UK) Ltd
Ajmal House, Hayes Road, Southall, London
Printed in Great Britain by Guernsey Press Co. Ltd.
Guernsey, C.I.

British Library Cataloguing in Publication Data
Horne, Donald
   The public culture.
   1. Culture
   I. Title
   306   HM101

ISBN 0 7453 0067 7

Contents

Part One: The Public Culture

1. *We Are All Intellectuals*   *1*
   Constructing 'reality'   *1*
   Creating 'nations'   *8*
   'The news' as legend and ritual   *16*
   Critics of existence   *22*

2. *The 'Language' of a Culture*   *25*
   The industrialization of culture   *25*
   The obsession with ownership   *32*
   The obsession with 'research'   *38*
   The 'language' of a culture   *42*
   Getting on with the discussion   *47*

3. *The 'Enchantment' Of Modern Societies*   *50*
   Why do we obey?   *50*
   The public culture   *53*
   The 'myths' of modern enchantment   *57*
   Dominance in a public culture   *70*

Part Two: 'Myths' of the Public Culture

4. *'Myths' of Industrialism and Modernity*   *75*
   Ingredients   *75*
   The accumulation of capital   *76*
   The accumulation of labour   *81*
   'Myths' of modernity   *87*

5. *'Myths' of Race, Sex, Nation*   *92*
   The logic of race and gender chauvinism   *92*

Chauvinism and industrialism   *96*
Icons of subjection   *102*
'Myths' of nation   *108*

6. *'Legitimations'*   *119*
Capitalists and Communists   *119*
'Myths' of free enterprise   *123*
'Myths' of collectivism   *133*

7. *The Variant Repertoires of the Public Culture*   *140*
Repertoires   *140*
The religious culture   *141*
The neo-traditional culture   *150*
The ethnic compromise   *158*
The labour culture   *166*
The critics' culture   *174*
The modern phenomenon of 'high culture'   *183*

Part Three: A Declaration of Cultural Rights for the Citizen

8. *Who Wins? Who Loses?*   *189*
A show for the victors?   *189*
The alternative and the oppositional   *195*
The momentum of industrialism   *199*
'Legitimations' of power: sex, race, ethnicity   *202*
'Legitimations' of power: class   *207*
'Legitimations' of power: the neo-traditional   *213*
'Legitimations' of power: political 'myth'   *215*

9. *Constructing New 'Myths'*   *218*
Changing 'reality'   *218*
New 'worlds'   *223*
The protest movements   *227*
A declaration of 'cultural rights'   *232*
Who are the 'myth'-makers?   *237*

Select Bibliography   *246*
Index   *254*

Part One:

The Public Culture

_____

1. We Are All Intellectuals

Constructing 'reality'

In one of the most famous stone gardens in Kyoto, I was listening to the interpreter explain how every ripple in the pebbles had a special meaning. A group of Japanese tourists came in, lined up along a wall and began a characteristic modern ritual. In turn each of them approached their guide and, standing on exactly the same spot, positioned a camera. The guide's lips would move with the repetitiveness of a priest repeating exactly the same words to each communicant. The camera would click. The next tourist would come up. After watching this I asked my interpreter what the religious phrase was that the guide was repeating. She said, 'What the guide is saying is, "F-stop 2.8, shutter speed 250".'

The camera provides one of the most significant paradoxes of modern industrial societies – our ability to feel free, when in fact we are, most of us, all doing the same thing. When we hold cameras in our hands we hold an enormous potential to be artists, to create 'reality' in our own way. Yet, as if by choice, almost all of us use this potential to portray existence in exactly the same manner as everyone else. Although, with these ritual acts of stereotyping, we can feel we have choice (it is we who are making the cameras click), it is as if we are using these small black boxes to demonstrate our faith that there is only one truth.

Consider, throughout the modern industrial societies, the similarities of 'family photographs'. No matter what the society, a wedding can scarcely be said to have taken place unless the participants are photographed. A baby is not properly born until it is 'snapped', and not to photograph it regularly thereafter can seem a form of child neglect. Merely to display a family photograph album can have a high symbolic effect. If, after a certain period of trial, some newcomer is seen as possibly becoming 'part of the family', the family albums are taken out and presented as evidence of trust and sometimes as a test of the newcomer's intentions. Simply by holding the family albums in their hands and turning over the pages, individuals in a family might reassure themselves that their family has a structure and a history. If there has been a long delay since the last meeting, and in reality not much remains in common between two members of a family, looking at the family albums might provide greater emotional satisfaction than the reunion itself.

Given these declarations of faith, we can ask: what are the family photographs saying about the world? They present a view of the world that is made up mainly of celebrations of the importance of the family and of holiday-making, and these celebrations are made in three prevailing aesthetic forms: the pose, in which people attempt to make their faces and postures conform to certain post-medieval European painting conventions; the landscape, in which nature is presented in nineteenth-century European painting conventions of what made a good picture; and the tourist snap, in which a tourist object, whether Old Master or motel, is 'acquired', and taken home in a photograph. Sometimes all three might be combined: a tourist might pose in front of a motel in the general setting of a landscape.

Photography pays tribute to post-medieval European conventions of beauty. What is conventionally seen as the ugly is not photographed. Indeed, even the conventionally beautiful often existed only in the photographs themselves – through the special techniques of the pose or the techniques of selective arrangement in photographing landscapes or monuments. Photography instruction books give routine suggestions about how to make nature appear like a European painting – for instance, by the selective close-up from a telephoto lens or by framing a distant scene with some foreground landscape. In this world, not unlike a gallery of paintings in a nineteenth-century palace, there is no place for working life – not even the arcadian views of work that are found in some eighteenth-century paintings. Workplaces do not exist: no factories, no offices. Even housework does not exist. Nor does any kind of human distress. (A photograph of part of the 'Old Town' in some city – an alley in Naples, for example, with the washing hanging out – is not a photograph of poverty, but of the 'picturesque': it is like a painting.) Nor is there representation of human discord. And while family albums record births and marriages, they rarely recall funerals. Death is taboo in family albums. The world shown in the family albums is one of beautiful objects and posed individuals. Apart from portraits of families minding their manners, there is no indication of the *social* character of human existence: all the complexities of life in modern industrial societies are excluded.

One of the principal themes of this book is the question of how it is that almost all of us can, as it were, engage in acts of complicity in which, by what we see as acts of individual enterprise, we all do much the same thing – in this case, pretend in our photography rituals that society very largely is not there. But before continuing this theme it is necessary to state, as simply as possible, how the 'realities' by which we see existence are not *really* 'reality', but an intellectual creation.

Cameras are prime vehicles of modern 'reality'-making. Photographs – simply because they are *photographs* – are seen as necessarily 'true'. It has been one of the faiths of the modern age that the camera cannot lie. So, as well as their statements about family and society, family albums, along with the whole belief in photographs, are statements about the objectiveness of reality – as if there is a definite, definable reality out there and it is the intellectual and artistic task to discover it, and to represent it accurately.

Cameras, of course, can, and do, lie. Like any other attempt to represent 'reality', photography can be, and often is, deliberately faked – sometimes unscrupulously, as often happens with the news media and in propaganda and advertising, but usually because much of the art of photography is a form of deliberate faking that can seem so natural that it doesn't seem like faking. The larger point is that 'reality', in the sense of a representation of existence, must always be created.

These creations begin with the conventions of our senses. Humans create a world of colour and smell and taste and heat and sound, for example, because these are the ways the human body's sensory apparatus interprets existence. But existence is not 'really' a matter of colour and smell and heat and taste and sound: 'colour' is a reaction by our retinas to light 'waves' (themselves unimaginable except in mathematical terms); 'heat' and 'sound' are reactions of our nerves to heat 'waves' and sound 'waves' (which are as unimaginable as light 'waves'); 'taste' and 'smell' are reactions of nerves in our mouths and noses to molecules (which are also unimaginable except mathematically). If we had a different sensory apparatus, our bodies would construct a different kind of 'reality'. Our senses give us, as it were, a hypothetical relationship to existence. They are part of a theory of 'reality' without which we could not continue to act, or to stay alive. But the hypothesis of 'reality' provided by the senses is not existence itself: it comes from the intellectual concepts provided by our senses. Antonio Gramsci said that we are all intellectuals, and so we are, but in an even deeper sense than Gramsci intended. It is with the sensory apparatus of our bodies that we first become intellectuals; it is through our very nerves that we first conceptualize existence into hypothetical 'realities'.

The more ordinary meaning of intellectuality – and this was the one Gramsci had in mind – comes when, to the hypotheses of reality provided by our nerves, are added the hypotheses about existence we learn from our cultures, the repertoires of collective habits of thinking and acting that give meaning to existence. In this sense we are all, even more clearly, intellectuals. Without the conceptualizations of culture we could also not exist. And these concepts are also, all of them, not existence itself but socially constructed 'realities' that provide us with theories about existence, from which we can then think and act. That some of them may be quite false does not affect their strength in providing a basis for thought and action. For example, in a world where the normal explanations of existence were supernatural, a person wanting something might have offered a sacrifice, or prayed to an image, or a shrine, or a relic. That seemed to be the way to get things done. In a modern industrial society where explanations of existence are scientific and ways of achieving things are seen as political and economic, a person wanting something done is likely to see it as a question of causality, to be turned into action by politics or economics. Whether we imagine we get things done by praying or by economic blueprints, it is the perceived 'reality' that suggests to us how we should behave. I have put the world 'reality' in quotation marks as a reminder that we create 'realities' (hypotheses about existence), but then act as if they *were* existence.

The family album is a manifestation of the camera as one of the few cultural techniques in a modern industrial society in which ordinary people, if in a most confined and attenuated manner, have an active role in perpetuating in an art form some features of their own culture. In societies where a participatory performing culture survived, such as that of the Australian Aborigines, the people, in dance and song, in instrumental music, drama and recitation, and in painting, themselves perpetuated the meaning they gave to the world. The people themselves made their own 'art' (although to them there was no distinction between 'art' and the rest of their life). When they performed their festivals it was their equivalent of what we would now see as a multi-media presentation in a civic cultural centre – except that their presentation was not for an audience. In a modern industrial society our festivals are performed for us, usually on television screens. At least when we take a photograph we hold a camera in our hands.

As an Aborigine did when painting, with our own hands we help perpetuate a part of our cultural repertoire: we are affirming a particular 'reality'. If we are photographing a 'landscape', for example, we are helping to perpetuate a way of looking at things that began in European painting several hundred years ago, at first in backgrounds to portraits, or in background scenes through windows, and then, with greater confidence, over whole canvases, so that landscape became a theme in itself. Landscapes or, more exactly, *certain* landscapes became 'beautiful'. Subsequently, the contemplation of them became morally regenerative. But there are no 'landscapes' in nature. A 'landscape' is simply one way of looking at the world.

Aborigines had a much greater sense of belonging in their environment than people in modern industrial societies, or the Renaissance painters who began the 'creation' of landscape. The environment was part of Aborigines and they were part of it. Their physical surroundings were the scenes of Creation. When they walked from one sacred place to the other they were, in Judaeo-Christian terms, walking through the Garden of Eden. Therefore Aborigines had no conception of 'landscape'; they did not see some aspects of their physical environment as 'beautiful' and not others; they did not have the sense of scrutinizing and *managing* the environment that European landscape painting entailed. They did not have the sense of separation from the landscape that this involved, nor the sense of naturalistic representation in which all that matters is what meets the eye.

Existence does not 'express' itself. We speak of an 'event' or a 'process' for example, but in existence there are no 'events' or 'processes'; these are simply conventions we can use in creating 'realities'. Even as concepts they are not self-contained. There is human selectivity in all representations of 'reality'. There is 'bias' in all ordering of experience. If that were not so, what would we order experience *with*? The very idea of intellectuality – of conceptualizing – is one of bias-making. The question is: *which 'bias'*? We approach existence with certain conventions of what matters and how to represent it. It is the nature of these conventions that can determine what we make of existence.

Take another example from photography: the school photo-graph. Imagine a classroom and imagine some of the possibili-ties there are for a photographer, both in what to point the camera at and how to manipulate the camera when it is pointed.

The camera might be pointed at both teacher and students: it might then be manipulated to make teacher and students seem a happy community, or it might isolate the students so that there is a gap between students and teacher and this represen-tation might be done in such a way that it is the students we feel sympathy with in their isolation; or it might be the teacher with whom we are directed, by photographic convention, to be sympathetic.

If the camera is pointed only at the students, by treatment it can suggest communality but it can also suggest individualism or loneliness or hostility; it might show the students interacting, or it might show them bored; it might concentrate on one student with head bent industriously over a book; or on another student wistfully looking out of the window; or on two students sharing furtive friendship in the hostile surroundings of the classroom.

The camera might not focus on students or teacher at all, but on the texture of the wall, suggesting a certain mood. Or it might concentrate on writing on the blackboard, or objects on the walls. Again the questions would be these. *What* writing? *Which* objects? *Which* photographic style? Perhaps only a stick of chalk might be photographed. But a stick of chalk is one of the many symbols of modern classroom cultures, rich in potential meanings. The chalk might be photographed unused, in a cold style, suggesting impersonal authority; or worn down to a stub, photographed in a warm style, suggesting a happy day's teaching.

The camera might not be used in the classroom at all, but out in the playground, where selections of what to point the camera at, and how to point it, would determine which of the many moods of the playground was to be represented: or the camera might be moved to the staff common-room, or to the principal's office, or the janitor's room, and each of these would provide its own range of styles. Or it might be pointed at the school buildings, and the selection here could draw on that wide range of photographic techniques that can make buildings symbols of human emotions. In fact what is most likely to happen is none of these. What is most likely to happen is that once a year the class will be lined up in a class photograph, with its conventional projections of solidarity and conformity. Throughout the industrial societies there are class photographs, all saying much the same thing. They may be the only photographic record many of us have of our schooldays.

Creating 'nations'

One of the most remarkable examples of 'reality' creation lies in the process of what some United States social theorists call 'nation-creating'. A new nation-state is formed: what 'character' will it have? The answer may seem obvious, but it isn't. There are many characteristics a new nation-state might be seen as having. Only some of them prevail. In the processes that precede the formation of a new nation-state great acts of imaginative construction occur, out of which the image of the new nation is born.

One way of studying this phenomenon of creating a certain identity for a newly formed nation-state is to visit a history museum in one of the 'new nations' of Europe (some of them, in fact, old nations restored) that were taken out of the old dynastic empires: museums in Ireland, Norway, Finland, Poland, Belgium, Romania, Bulgaria, Czechoslovakia, Greece and the republics of Yugoslavia all tell similar stories. In museums in each of these countries is laid out, in glass display cases and on walls, much of the history of how an 'identity' for that particular nation was created, usually by humanist intellectuals, who saw nationalism as a form of liberating self-expression.

In Bucharest, for example, the History Museum of the Socialist Republic of Romania shows the beginning of the most significant of all the national-identity creations – the invention, out of the languages and dialects spoken by the peasants, of what later came to be considered as the one national literary language, in this case the language that came to be known as 'Romanian'. A prize exhibit is a letter, dated 29 June 1521. This is the first preserved text in this new literary language, the first evidence of the 'Romania' that is to come. Then follows evidence of the spread of the new language – early translations into this language, first chronicles written in it about the territories that will later be 'Romania', first textbooks written in 'Romanian'. When the museum reaches the nineteenth century, reminders are flourished of the 'Romanian' culture that had been newly invented by Enlightenment intellectuals who wished to create a Romanian nation through such embodiments of the human spirit as literary societies, choir singing, amateur theatricals, regional cultural associations, newspapers and above all through an education system conducted in the Romanian language – necessary not only for unity against the occupying Ottoman Empire but, even more, against the Greeks, who were fighting for cultural as well as economic dominance over most of the European parts of the Ottoman Empire.

With independence, the museum shows new evidence of nation-'creating': the creation of the concept of a Romanian 'economy' is summoned up in relics such as inkpots and title deeds recalling acts as symbolically significant as the establishment of the first cement factory and the establishment of the National Bank. A theodolite recalls Romanian engineering skills. Meanwhile the proofs of Romanian intellectual culture multiply in the display of other relics – the crown of laurels given to a Romanian music composer in Rio de Janeiro, the eyeglasses of a poet, a cup won at Montpellier in a literary contest, the cloak worn by an actor in a Romanian play. All of these come together to demonstrate that the newly formed Romania was a modern nation.

In the art museum the idea of Romania is personified as a large-breasted female shown in the act of breaking her chains. The idea of a nation is also translated into 'the typical

Romanian landscape' with its ox-carts lumbering down country roads (a landscape that is much the same as the landscapes of adjoining countries, but is nevertheless seen as truly Romanian), and it is turned into 'national character', in the form of paintings of the wisdom of peasants, some of whom at that time might scarcely have known they were Romanian.

The men who made these paintings all knew they were engaged in creating 'Romania'. How this happened is shown in a special museum honouring Theodor Aman, one of the leaders amongst these creators. It is a kind of laboratory in the creation of national identity, showing how Aman experimented with one form, and then another. It shows his wooden carving phase, when he found the Romanian character in traditional carved objects; his historical phase, when he painted patriotic frescoes of the past; his oriental and classical phases, when he looked to both east and west to discover secrets of the Romanian character; the still lifes, in which he found Romanianness in physical objects; and then the scenes from village life in which he finally found the truly Romanian.

A national architecture was then discovered, in which it was the porch that was seen as typically Romanian. Whether the porches of peasant cottages or churches or the belvederes of palaces, all were seen as showing an opening out to nature and a freedom of spirit typical of the Romanian character and not to be found, it was claimed, in any other European nation.

Many assertions of a Romanian past were made: the immediate past of heroic struggle against the Ottomans, recalled in captured cannon, maps used by great commanders, banners borne aloft by heroes; then there is the past of medieval culture, shown in the famous external church frescoes of Moldavia, or elaborate wood carvings from the period when, it is claimed, Romania was the artistic centre of south-east Europe; monumental paintings recall the past of medieval valour when Romanian princes held back the Turk; further into the past, there is Romania's claim to be the only true heir of Rome in south-east Europe; and further back than that, there are celebrations of the great Dacian civilization that preceded the Romans.

As with all other nation-states, whether old or new, the national identity projected in these images was only one of the many national identities that might have been claimed for Romania. There were many other potential 'Romanias': its subsequent history has demonstrated that. The Romania that was created was one that suited the liberal imagination of nineteenth-century Romanian intellectuals. Many, or even most, of the ordinary people of the new nation-state may scarcely have been aware of the 'Romania' that had been created for them, and amply bosomed women striking off their manacles or honest ox-cart drivers on winding country roads were not representative of the new ruling groups that began to do well out of Romania. But the invented 'Romania' of nineteenth-century intellectuals went on serving these successive ruling groups. This concept of 'Romania' became reinterpretable, shifting in functions and meanings. One of the greatest creations of Romanian cultural nationalism was a painting by Nicolae Grigorescu; it showed a woman in a pure white kerchief, wise and trusting with steady eyes and smooth skin. The *Peasant Girl of Musecel* has served them all – merchants and nobility, racketeers and idealists, King Carol, the Iron Guard, President Ceauşescu.

Another example might be taken – the 'creation' of the various imperialist cultures that developed in Europe in the nineteenth century to explain and justify European world dominance. Of these, by far the most thoroughly orchestrated – in rhetoric, in music, in visual images, in literature and in the writing of history and geography, in education programmes and in rituals, costumes and ceremonials – was the British version of imperialism that gave a new national identity to England. It is no longer credible, as the hymn 'Land of Hope and Glory' claimed for the British, that 'wider still and wider would their bounds be set, as God who made them mighty made them mightier yet', but, although to outsiders such a claim might seem merely bizarre, 'Land of Hope and Glory' was the song that the British sang to the world's television audiences at the time of the Malvinas confrontation. Those who sang it had the appearance of clockwork toys. When they were wound up, they did the dance they were constructed to do. They were acting from the 'realities' that defined the nation-state to which they belonged.

However, in terms at least of size and importance, and perhaps also in other ways, the two most significant nation-states in which national identities were articulated are those that most emphatically defined their nationality in political terms: the Soviet Union and the United States. The cults of British imperialism drew on older material stretching back through romantic visions of Anglo-Saxon Witanegemots to the legends of 'Queen Boadicea' fighting the Romans. The claims for national identity of the Soviet Union and the United States were based on the idea that each of them was an entirely new form of political organization. The very names they were given – 'United States', 'Soviet Union' – suggested not a people, but a form of government, and a form of government that, like the 'Central Kingdom' of pre-revolutionary China, could allow territorial additions as the world progressed. In these claims to national identity, each nation claimed that it had produced a new kind of person (an 'American Man', a 'Soviet Man') and a new order for humankind ('the American Dream', 'the Soviet Way'). Out of concepts of the state, they both produced civil religions in which both have spoken, in secular terms, of the destiny of the nation as that of the world.

When the city of Washington was planned, it was designed to demonstrate the magnificence of a political idea, the republican ideal, with its basis in 'the people'. The dome of the Capitol, the palace of the representatives of 'the people', was to dominate the city and the great area of the Mall stretching out in front of it was to give this ideal emphasis. This was to be the heart of the United States. Nearby, government buildings still proclaim public virtue (in various varieties of the classical): the president's mansion, by its very modesty of size and the way in which it can be looked at from all sides, can be taken to symbolize open and accessible government; and, in their three memorials, the spirits of Washington and Jefferson and Lincoln can appear to continue to be inspirers of the people. By and large, when sightseers go on a 'tourmobile' tour in Washington, they are making a pilgrimage to the political statements that appear to define the United States.

In Moscow, there is an ambiguity. Red Square and its surroundings are 'Russian' as well as 'Soviet'. But they have been given a new and awesome political solemnity. Among the silver firs beside the warm brick of the Kremlin walls with their towers canopied in green and gold lie the bodies of revolutionary heroes and martyrs; the tomb of the unknown soldier is also there, its red granite trimmed with black, and on top of it an eternal flame brought from the eternal flame commemorating the revolutionary martyrs in the Leningrad Field of Mars; along the wall, long slabs of red porphyry contain caskets of soil from the Soviet's hero cities; and commanding the Red Square itself is the understated solemnity, in red and black, of the mausoleum of Lenin.

In their habit of continuing to define themselves by sacred (if secular) texts, the two nations are also similar. This is obvious in the case of the Soviet Union, where the words of Lenin, and of Marx and Engels, as interpreted by Lenin, are such necessary explanations of everything that matters in life that even a museum can be designed around the words of Lenin. In the Central Lenin Museum in Moscow the theme unifying the relics in each hall (desks, armchairs, famous photographs, maps, old clothes, posters, etc.) is the development of one of the great ideas of Lenin. In the United States, the sacred secular texts are somewhat wider and political discourse is possible without them, but in moments of significance they are still much drawn on. In Moscow people make their pilgrimage to the Lenin Mausoleum; in Washington, one of the significant highlights is the temple, approached by awe-producing monumental steps and guarded by United States eagles, where original pages of the Constitution are enshrined in their tabernacle. In the political controversy in 1984 about religion and politics, opponents of President Reagan would attempt to defend the 'great party of Lincoln' from the fundamentalists by asking what Lincoln would have said if he were alive today and then providing impressive words from Lincoln texts. In response, the president quoted the Mayflower Compact, the Declaration of Independence, the *Federalist* and words from James Maddison and George Washington. No other modern industrial nation-state has any approximation to the definition of itself by sacred texts and political heroes as is found in the United States and the Soviet Union.

The Museum of Natural History in Los Angeles provides an excellent example of the spell-binding power of an official version of a national identity. Los Angeles is a multicultural city; in numerical terms there is no dominant ethnic group, but as things are going now the largest single ethnic group will not be 'Anglo', but Latin. Yet the Museum of Natural History still calmly displays the development of the United States as the development of an identity established by emigrant English. One of the two principal history halls is called 'The American: This New Man'. It begins with a tapestry paying tribute to George Washington, and a display of the clothes of Thomas Jefferson. It is with them that 'American' history begins. (The official guidebook says: 'The United States survived and prospered because the people developed those characteristics which have become synonymous with the American way of life – individualism, self-reliance, initiative, co-operation and confidence.') The only reference to ethnic diversity is to be found in the other history hall, 'The Garland Hall of American History', where, among the mementoes of cowboys and homesteaders, there stand two dummies, wanly dressed and labelled 'The Immigrants'.

The Mexicanness of Los Angeles, and of California generally, has traditionally received no place in California's public identity. In fact, by a kind of sleight of hand, a diversion was created by concentrating on a glamorized *Spanish* past rather than on the *Mexican* and *Mexican American* past, present and future. In a hall in the Natural History Museum, there are reminders of romantic Old Spain – the armour of a conquistador, a model of a galleon – and the museum labels use good Californian tourist words like *presidio*, *adobe*, *pueblo* and *rancho*. But all this is fenced off as part of 'the long ago', as part of a wider illusion.

Throughout California in the late nineteenth century there developed a cult for the ruined buildings of the Spanish missions developed by the Franciscan Father Serra in California's Spanish period. It was a cult favoured by Protestant intellectuals and business men, who almost forced on the Catholic Church the task of reconstructing the ruins. There was a strong market for romantic books and paintings about imagined life in the missions. Annual pageants were performed. The word 'Mission' was used in their brand names by many business firms. The cult has passed its peak, but tourist business is still attracted by the reconstructed mission buildings. (Some of them have phoney relics of Father Serra; all of them have phoney gardens; and some of them are given richer meaning by the surrounding commercial promotions. The Mission San Juan Capistrano, for example, is surrounded by a 'Mission Inn Motel', a 'Capistrano Traders Post', a 'Father Serra's Restaurant and Deli' and a 'Mission Mug Shoppe'.) And there was also, of course, the development throughout southern California of the 'Spanish Colonial' architectural styles that followed the 1915 Exposition at San Diego, where, to create a difference from a similar exposition being held in California, it was decided to make all of the buildings 'Spanish' in style, and that received an extra boost after an earthquake in the 1920s when the authorities of Santa Barbara decided to 'go Spanish'.

Yet despite all the romantic novels, paintings, pageants and plays, the development of a Spanish mission tourist cult and the spreading of Spanishness with white stucco walls and red roof-tiles into the suburbs and shopping places of southern California, no real attempt was made to teach Spanish in schools until after the Second World War, and no attempt is yet made to teach Mexican history. The mirage of pseudo-Spanishness helped preserve a basically Anglo 'reality' which excluded the presence of the exploited Mexican American farm labourers and the shabby *barrios* where Mexican Americans lived in the Anglo-dominated cities.

When the time came in the late 1960s, with *El Movimiento*, a militant liberation movement in which some of the newly awakened Mexican American youth tried to break down their exclusion from Californian public identity, it was significant that they chose to do this by presenting a counter-'reality' – sometimes peacefully, as in the establishment in San Francisco of a Mexican Art Museum, sometimes militantly, as in the seizure of a building in San Diego (well placed strategically, near the Spanish Revival buildings of the 1915 Exposition) which they then turned into a House of People's Culture, but most notably in flaming Mexican posters and, above all, in murals, in the Mexican tradition. A Mexican American 'reality' had been excluded from public proclamations of what it meant to be a Californian, thereby limiting the self-perceptions of Mexican Americans as well as the perceptions of Anglos: the Mexican Americans seized the walls of Californian cities and proclaimed their own 'reality'.

'The news' as legend and ritual

As well as classroom photographs, family albums and symbols of nationality, one of the many other ways in which the 'realities' of modern nation-states are maintained in ways not known before is 'the news': 'the news' as a surrogate form of conversation (so that a national telecast became a kind of national conversation); as a particularly complex form of legend-making; and as a type of ritual that brings people together even when they are walled into their own homes.

A prime way of maintaining a 'reality' is by conversation and, recognizing that it is in our talking to each other that we maintain and at times change 'reality', one can find in 'the news' a form of surrogate conversation which allows others to do the talking for us (and which, if we are ourselves talkers, can also give us something to talk about to others). A common way in which we give meaning to existence when talking to each other is by telling anecdotes; in fact, most of us fill out large parts of our lives by telling each other simple little narratives to such an extent that one can approach a society simply by asking: what are its characteristic anecdotes? In this sense, most of 'the news' is highly 'conversational'. It consists mainly of the presentation of anecdotes in the form of 'events', even if in the Communist countries there is a greater attempt to place these 'events' as part of processes (to such an extent that at times the reporting of an 'event' may have to wait until the authorities can decide how to place it in history).

However, many of our conversational anecdotes lack the immediacy of 'the news'. A better parallel is with that form of conversational anecdote known as 'gossip' – short, concrete, spicy. As Thoreau once said, 'To a philosopher all news, as it is called, is gossip.' What makes some 'news stories' so powerful is that we feel the special excitement of being in the know so intently that we are eager to pass it on to someone else. Even more magic is given to 'the news', however, by a special form of gossip – the rumour, an anecdote or set of anecdotes that, in a situation we can't understand, can explain everything.

However, 'realities' can be maintained even more by what is not said than by what is said, and magic is given to 'the news', as to conversation, by what it does not need to say. It is what is *so taken for granted that it need not be said* that can be most significant. There is much criticism in the Soviet press of many aspects of Soviet life – but no criticisms, as such, of the Soviet system. The United States press justifies its existence by criticism – but there is scarcely any criticism of the underlying assumptions of American individualism.

Two other features of 'the news' give it much the same 'reality'-maintaining function as an Aboriginal festival: the emphasis on personalities in its story-telling and legend-making, and its attention to theatricality and ceremony.

In its emphasis on personalities, 'the news' helps perpetuate mythic stereotypes. Just like tribal story-telling around a fire, this confirms our feelings about what it is that makes a 'good guy' or a 'bad guy'. Some of these mythic figures become world characters whom we use for our purposes: names like 'the Ayotollah', 'John XXIII', 'Nixon', 'Lech Walesa', 'Kennedy' for a season become as legendary, standing for good or for evil, as do characters in an Aboriginal tale. These and their domestic equivalents are 'staged' personalities, the product of deliberate illusion-making, but when a Hopi dancer dresses up and impersonates a *kachina* (spirit), although this is also deliberate illusion-making, it is none the less effective for it. In fact, in the liberal-democratic countries information about the contrivances in the staging of public personalities – so that they can appear to be an intimate part of our daily life, coming into our houses regularly for a chat – can add to their magic. President Reagan kept much of his charm to supporters even though the media regularly gave them details of the contrivances by which he was deluding them on television: the very ingenuity of these illusions could engage the imagination by their expertness.

It is even more obvious that modern 'news', above all on television, brings 'reality'-maintenance ceremonies into people's lives in those great celebrations in which, as Murray Edelman says, *in Politics as Symbolic Action*, 'Institutions, like individuals, must parade and display their glamour if they are to keep their glory alive.' A May Day march in Moscow, an Academy Awards ceremony in Hollywood, a World Cup final, a British royal funeral, an Olympic Games opening: these are all reminders of what can seem eternal values, and while they may not be felt with the immediacy of those who participate directly in a High Mass or a corn dance, the contrivances of television, with its ability to show much more than any one individual can see, can provide a super-'reality'.

These stories that are told to us every day, and that on radio and television are often acted out by the very characters themselves (sometimes 'live'), provide a familiar community drama in which we can all feel present, if vicariously; but what is different about them is that although they have the effect of legends, they are not old stories retold. They are *news*. In form they aren't set-piece legendary tales, passed down in traditional enactments from generation to generation. On the face of it, they say something new every day, and this is taken out of 'events' from the last day, or even the last hour, in a series of editions, bulletins, newscasts and updates that provide one of the many novelties of modern industrial societies – the belief that existence is made up of daily, reportable segments. Yet where they become 'legendary' is that these enormous improvisations, made up daily or even hourly out of what are seen as passing 'events', can go on saying much the same things – projecting much the same 'realities' – year after year.

One qualification must be made: there is more contrivance in the manufacture of 'events' than may meet the eyes of those who grow up with the convention of 'the news'. This goes beyond the inevitability of 'manipulation' in which 'the news' is necessarily 'created', since it involves selection in both what is seen to be 'news', and how it is to be presented. There is also a special kind of fabrication in much 'news'-making, in that the news is 'made', in what the culture critic David Borstin in *The Image* called a 'pseudo event', either an event put on by some publicity-seeker for the particular purpose of 'making news' that would be reported, or, more usually, an event created by a journalist. Of the latter, the paradigm example is 'the interview' – a cultural form invented on 13 July 1859, when Brigham Young was asked some questions in Salt Lake City and the answers were printed in the New York *Tribune*. A good example of joint complicity between journalists and publicity-seekers is 'the photo opportunity' in which a publicity-seeker contrives a special publicity backdrop that makes a good newspaper picture or a good television 'grab'. Thus, during the presidential primaries in the United States candidates fly east and west, north and south, followed by cameras. Their daily task is to pose in significant backgrounds that will make special appeals to special groups of voters. They might eat bagels or tacos or sushi or dim sum in the appropriate ethnic neighbourhood. Or they might stand beside putrid ponds, inveigh against toxic waste and philosophize about the environment. Or stride around steel mills, coal mines or container ports wearing white hats and talking about unemployment. Or play basketball with a neighbourhood team in order to philosophize about family and the neighbourhood. Or dress in white laboratory smocks to inspect high-technology tomatoes. Or stand in front of a famously overcrowded bridge, or on a commuter's ferry, to discuss transport problems. When campaigning in New Mexico, Gary Hart stopped his motorcade just outside a town, got on to a white horse and rode into town like the good guy who was about to clean out the bad guys.

But despite these many contrivances, 'the news' must also respond to the unexpected and the uncontrived. This makes it different from all traditional legend-telling. 'The news' repeats the old verities every day, but it does so by telling constant new stories.

Overall, despite many differences, this 'reality' can show one similarity: whatever the political system of a modern industrial society, its elements come together to form recurrent images of what makes up 'the nation'. It does this partly, day by day, by reminding us what kinds of people are important in the nation, what the nation's significant social stereotypes are, what the nation's principal 'issues' are and what (to use the phrase of the culture critic Herbert Gans in *Deciding What's News*) the nation's 'symbolic complexes' are: these are the lenses through which 'the news' both separates out a society into recognized components and blots out the existence of some aspects of the society. In speaking of the United States, Gans refers to symbolic complexes such as 'Government', 'Business', 'Labour', 'Law', 'Religion', 'Science', 'Medicine', 'the Arts' as being the kinds of elements into which people in the United States have been taught by 'the news' to sectionalize society. One could make out equivalent lists for other modern industrial states, whether capitalist or Communist. The essential points are that these elements are seen as separate, without inter-connections, and, even more significantly, these are the only elements that *are* presented. As Gans points out, categories such as class structure, power structure and oligopoly are not recognized by 'the news'. What comes through as central in modern industrial societies in 'the news' (central at least in prestige) is *the government*. The other grave public matters are politics (if it is a country where there is some openness in politics, and even in such a country 'politics' is defined in a restricted way), 'the economy' (as defined in that country), and various exemplary tales going under the name of 'foreign affairs' that function to maintain a certain limited view of the world. The great drama, endlessly playing, is that of maintaining definitions of the nation and its social order: definitions are being repeated daily, hourly, of what the nation and society are.

As in any story of good and evil, there are continuing themes of order and disorder. Great threats from abroad, and, at home, huge conspiracies. In liberal-democratic societies there is a certain defined area of political struggle – between the accepted political parties – but this struggle also helps explain and justify order by displaying that the society is *liberal*-democratic; any political struggle beyond this is likely either not to be reported, or reported as deviant or threatening. Although some of these deviant activities may later gain some acceptance, they will be replaced by new threats.

In all societies, however, 'the news' is likely to take for granted certain basic assumptions about the economic and social order and, indeed, the meaning of existence. As Jacques Ellul put it in his book, *Propaganda*, 'Our many media messages are really in basic accord with each other and lead spontaneously in the same direction.' They produce 'a general conception of society, a particular way of life'. Even the very idea of 'the news' as bits and pieces of 'current affairs' presents a view of the world that is a distraction from thinking about fundamental questions of the human condition. The more we know, the less we know. And we are not invited to examine the basic assumptions of the social, economic and moral order. On these there might be a significant silence, protected by the surface noise of 'the news'.

It could be argued that a prime function of what is spoken of as 'the news' is not to 'inform' but to act as a *ritual* – a ritual in which there are both daily re-enactments of conventional 'realities', and at times (sometimes slow, sometimes fast) the inauguration of new 'realities'.

In the sense in which the word is often used, there are two tests of a ritual. It should be *instrumental*, appearing to be a way of getting something done (in this case, to become 'informed'), and it should be *expressive*, drawing attention to values and beliefs that hold people together. 'The news' fills these two requirements. It is true that watching or reading 'the news' does not involve personal activity in the rituals in the way that voting or performing a rain dance does, but participation is often surrogate in modern industrial societies.

For many people 'the news', as a ritual, plays as regular a part in life as the patterns of daily prayer in religious societies. People pay their formal devotions to 'the news' by reading a newspaper or listening to the radio or watching television (sometimes all three, perhaps simultaneously). They may pay special devotions to 'the news' during the day. At night the television 'news' can be the equivalent of family prayers.

Critics of existence

We live hypothetically. From the inventions of our cultures we create 'realities' that divert our attention from the 'meaning'-lessness of existence and provide the frameworks from which we can think and act. It is from this that there comes the peculiarly human possibility of liberation: we expect from life more than we can ever get. But we can get some of what we expect.

It is true that these 'realities' are also constrictive. But if our imaginations were not constricted we could not exist: we would have nothing from which to think and act. In a secular form of buddhism, the nothingness of nirvana would come from a contemplation of existence so infinitely complex that the self would cease to be. If there is everything, there is nothing.

But even if out of physical necessity we simply must accept

most of the limits of our own creations, and even if social forces push us towards 'realities', there is always at least the physical possibility of what one might call 'criticism': we can question existing 'realities' and we can be conscious of creating 'realities' of our own.

Since we *do* live hypothetically, some of the 'realities' from which we think and act can, as it were, be 'disproved': they don't work, or they cease to work. Even if they don't work, of course, we may go on believing them. Prayer for supernatural intervention in earthly affairs has never worked, yet belief in prayer as the way of getting things done has provided 'legitimations' so complex that they have provided much of the bases of most past cultures, just as in modern secular societies belief in politics and economics as ways of getting things done have produced 'legitimations' so complex that they have provided much of the bases of most modern cultures. When 'realities' are challenged by changing circumstances they may prove too stubborn to adjust: people prefer to retain unworkable 'realities' to changing their ways. The 'realities' of nuclear deterrence could lead to the destruction of our species.

But even while human societies can cling to 'realities' that do not work, the *possibility* of criticism is there: at least some people might see that some of the 'realities' of their society are, as it were, disproved. In response, they can help construct new 'realities' – or, if you like, they can try out other hypotheses as a base for thought and action. (In fact 'hypothesis' is far too rational a description for what goes on in scientific research, let alone the enormous number of interactions of human societies, but it is a usefully simplifying concept, showing how human existence must necessarily be fragile and experimental.)

The possibility of 'criticism' exists not only in recognizing that a 'reality' may not be working. It exists generally. Just as we are all of us intellectuals, we are all of us critics. However much there may be a sharing of 'realities', each person's mixture of 'realities' is at least marginally individual. We are all of us – but to enormously differing degrees – evaluating our own experience.

But what if we were all 'critics' in the sense that we had all developed a special self-conscious interest in constructions of reality, and we had all accepted, self-consciously, a concern with theorizing about humanity and its environment, and we were all ready to try to make some sense to each other as, like patients lying in a hospital ward, we shared some of our secrets and spoke a little of our common predicament? In such circumstances we would not be primarily critics of *texts*. We would be critics of *existence*, leading an examined life in which two great questions would constantly arise (and would never be finally answered): *What can we believe? How can we describe existence?*

As critics of existence we would normally use texts not as matters of final interest in themselves (something that you give a mark to, like a university exercise), but as guides in building our criticisms of existence. In this we would lose the sense of individualism in which we evaluate each other in terms of originality, a practice that can lead to habits of immense and chilling caution. We would see criticism and speculation not as questions of *personal* originality and prestige, but of a *collective* originality, so that in intellectual discourse it might not be personal ambition but common concern that prevailed. We would see the potential creativity of error and absurdity (opening up our minds, getting discussion going). It might not be seriousness that prevailed, but irony and wit – irony as a way of reminding ourselves of the ever-present possibility that things might come out differently from how we had intended them; wit as a way of distancing ourselves from the 'realities' we create for the sake of discussion, so that we could remind ourselves that they *were* only hypothetical.

But, as things now stand, while in terms of physical possibility we can all be critics, and in terms of individual personality we *must* all be critics, some of us are much more critics than others.

2. The 'Language' of a Culture

The industrialization of culture

The human predicaments this book is concerned with are those that come from the maintaining and the changing of 'realities' in modern industrial nation-states. In some ways these processes are as old as myths and legends, images and words. But, more often than not, they are now carried out in new ways, with low levels of participation but with high levels of reach. And, while some of the 'realities' that are being maintained are older than the formation of modern industrial nation-states, some are uniquely related to modernity, industrialism and nationality.

The book is concerned with stability and obedience. In particular, it is concerned with the kinds of ways in which the existing social order in modern industrial states is maintained not only by coercion but by the dominance of certain 'realities'. It is, therefore, also concerned with privilege, with the question of how the 'realities' that dominate a society may favour one economic class over others, one sex over another, one ethnic group over others, one racial type over others, one region over others.

It is also concerned with strategies for change, with the question of what part 'reality'-creation plays in strategies for changing a social order. And, too, it is concerned with that deprivation of 'cultural rights' in modern industrial societies in which 'art' and 'intellect' are seen as entities separate from ordinary life, specialist matters in which ordinary people have no part.

If it is kept at a fairly mechanical level, engaging in the first part of that task – telling the story of the industrialization of culture – is easy. That is no reason for not telling it.

Traditionally, the story can be seen as beginning with one of the first examples of modern mass production – the printed book. The printing press was one of the first modern machines and its arrival in Europe in the mid fifteenth century made possible the great religious and then the great secular revolutions that followed. At first, as the old elites fell on one another, the printed book was their instrument, then, by the time two of its typical forms had become the three-volume novel and the circulating library, it had become associated with the coming order. Some of its forms – the novel, for example, or the encyclopedia – still reflect this origin. With the development of mass education (made feasible through printing), new markets developed, at first through 'penny fiction', cheap textbooks, and public libraries. Then, when the market diversified, books became big business. There were ever-growing demands from the educational institutions; there were large demands for technical books, from legal reference works to cookbooks; there were specialist high culture and popularized high culture markets; and, in what Malraux described as 'the industrialization of fantasy', there developed an enormous use of resources in the production of mountains of trash.

Also associated with the coming social order was the invention of newspapers and magazines. Even now, in the Communist countries also, as with books, the structure of newspapers largely reflects the forms of their origin. The 'popular' newspaper – relying on street sales rather than subscription – was developed in the United States and spread throughout the world. Printing became faster and cheaper when the old flatbed press was replaced by the rotary press with its continuous supply of paper from rolls. Paper itself was made cheaper by producing it from wood pulp rather than rags – vast forestry industries were formed to feed the presses – and the setting of type was made cheaper by the development of the linotype machine; the telegraph enormously increased the newsiness of news and so, in its turn, did the telephone; the development of the railway and, later, the motor industry increased the number of people a newspaper could reach. Now the newspaper, with its encapsulations of existence in terms of headlines and 'news stories', provides entirely modern ways of looking at the world.

By the middle of the nineteenth century illustrated magazines began to join the increasing output of newsprint. The mass-sale popular magazine joined the mass-sale newspaper. Towards the end of the nineteenth century, at first in Paris, the street poster also developed a pictorial form; in the twentieth century, because of its simplicity, it became one of the most effective of all devices for what is now known as propaganda. Meanwhile, with the application of the lens in a dark box with light sensitive chemicals, the camera had been invented, and when photo-engraving replaced woodcuts and etchings the photograph began to lend newspapers and magazines their stunning sense of reality, as credible in effect as it can be spurious and, like the headline and the news story, providing an entirely new way of looking at the world.

Meanwhile, in the United States (where most of these developments first matured), Tin Pan Alley produced a mass production of 'the song hit', made profitable by the commercialization of music in sheet music and later in pianola rolls. Also in the United States, the phonograph was developed, and the record industry; then the long-playing record; later, the cassette and the compact disc. The enormous range of popular music (so much of it of United States origin) now spreads into almost every house in industrialized countries and can even follow people, if they are properly wired up, as they sit in the sun or walk down the street. At the same time the 'popularization' of 'classics' on cassettes means that people can listen to a Bach Mass in the bath, or hear Renaissance court music or the music of Tibetan stone bells while driving along a freeway to the office.

In 1895 Marconi experimented with the first wireless telegraphy; in 1904 the British developed a vacuum tube that could detect wireless messages; in 1906 there was the first transition of a voice through wireless 'waves'. At first, as earlier with the telegraph, it was the military and commercial uses of wireless telegraphy that predominated: then in the 1920s the radio began to penetrate people's homes. Two of the most successful political propagandists in the 1930s found different functions for it. In Germany, Goebbels used it, as Marshall McLuhan later put it, to beat 'the tribal drums': intended to provide a national unity, the radio played in the streets (as it played in Stalin's factories) and 'radio wardens' were appointed by the Nazi Party to spy on people's habits as they 'listened in'. But in the United States President Roosevelt, in his 'fireside chats', exploited the intimacy of radio: it was as if the president was sitting with the people and philosophizing with them in their sitting-rooms. Later, with the transistor, the radio became a potentially permanent companion. There was no occasion when it need not be nearby.

At the time it was giving newspapers and magazines a sharper sense of actuality, the invention of the camera was also making possible the cinema industry, led, at least in commercial terms, by the Hollywood film factories whose fantasies manufactured new stereotypes of reality. Cowboys and Indians became a children's game over most of the industrial world. In the late 1920s the principle of the camera was joined with the principle of the phonograph, in the invention of talking pictures, but it is when these principles were combined with the principle of radio to produce television that the most complex of all the media appeared, combining the intimacy of radio with the actuality of film to produce the most effective of all illusions.

Sometimes the story ends here. But we should also add the vast school-building programmes and teacher-training programmes that produced systems of universal education, and the universities and technical and professional colleges that, whether in capitalist or Communist societies, maintained the principles of specialization and provided credentials for careers, and also, as the sociologist Edward Shils put it, 'universitized' knowledge so that it could seem a specialist matter pursued by a select few in separate and non-communicable 'disciplines'. To this then add the great industries of 'popularization' of 'classics', some supporting specialization, but some challenging it: the public libraries; the museums; the paperbacks and records and cassettes and art books and colour prints; the drama, ballet, opera and music groups supported by public funds; the evening classes and other non-specialist study groups. And, to all this, add the invention of modern spectator sport, with the construction of large sports grounds provided with audiences by the new public transport systems – and the division of life into 'teams' with such enthusiasm that, for many, sport can become one of the richest parts of existence, the true 'reality', full of meaning. There is also, if for a smaller number, the development of participant sport, with its great allocation of resources to facilities and equipment as ordinary people took over from the rich their previous monopoly of this type of pleasure. By now the idea of 'leisure' had been created, with, as well as sports, television and so forth, other organized diversions – places to dance, the manufacture of indoor games, provision for gambling (whether legal or illegal), specialist clubs, places to eat and drink. Part of 'leisure', as perceived, became 'the hobby'. 'Work' was seen as something for which one was paid, thereby providing the only true means to human welfare and dignity, but for most people something over which they had no control, something they simply had to learn to bear: the work that really interested someone (a 'hobby') could be seen as a lesser, spare time indulgence, not work at all really, an indulgent reward. Life outside work had been 'privatized' and the provision of culture facilities had partly become domestic: 'home craft' could become an important part of life and, in the places where town planning allowed it, gardening. Add to all this the spreading, at least in the capitalist states and to some extent also in the Communist states, of shopping as a great declarer of meaning. First, new institutions – department stores, mail order firms and chain stores were created; then the 'supermarket', the shopping centre, the shopping mall, all of them great display places of icons rich in reminders of 'realities'. In the capitalist countries, there was the creation of brand names (a new type of encapsulation of values) and the coming of mass scale advertising, which became, above all else in the capitalist countries, the public iconography of society. Then to all this add the great significance of the annual holiday, a festival of regeneration supported by enormous building programmes, and in particular that modern pilgrimage, the organized sight-seeing tour. To all this add the civil religions that, in varying forms, developed in each nation-state – the national days, the processions and ceremonies and the great value-affirming special occasions, now made larger than life by television. Then add the idea of propaganda itself.

'Propaganda' is not a new idea. The word was first produced in the Catholic church to describe the propagation of the Christian faith. The activity itself began long before that – but what is quite novel is the enormous deployment of resources and the open development of the professionalization of deception. In the liberal-democratic capitalist societies the word 'propaganda' is not now generally used to describe what happens in those societies; but in one-party states, just as in the Catholic church, 'propaganda' is an entirely honourable process (whatever its deceptions) concerned with a task given by destiny – the spreading of secular faiths. Lenin articulated famous principles of Communist propaganda, with a division between the spreading to a few of the whole Marxist view of life and the 'agitation' that can mobilize the masses by theatricalizing one or two simple issues. In their heroic stages this helped sustain Communist parties throughout the world as somewhat similar organizing principles had once sustained the Calvinists. Now it also helps sustain the Communist states, with deliberate manipulations by members of the vanguard party designed, it is said, to extend the true consciousness of the working class, a process in which allowing the propagation of a variety of beliefs can seem, as it did in the Catholic church, an encouragement of falsehood and error. To people in the liberal-democratic capitalist states the other users of propaganda have seemed to be 'the dictators', with Hitler and Goebbels as paradigms. ('The masses are feminine in their attitudes, motivated by feeling and sentiment.' 'The thousand-fold repetition of the most simple ideas can force a doctrine upon a whole people.') But the propaganda of modern states might be better seen as beginning with the manufacture of racist imperialisms in the nineteenth century – it was the British who were the most successful and the most unscrupulous propagandists in the First World War – and it is commonplace that liberal-democratic governments can also lie and suppress in a good cause. The fighting of elections in such societies is based on whole 'sciences' of the practice of deception.

To a Communist observer, 'the news' and the rest of the 'culture industries' in liberal-democratic capitalist societies have such common emphases that they can also seem to be deliberately propagandist. Whether this is done deliberately or not is a matter for argument but there is no doubt about the deliberation that goes into concocting the seductions of advertising. This is an industry based on a perhaps unique acceptance and even self-congratulation of its own deceits. Yet its effects should not simply be measured in their success in helping the sales of this or that, but, as Jacques Ellul argues in *Propaganda*, in the way in which, taken as a whole, above the individual intentions of advertisers, advertisements come together to produce a social propaganda, without the appearance of propaganda, and without deliberate propaganda action. In the United States, for example, advertising speaks not only for the goods and services of individual advertisers but also for 'the American way of life'; that is, the notion that everyone has the freedom of choice. And in all the capitalist societies it reflects certain prevailing views of what the nation and society are: it projects a world of the middle class, of fixed gender roles and established ethnic prejudices; above all, by its very presence advertising propaganda says that the consumer ethic gives life meaning and, with all these ads jostling each other, it also says that it is freedom of consumer choice and a competitive market economy that guarantee life, liberty and the pursuit of happiness.

In discussing the industrialization of culture there can be two obsessive approaches that now run the risk of concealing more than they illuminate. One is an obsession with ownership. The other is an obsession with research.

The obsession with ownership

In the liberal-democratic capitalist societies the culture and information industries are usually either big business or a part of government. In the Communist societies they are likely to be accepted as one of the most significant parts of the regime. This high centralization of the information and culture bureaucracies helps explain the survival of modern industrial nation-states. How could these nation-states operate, as they are now, without these cultural forms? These forms help maintain the stability of these states by defining the world in terms of certain 'realities' and also by diffusing, as it were, new kinds of 'instructions' about what matters and how people should behave (because things can remain 'basically' the same in these states only if they also marginally change, adjusting to new circumstances).

From this centralization some critics assume that the technology itself has demanded these corporate mega-structures. But, while a machine can limit or expand human potential, it cannot *demand* anything. It is itself a product of social circumstances, but it can also become a definer of social circumstances. Even when much of media technology is now so concentrated, this is no argument that the technology itself demands that its uses should be concentrated. Under a different social order there might still be centralized technical production, but from the one centralized collection of machinery there could be diverse uses. More than one newspaper, for example, can come off the one printing complex. More than one organization can produce programmes on the one broadcasting station. There is nothing about largeness that necessarily demands monopoly.

In the Soviet Union the state attempts to control the use of duplicators. For the very reason that the security services in all nations spy on perceivedly deviant telephone users because of the personal accessibility of the telephone, *any* personally accessible media can provide access to alternative or oppositional voices – typewriters, photocopiers, duplicators, small offset presses, cassettes, video packs, badges, posters, community radio. A well-chosen slogan, put up on walls at the right time, can help change some aspect of the 'reality' of a city. In her book *Committing Photography*, Su Braden suggests how the camera could be used by ordinary people if they chose to use it, to create a new, and oppositional, workers' 'reality'. Among the examples she gives is that of a pictorial booklet about a run-down dockyard area in Liverpool. It was produced by local people to such effect that the small arts grant given to the group was withdrawn.

To some culture critics, ownership is virtually the beginning and end of the discussion. Having recognized that the industrialization of culture plays a part in the 'social control' of modern industrial societies, they can feel that all they need then do is to establish who owns the 'information' and culture industries, and that's that. These owners have certain interests, so they run the information and culture industries to suit their interests. What else would you expect? What else is there to know? To critics of capitalist societies it is obvious that the culture industries are owned by the capitalist class, or controlled by organizations within the apparatus of state that serve the capitalist class. To critics of Communist societies it is equally obvious that the culture industries in those societies are, in effect, 'owned' by apparatchiks who run things to serve their own interests.

Overall, the crudity of this approach is useful, and can offset too many subtle ifs and buts. There *are* biases of power and privilege in societies. In the myriad of social conflicts there are always winners and always losers, and 'legitimations', to use Max Weber's term, grow up around the winners and explain the world (create 'realities') in ways that justify them. The winners will look to preserving what they see as their interests. To do this, if necessary, they will be ready for conscious deceits, acting not only from self-preservation but also from the justification that their power comes from God or the demands of human destiny or that their interests are really the interests of all, or of a chosen class, or of a master race, and that their power is a *burden* which they must not shirk.

But, having recognized these overall shapes, one must then also examine the two essential quibbles that must be applied to any discussion of interest and intention. The first is that although, from a wide viewpoint, a certain group of people may appear all to be in the one metaphorical boat, this does not mean that they all want to sail in the same direction. A classic case is that of a 'capitalist class'. Look at it close up, and its members are in conflict. So long as the society has not reached the capitalist goal of perfect monopoly, there are great marketing battles within industries and lobbying and battles between industries (between exporters and importers, for example) and contradictions such as those between the 'work ethic' and 'the consumer ethic'. It is true that if capitalism itself seems endangered, then the capitalists are likely to see a common threat (although even here there may be different perceptions as to whether there *is* a common threat, and even if there is agreement on that question there may not be agreement on what should be done about it); but the assumption of a general common interest and nothing else can miss all the subtleties of the 'contradictions' in capitalism. Yet studying these 'contradictions' is essential to the study of capitalism. And to those who want change, it may be that only from these 'contradictions' can the conditions for what they see as fundamental change arise.

The second necessary quibble is that intentions are not enough. Whatever it is that the owners of the information and culture industries intend, the consequences of their actions might be quite different from what they mean to happen. The complexities, ambiguities, mysteries and intractabilities of societies are so great that the paradox of unintended consequences casts its large shadow over all social speculation. Those who seek change are faced with the paradox that their actions may produce effects other than, or even opposite to, what they intended. Equally, those who want things to stay the same are faced with the paradox that struggling to keep things the same can also produce effects other than, or even opposite to, what was intended.

There is another range of quibbles about ownership. Legally, in the Communist societies, all productive property is owned by 'the people' – other than certain types of small business, or collectively or co-operatively owned property, or property owned by the party or other organizations acting on behalf of the people. So the information and culture industries are owned by 'the people'. ('State property, that is, the common property of the Soviet people, is the principal form of socialist property,' says the Soviet Constitution. In the Yugoslav Constitution, with its declarations of 'self-management by the working people', property is declared to be 'socially owned'.) And in the capitalist societies, some of the information and culture industries are owned by the state and most of the others are legally owned not by individuals but by agglomerations of shareholders, most of whom have no effect on what is happening in the corporations in which they are nominally the joint owners other than potentially being able to consent to a takeover. So, in both capitalist and Communist countries the large information and culture bureaucracies are likely to be controlled by salaried bureaucrats different from the legal owners and very largely unanswerable to them. It is true that in both forms of bureaucracies, actions will be taken in the name of the owners: but this is different from owning.

Owning can be of immense importance in determining personal attitudes – to become an owner can mean becoming a different person – but in analysing modern industrial states an over-emphasis on owning can lead to over-sophistication when analysing capitalist states and no analysis at all of Communist states since, if ownership is the beginning and end of analysis, there is no theoretical basis for analysing them. Here the Hungarian intellectual and former prime minister Andras Hegedus is illuminating. In his book *The Structure of Socialist Society* he abandons what he sees as the vulgar Marxism of a pure dichotomy between two classes based on ownership, and looks for approaches that can be useful in analysing complex modern industrial societies – where private ownership is limited but where there nevertheless remain great social divisions – and capitalist societies, where he sees 'hierarchically articulated bureaucracies acquiring independent functions and interests and serving the propertied interest only through complex intermediary mechanisms' so that 'the capitalist class, apart from a narrow section, tends to lose its real social function . . . like aristocrats in the eighteenth century attaching themselves to the new absolutist bureaucracies'.

There is another difficulty about turning ownership into a simple major premise from which everything else can then be deduced, and this is also a matter in which one should be looking for forms of analysis that will suit both Communist and capitalist modern industrial states. It is this (a point to be merely asserted here, and argued later): in all the modern industrial societies there are people whom I will later call 'the critics'. They might be seen as the heirs of fifteenth- and sixteenth-century humanism, the seventeenth-century scientific revolution and eighteenth-century enlightenment, and they believe in discussion. One way or another, they hold the notion that criticism is an improving force in society, perhaps good in itself but in any case essential for social efficiency. Some of them believe that only a free market of ideas can produce optimum social satisfaction: more usually they will accept a free market of ideas within a range restricted by what they see as the prevailing values of a society. But within that restricted range they still see criticism as essential. They are joined by 'creative people'. (In practice, one person might be both 'critic' and 'creative'.) The 'creative' are those who produce the goods and services of what we think of as arts and entertainment, and these goods and services hold the potential to produce trouble for an established order. This comes from the very nature of these activities, because within them there must be a conscious concern with illusion-making. They are the most self-aware of the crafts of 'reality'-creation: their continuous conscious preoccupation with *form* in itself holds dangers for an established order. Do something differently, and you have produced a new world. Thousands of paintings of crucifixions survive in the art museums of Europe and the Americas: they are all connected with the death of Christ, but in their differences in style they say many different things. Pass through a large art museum and examine, chronologically, the style of the crucifixions and you learn a great deal about changes in European perceptions of 'reality'. The culture industries cannot exist without 'critics' and 'creative persons', yet their view of things need not match those of the controllers, as Stalin knew when he insisted on personally reviewing so many Soviet films, or as Hollywood writers discovered from their dealings not only with producers and directors but also with the Hays Office and then the House Committee on Un-American Activities. Even when, with many of these tensions, the controllers win, they have had to win against resistance and if the controllers weaken in their bullying, the 'critics' and the 'creative persons' are again inclined to become the maintainers of overt traditions in the culture industries, their skills and styles becoming the institutionalized conscience of those industries and, often, their principal form of prestige. When Communist functionaries, frightened capitalists, fascists, militarists or ultra-Christians wake from their nightmares and denounce the culture industries as controlled by a 'liberal' conspiracy, they may be exaggerating, but their noses, in sniffing for an enemy, are sniffing in the right direction.

To sum up, on this question of ownership there seem three main points. The first is that an overriding concern with ownership can make impossible a looking for similarities between capitalist and Communist societies: it takes that difference for granted, without any further discussion. It can also overlook the subtleties and ambiguities that can come from the tensions between those who control these industries and those who work in them. And either it comes with a crude theory of social change – that general social change will necessarily occur with change of ownership, or even can occur only with change of ownership – or it has no theory of social change at all. (It could, of course, be argued that to leave social change as something that happens of its own accord with a change in ownership is, in effect, to have no theory of social change.) But the greatest of all criticisms of *a priori* arguing from ownership is that it blinds the observer. If one wishes to see what is produced by the culture industries one does not have to deduce this from first principles about ownership. One should open one's eyes and look.

The obsession with 'research'

When we do open our eyes, what is it that we should be looking at? Considering this question has produced an enormous debate that runs through whole parts of the discussion on modern industrial societies. Before offering an answer, there should be a reminder of where the debate on 'mass society' and 'mass culture' has been.

In his book *Keywords*, Raymond Williams discusses how the word 'mass' can be seen as good or bad. 'Mass' can indicate a positive or potentially positive social force, as in 'the masses', 'mass movement', 'mass meeting', 'mass protest': it can be good to engage in 'mass work' or to belong to a 'mass organization'. But 'mass' can also be a bad word – as in 'mass production', for example, or 'mass suggestion', or 'mass taste', or 'mass communications'. It can be good to hold a 'mass meeting'. It can be bad to control a 'mass market'. One can have a 'mass protest' (good) against the 'mass media' (bad).

'Mass society' has always been seen as bad. In fact the subject of sociology began as a criticism of the new mass societies, sometimes with an extraordinarily early percipience, as when

Comte, in the 1830s, detected modern specialization and prophesied that it would drive people apart, or when the young Marx in the 1840s wrote of the perils of 'alienation', in which workers, having lost control over both how they worked and what they produced, would themselves become commodities, like other commodities. Tönnies in the 1880s saw a breakdown of traditional, organic community (*Gemeinschaft*) with its strong sense of tradition, mutual association and locality and its replacement by a contractual society (*Gesellschaft*) of isolated individuals, driven apart by a competitive anonymity; Durkheim, in the 1890s, produced the word *anomie* to describe the state of isolation into which people would be driven by the new order of work specialization, social differentiation and individualism; Weber found the new bureaucracies dehumanized by their own expertness.

In the 'mass culture' discourse that began to develop in the 1930s there were conglomerations of agreement, at least about the headings of discourse, among the romantic conservatives who saw 'mass culture' as one of the degrading results of democratic levelling, the radicals who saw it as a product of capitalist greed, and the liberals, radicals and conservatives who saw it as a potential for 'totalitarianism' (which they defined according to taste). All of them detected the isolation of competitive individualism (or 'atomization') as one distinguishing characteristic of 'mass societies'. Conservatives may have done this by regretting the passing of an organic medieval community (of a kind that never existed) and radicals by regretting the disruption of the solidarity and gregariousness of the common people (which may also have been over-romanticized) but they were both likely to see the 'mass' of a 'mass society' as made up of anonymous individuals, isolated by the breaking of the old associations of extended family and neighbourhood and now uncertain about how to behave with each other because they had lost common, integrating values: condemned to shadowy, tenuous relationships, they were, in David Riesman's phrase, a 'lonely crowd'. Life was seen as mechanistic and, as in Charles Chaplin's *Modern Times*, work was seen as remote, standardized and alienating, leaving the greater part of the human personality frozen in a dehumanized, over-rational bureaucratic society in which were destroyed the strong, independent institutions in which people had previously been able to have some connection with events. Isolated and uneasy in their relationships with each other, the people were given over to the decisions of 'power elites' commanding large corporate organizations over which there was no possibility of popular intervention.

Fed pap by the 'culture industries', a 'mass audience', homogenized, dehumanized, trivialized, volatile and open to passing fads and fancies, was uniquely manipulable by those who held power. Hence (according to how you looked at it) the success of Communism, or fascism, or monopoly capitalism.

Whether one accepted it all, or only parts of it, this type of general theorizing was of absorbing interest to those who cared about what was happening in the modern world. But an enormous and trivial diversion was created from these serious concerns by the dominant sociologists in the United States who became so concerned with specialist number-crunching that a conspiracy theorist might well have found the explanation in a capitalist plot. (However, another explanation is that, often, capitalists do not have to plot: their view of 'reality' can so permeate a liberal-democratic capitalist society that a lot of the work of the capitalists is done for them.)

The long season of number-crunching opened with the publication, in 1944, of what was to become a research classic, *The People's Choice*, a book based on a series of surveys carried out in a small county in Ohio during the 1940 election campaign, when a staff of interviewers visited every fourth house, interviewing 3,000 people from whom four groups of 600 were chosen, three of them 'control groups' and the fourth 'a panel'. There were two useful contributions from this famous work and from the works that followed it. One was that they suggested that even in a mass society people were not entirely empty-headed and that how they reacted to election propaganda depended on what was in their minds already. The other was the acceptance that even in a mass society people were social animals, reacting socially and not simply as individual isolates. But as the surveys went on and on, becoming narrower and narrower, more and more costly and more and more scientistic (assuming that only inductive methods can produce knowledge) they came to be interpreted as meaning that election campaigns really didn't have much effect (whereas one could argue the opposite – that the surveys showed how it was that election campaigns *were* likely to affect voting). The claims went further than that. In 'the law of minimum media influence' it was argued that the media didn't really matter much in anything: the media simply told people what they believed already. It is a superb example of the blindness that can affect scientistic enquiry that 'the law of minimum media influence' was being developed in the very years when Senator Joseph McCarthy was terrorizing United States politics. McCarthyism was not researchable.

To obtain research grants and advance academic careers, the kind of research that was being conducted *had* to be narrow, otherwise it would not be scientific. It was confined to observable changes in electoral behaviour within a limited time-span and this meant that it ignored all other social behaviour and that, even so far as electoral behaviour went, it was searching too narrowly. Shifts in perceptions of 'reality' usually occur over a longer period than that of personal behaviour during an election campaign. But it was typical of the intellectual shallowness of this research that the very possibility of there being different perceptions of 'reality' was not considered. There was an exclusive emphasis on attitudes, not on how people saw the world (knowledge), and even so far as the idea of 'influence' was concerned there was an obsession with one-to-one change – something happens in a campaign and it alters some voter's attitude. It left unconsidered quite different theories of influence: of the importance of reinforcement, for instance; even more, of the importance of definitions of what matters in politics – these can virtually monopolize political discourse; and, even more important, dominant

definitions ('realities') of the world at large. The triviality of
this research was matched by the triviality of a great deal of
United States 'political science'; 'political science' was not only
scientistic, with high, scientific standards of research that
necessarily limited research to the trivial, but it could scarcely
get its mind off elections, as if they were the only social conflict,
whereas one of the functions of elections can be to conceal
social conflict or to reduce conflict to what is safe.

What most of these surveys actually demonstrated, and
continue to demonstrate, is that media influence is not
researchable in any serious sense. If it is correct to speak of the
'language' of a 'reality', we must try to see that 'language' as all
in one piece. If we are concerned with the media we cannot be
concerned only with the media. As Michael Real suggests in
Mass-Mediated Culture we must also be concerned with what it
is that the media mediate. We must have some overall theory of
the shaping of 'realities' in a modern nation-state, in which we
look for the 'languages' of its cultures.

The 'language' of a culture

Photo albums or national flags or television newscasts are as
much part of the 'language' of a culture as words. When we
look at the Acropolis or the Kremlin or the ruins of Auschwitz,
or at the Matterhorn or the Sogne Fjord or Mount Fuji, or hear
the 'Marseillaise' or the 'Internationale' or 'The Battle Hymn
of the Republic', we are 'reading' these sights and sounds. Lake
Baloton is as much a part of the Hungarian 'language' as is
Hungarian. The Ramblas is part of the 'language' of Barcelona.
Guinness stout is part of the 'language' of Dublin. A *fado*
performance in Lisbon is more than a song; it is a declarative
form, seen as defining the Portuguese, just as the strumming of
a *gusle* can be seen as defining a traditional idea of the Serbian.
A meat pie eaten in the street is part of the 'language' of
Melbourne, just as a raw herring eaten from a street stall is part
of the 'language' of Amsterdam. Brands of cigarettes are part
of the 'language' of every modern industrial society.

But the social world isn't just full of the signs of a cultural 'language'. As the Italian culture critic Umberto Eco puts it in *Semiotics and the Philosophy of Language*: the social world *is* signs. To behave socially, we constantly invent the signs of our culture so that they *become* the social world. We act (although in vastly more complex and ambiguous ways) as a dog does when it picks up scents. We react to them, and, perhaps without thinking, perhaps after thought, we act.

But the 'scents' we pick up are not part of the physical world. They are meanings that have already been 'invented' socially by other humans. We may be told what to do by these 'scents'. But they are also part of our own invention. It is in this sense that things are what we make them. Imagine a photograph of a young man and a young woman sitting side by side, slightly smiling. Beside them is a gleaming, circular, open-ended container and resting in it, although partly obtruding over the edge, is another gleaming object, long and cylindrical, tapering at one end, with a small object of a different substance, not gleaming, fastened to this tapered end. Attached to the long cylindrical object, again on a different substance, is some writing. To an observer from a totally alien culture this photograph would not have any meaning. Even the interpretation of the smiles would depend on what smiling was taken to mean in that culture. If the photograph were the only evidence of life in a modern industrial society, the only meaning that could be given to it would come from the conventions of the alien culture and would almost certainly be absolutely wrong. But within our society the meaning of this photograph would be quite clear. The gleaming, circular, open-ended container is a metal ice bucket. The long, cylindrical object tapering at the end is a bottle. The small object of a different substance is a cork. The substance with some writing on it is a champagne label. The emotion that causes the two young people to smile is anticipation.

To say this is to describe what the separate objects in the photograph *denote*. However these elements also join together in an act of symbolic synthesis that is so commonplace that it comes through as clearly to us as a word: these denoting elements fuse into an image that *connotes* privilege, pleasure, anticipation, perhaps celebration, and also some degree of sexual innuendo. Yet this connotation is, as it were, very finely tuned. Change one of the elements of denotation and we tune in to a different meaning. Make the man older but keep the woman young, for instance, and the sexual innuendo would change; it would be likely to change even more if it is the woman who is old and the man who is young. The sexual innuendo would disappear, to be replaced by other meanings, if both the man and the woman were made old; or, if, instead of a man and a woman, we have two men; or two women; or a family; or an assorted group of adults. The meaning would again be changed if it were still a young man and a young woman who were sitting there smiling, but the champagne bottle was empty and lying on the floor. There would be a further switch in meaning if the champagne bottle were both empty, and smashed. Change the champagne bottle to a can of Coke, and the meaning again changes. With a bottle of whisky or a bottle of vodka, the meaning would change again. Imagine the young man and the young woman sitting there smiling: on the floor is an empty and broken vodka bottle.

There are many examples of how culture critics have 'read' one aspect of the 'language' of a culture in this kind of way. To Ariel Dorfman, in *The Empire's Old Clothes*, the comic strip Babar the Elephant is an articulation of the European imperial imagination. To Roland Barthes, in his essay 'The *Blue Guide*', a tourist guide to Spain in its concern with scenery connotes bourgeois moral uplift, and in its concern with monuments connotes a bourgeois concern with the accumulation of goods. To Michael Real, in *Mass-Mediated Culture*, Disneyland is a sacred site displaying United States self-images, and also a morality play structuring personal values. To John Berger, in *Ways of Seeing*, the Old Master nude in an art museum is a sign of the submission of women to the demands of male spectators. To Meaghan Morris in her essay 'Sydney Tower', the building of a tourist tower in Sydney can be seen by Sydney people as a sign that their city is now a technologically mature community – because it can do what has already been done overseas.

In *Structuralism and Semiotics*, Terence Hawkes says; 'Nothing in the world can be merely utilitarian. Even the most ordinary buildings organise space in various ways, and in so doing they issue some kind of message about the society's priorities, its presuppositions concerning human nature, politics, economics, over and above their overt concern with the provision of shelter, entertainment, medical care, or whatever.' One can learn to 'read' buildings and ask: 'What do these buildings "say"?' Consider, for example, the entirely different declarations made by the buildings of a medieval town and a modern city, or by an eighteenth-century palace and a contemporary office tower. Or the difference, within modern cities, between, say, Chicago (as the crucible of modern city architecture, the most traditional of modern cities) and Los Angeles, a non-city city of freeways rather than pavements. Or consider the wealth of meanings contained in the phrase 'the corner store'. Or the different meanings contained in the phrases 'suburban street', 'community housing scheme' and 'city ghetto'. A market building, whether a simple, covered place where peasants bring what they have to sell or the glass palace of a United States shopping centre, makes a universal declaration – the market is one of humanity's oldest surviving social forms – but other forms of communal buildings can be seen as expressions of national particularity. To many Swedes, Swedish ideals of communality, harmony and self-improvement are symbolized in the popular intellectual centres of the *folket hus* buildings. To many Australians, at least for a period, the particularity of Australia was seen in the lavish 'clubs' in the state of New South Wales, popularly owned institutions that developed Las Vegas modes of architecture when poker machines were made legal, and became symbols, especially to visiting British journalists, of the depravity of Australian democracy. To some Bulgarians, Bulgarian aspiration can still be found in the 'the reading room', a type of what we would now call a 'cultural centre' that was first developed by

Bulgarian nationalists under the Ottomans. British people are likely to see themselves defined in 'the pub' (a form of communality of which there are failed imitations throughout Europe, North America and parts of Asia: in Istanbul there is a 'Sultan Pub'). When people wish to compare the two Berlins they are likely to contrast the bustle of the Kurfürstendamm with the quiet of the Unter den Linden.

But different people find different meanings in the Kurfürstendamm and the Unter den Linden. To some, the urgency and bright lights of the Kurfürstendamm are a symbol of the prosperity of free enterprise; to others they are a symbol of the depravity of commercialist triviality and capitalist greed. To some the pace of the Unter den Linden is a tribute to sober good taste and order; to others it is a sign of totalitarian suppression. To Swedes, or most Swedes, a *folket hus* building can seem a symbol of communality and civilization; to outsiders it can seem a symbol of cold Swedish impersonality, or even the perils of Swedish socialism. 'Suburban street' and 'community housing scheme' can be as much terms of abuse as of praise; to some, 'city ghetto' may mean the only approximation to a romantically desired *Gemeinschaft*, a sense of organic community, to be found in an otherwise anomic city of isolated individuals. To Chicagoans, there can be a sense of deprivation in the world of the Los Angeles freeways, on which one skims over the city, glimpsing shabby palms and makeshift rooftops, and on which the only significant changes in texture are the waltz-like sweeps from one freeway to the next, until one descends, briefly, to travel on 'the surface'. This can seem individualism gone crazy. But in Los Angeles it can seem both freedom – getting somewhere fast – and a co-operative enterprise in which the freeways work only because of the intelligent co-operation of the drivers.

In *Semiotics and the Philosophy of Language*, Eco recognizes that merely to survive in society we put in much daily interpretative work 'reading' social signs, in some cases so quickly and naturally that we do it without thinking but, in other cases, with uncertainty and anxiety. The same signs do not say, to everybody, the same things. Apart from those whose nervous systems are 'abnormal' we all receive much the same 'signs' from the physical world: if sensory systems are similar the 'realities' they create are similar and, apart from some artifices such as absorbing hallucinogens or wearing tinted glasses, there is nothing we can do about it. But the realities created in the social world can be marked by contradictions and ambiguities. Not only can there be differences between groups in the realities they invent in their cultural language, so that the same building, or words, or song can mean different things: there can also be differences between individuals within a group. We all live with ambiguity.

Getting on with the discussion

If one accepts the idea of looking for the 'languages' of dominant cultures, what happens next? In recent years there have been two particularly useful areas of speculation about the shaping of 'realities' in modern industrial societies that both suggest a way.

The activities in one of these arenas, that of semiotics, the study of signs, can, with the associated doctrines of 'structuralism', pass far beyond ordinary intellectual understanding. There are elegant exceptions – Umberto Eco's work, for example, simply requires careful reading and some of Roland Barthes's shorter pieces achieve the luminosity and clarity of an eighteenth-century essay. But semioticists (including Barthes in some of his other moods) can fall into higly technical vocabularies which demand that to participate in their mysteries one must pass through the painful initiatory processes of learning a new language. The initiatory processes of acquiring the language of structuralism are even more demanding because structuralism now has its heresies and to remain a structuralist one must also learn the equally difficult languages of these heresies.

Readers familiar with semiotics will already have recognized emerging in these first two chapters a primitive kind of semiotics. I intend to leave it at that, but perhaps I should state the gist of what I am getting at (with a few new points):

○ For humans to survive, they must create simplifications of existence. Without these, thought and action are not possible. I called these simplifications of existence 'realities'. The word is in quotation marks as a reminder that these are *perceptions* of existence, not existence. But I do not want to abandon use of the word 'reality' – it is a reminder that we *do* see them *as* existence.

○ These 'realities' are not symbolized only in words. The 'language' of 'realities' includes visual images, music, buildings, dancing, body language, textiles, political rhetoric, entertainment, even odours, and it is a language we learn, unlike the language of the senses.

○ It can be useful, at least as an abstract, analytical exercise, to imagine a difference – even if it is not a difference in practice – between 'denotation', in which a symbol, whether word, or visual image, or whatever, signposts an object, and 'connotation', where various denoting symbols come together to make a more complex statement. The example I gave was of a picture of a young man and a young woman, smiling slightly with, beside them, in a frosted ice bucket, an unopened bottle of champagne, a picture which has a general meaning, apart from its particular meanings. This distinction between 'denotation' and 'connotation' can also apply to a single object. For example, the name of a tree, or its visual representation, can simply signpost the tree: but consider also the richness of other meanings connoted, for northern Californians, by 'redwood'; for the English, by 'oak'; for the Danes, by 'beech'; for the Australians, by 'eucalypt'; for Greeks, by 'olive'; for Canadians by 'maple'.

○ Not only may the same object or events hold different

meanings for different kinds of people. Even among groups of the same kinds of people there may be contradictions and, even more important, ambiguities in 'realities'. The contradictions come partly because different 'realities' are constructed for different circumstances. The ambiguities come from the necessarily hypothetical and contrived nature of 'reality'-construction. Nevertheless, among these differences, there are overall groupings of similarity – or, as it was put in the last section, 'languages'. If different groups of people find different meanings in the one object or event, this means that they are speaking different languages.

O Since thought and action depend on these 'languages', if one is interested in questions of power and democracy in modern industrial nation-states, a useful question to ask of such a society is: What are its dominant 'languages'? And: Whose interests do they most serve?

3. The 'Enchantment' of Modern Societies

Why do we obey?

Two of the most important questions asked by Weber in his famous essay 'Politics as a Vocation' were 'When and why do men obey?' and 'Upon what inner justifications and upon what external means does that domination rest?' The first part of his answer was that we obey because of 'highly robust motives of fear and hope'. One should not underestimate the extent to which we do what we are told because we hope to get something out of it (even if it is only survival). There are sometimes special terror campaigns in a modern industrial society that force conformity through an organized brutality, as there was in the Hitler and Stalin regimes. Terror campaigns can also take selective and milder forms, as with the McCarthyist era (where the threat was mainly to careers, although there were deaths – like those of the Rosenbergs – and some gaolings). Sometimes physical terror is endemic, with both police and vigilant citizens enforcing it, as in many Latin American nations and, to a lesser degree so far as killings went, in the South of the United States before the civil liberties movement. Sometimes a society is tightly controlled by the police, as in the Soviet Union now or in Portugal under the Salazar regime. All societies are, of course, to some extent controlled by the police and in time of war or some other time of perceived emergency all states will justify increased repression. But as well as these physical constraints or physical terrors, there are also economic hopes and fears. A particular fear that can keep people in order in most liberal-democratic capitalist societies is that of getting the sack, or at least the fear that pay packets won't settle the bills. The particular hope that can keep them in order is that of getting a rise. But as well as these hopes and fears, people can clothe their obedience with a respect for the authority of those who give the orders, doing this by what Weber described as 'legitimations', which might be thought of as justifications of power and also as explanations of the world of a kind that make sense of that power by creating, as it were, a sympathetic 'reality'. Ingrained acceptance of the force of authority can sometimes be a principal basis of social order. In her book, *For Your Own Good*, Alice Miller suggests that Hitler was such an effective authority figure in part because the mass of the German people had been subject to pedagogic processes the first commandment of which was to break children's wills so that they would value into adulthood obedience over all other virtues, and praise those who enforced it, even when this caused them pain.

One can imagine three kinds of attitudes to obedience. Some people may be activated only by their own hopes and fears: they may despise those who are giving the orders, but, for reasons of survival, they do what they are told. A factory worker might feel like this, for example, or a soldier. Others may see it as so natural to do what they are told that they may scarcely be conscious of calculation. (Not a likely situation in a factory but imaginable perhaps among the family retainers of the rich, perhaps in family businesses and on farms – and certainly imaginable in an army, a church, a revolutionary party.) Others may be a mixture of both: they are keeping an eye out for their own survival (whether economic or physical) but they also respect the right of their bosses or their officers to give them orders, because they see the social order in a certain kind of way that makes sense of obeying such orders.

One point that comes out of this is that 'legitimations' of power are only *claims* to justification and explanation. (For this reason 'legitimation' will continue to appear in quotation marks.) However much they may appear to dominate a scene, 'legitimations' may or may not be believed. They are attempted explanations and justifications of power – but they are not necessarily instructions on how to behave that have become, as it were, part of one's body. The ideas of 'habit' and 'common sense' are also needed to explain why we obey – ways of thinking and acting that seem so natural that they almost feel part of one's body. Workers in a factory may despise the people who give the orders, but they obey them, naturally, with their bodies. Their bodies have become as habituated to factory work as soldiers' bodies to army drill – through those processes of what Michel Foucault called 'the normalization of individuals' without which modern industrial societies would not work.

It is in his recognition of the importance of both coercion (hopes and fears) and consent (not only 'legitimations', but habits and 'common sense') that Gramsci's work has, posthumously, been useful in theorizing about modern industrial states (although we should recognize that since Gramsci has been dead for 50 years he didn't produce a theory that accounts for everything about industrial states as they are now). As a revolutionary Marxist, his particular concerns were to account for the continued 'false consciousness' of the workers – why, given, in the Leninist sense, the leadership of a vanguard party, did the workers fail to achieve new 'realities'? – and to suggest new strategies based on his new theories. But even for people who are not Marxists, but who are nevertheless concerned with strategies for change in modern industrial societies, Gramsci's theories can make a good starting point.

Gramsci saw a 'dual perspective' in modern industrial states in which the supremacy of a social group manifested itself partly through 'dominance' (coercion) but also through an intellectual and moral leadership by that group ('hegemony'). The result was that the interests of that group and the groups associated with it could seem the natural interests of the whole society. This could mean that there was, as it were, a 'consent' to the general direction, or leadership, of the dominant group. His decision to call this process 'hegemony' was unfortunate since in ordinary usage the word has the connotation of 'dominance', while Gramsci was in fact using 'hegemony' to distinguish it from 'dominance'. What he was getting at is hard to translate, but I think the word 'directive' comes close – 'directive' in the sense that people are being shown what to do and how to do it, what to believe and how to believe it. Not necessarily, or even usually, by direct exhortation, but more by a process of permeation throughout society of ways of doing things and seeing the world (creating 'realities') that are in one way or the other supportive of the established order and the class interests that dominate it. The essential point is that *the ways of thinking and acting of the dominant group become the society's 'common sense'*. These become the natural way to behave. This is how Gramsci's theory accounts for stability in modern industrial states. His theory of hegemony is also concerned, however, with explanations of and strategies for social and economic change in which he sees a necessity for a change from one class to the other of moral and intellectual leadership (hegemony) as well as political and economic control (dominance). Before considering how it is that things might be changed, it is worth considering how it is that they can stay the same.

Because it is filled with Gramscian meanings, I will now abandon the word 'hegemony' – but maintain the idea that there are prevailing 'realities' in modern societies and although they are also, as Gramsci put it, 'armoured by coercion', they can be seen, along with coercion, as an essential characteristic of those societies.

The public culture

Perhaps this might seem to apply to all societies. But does it? In *Discipline and Punish* Foucault suggests that in the pre-modern societies the rulers displayed their power irregularly, through demarcations, signs, levies, ceremonies – among them the ceremonial theatre of punishment with its exemplary torturings and killings, conducted irregularly, in periods of intense terror. This could be sufficient for ruling: it could reach its apex in the great courtly displays, or in the suppression of a peasants' revolt when the bodies of peasant leaders were likely to be dismembered in ceremonies of some complexity and the pieces sent throughout a kingdom with considerable solemnity as a lesson to the others. It was a time, as Herbert Gans puts it, in *Popular Culture and High Culture*:

> when European societies were divided culturally into high culture and folk culture. The latter was sparse, homemade, and, because peasants lived in isolated villages, largely invisible. The former was supported by the city-dwelling elites – the court, the nobility, the priesthood and merchants – who had the time, education and resources for entertainment and art . . . Because of the low social status and geographical isolation of folk culture, they also had a virtual monopoly on public and visible culture.

There was not much concern with how the peasants lived or with what they thought – except from the church, and then often only in a desultory way. Thinking was not the business of peasants. Their role was to contribute to levies, whether of kind, or of labour, or in military service and, for some of them, to provide raw material in exemplary ceremonies such as nose-slittings, floggings, bone-breakings, eviscerations, beheadings, hangings and burnings.

We now live in a time when there is a demand for what at least appears to be a *shared* 'public and visible culture', in which both rulers and ruled can appear to be common, if differentiated, participants. Later we will examine many examples. I will give one now: among the principles of modern societies, whether capitalist, Communist or fascist, is that of 'work' as the only true means to human dignity and welfare. The mark of authority is not now the throne, but the *desk*. One of the most prestigious of all the photographs of the United States presidents is a photograph of a president, the Stars and Stripes beside him, in the Oval Office working at his desk. One of the ways in which the Watergate tapes profaned political decency was that such things were being said in *this* place, and being recorded by a tape recorder concealed in the leg well of *this* desk. Some of the most revered of the relics in the V.I. Lenin museums are the actual desks, or replicas of the actual desks, at which Lenin worked so hard for humankind. Under Mussolini, in the Palazzo Venezia some of the rooms were likely to be a blaze of light until late in the night: passers-by could look up and know that the Duce was there, behind his colossal desk, working for Italy. With a few exceptions the privileged do not justify their importance any longer by vast displays of frivolity and enjoyment, but by displays of hard work. In the days of Christendom, religious rhetoric saw a common binding of high and low in the fact that they were all sinners: now they can be seen as all hard workers. There are, of course, the unemployed, but the very name give to them – 'the *un*employed' – is a declaration of the importance of 'work'. All the modern industrial societies are bonded by adherence to principles of usefulness.

A way of beginning this discussion can be to think about the 'public cultures' of modern industrial societies. To begin with, one need not think about them with the Gramscian assumption that they are dominated by the 'realities' (whether in thinking or in acting) of one group. Instead, at first, the question can be left open. One can look at what the public 'realities' are, then examine later the question of whose 'world' it is that these 'realities' project.

How then can a public culture be described? It must be done in ways that will allow comparisons between different kinds of modern industrial states, whether capitalist or Communist, liberal-democratic, fascist, militarized, *étatiste*, or whatever. In all of them we might look in much the same places; obviously, affairs of state and the ceremonies of civil religion; equally obviously, the corporate institutions of the society – in all cases, the great bureaucracies of government, the financial, industrial and commercial organizations (whether owned by shareholders or the state) and the labour organizations (whether self-managed or not). In some societies there would also be the great party bureaucracies; in others at least the political parties themselves and their machines. Again obviously, public propaganda and 'the news' must be considered, the entertainment and education industries, the culture industries, sport and tourism, public art and architecture, 'leisure' and shopping. In some cases, the churches, and prestigious voluntary organizations. At present, these are the places to look in a modern industrial society for the public 'language' of that society.

Lists of the elements in the repertoire of a public culture are relatively easy to work out provided one accepts a certain level of abstraction (it *is* lists of collective habits we are talking about), and provided one jettisons all ambition for performing acts of measurement, and provided one abandons, at least at this listing stage, an instant concern with 'effects'.

We are concerned not so much with 'research' as with examples, and, of course, in looking for examples we are concerned with much more than political rhetoric. Examples of 'reality' maintenance can be found in the meanings now given in a coach tour of the battlefields of Verdun, or in the similarities between a spy drama about the KGB on United States television and a spy drama about the CIA on Soviet television; or in the way the annual Melbourne Cup race has become, in Australia, a national day, or in the way the Easter Mass in Sofia's Alexander Nevsky Cathedral has become an annual fashionable event with special passes and seating arrangements. The Christmas shopping festival in Tokyo can 'tell' us something. So can the skyline of a Stockholm community housing settlement or the expensive reconstruction of Old Warsaw. So can the bookshop in the British Houses of Parliament or a Fiat showroom in Turin, or the way a restaurant queue behaves in Dresden. Meanings can be found in the annual report of the board of directors of a Swiss manufacturing company and compared with the meanings in the annual report of a Yugoslav self-management corporation committee.

In looking for examples we can be as concerned as much with what is done as with what is said, because doing things can at times be an even more important form of 'reality' maintenance than saying them. For example, in most of these societies voting is an essential ritual, yet if you consider how all this voting proclaims 'realities' that are refuted by an examination of the actual operations of power you discover that voting *says* more than it *does*. Another example is work punctuality. By turning up to work on time, automatically, without questioning it, we make one of the fundamental declarations that distinguish industrial from other societies. Given this, one can again see how sometimes what is *not* said can be more important than what *is* said: it can show that something has become so ingrained as a bodily habit that it is taken for granted. It is not in the societies where there continue to be exhortations to arrive at work punctually that one can assume the work ethic to be most flourishing, but in those societies in which punctuality is so taken for granted that there is no longer any need for exhortation. In a communion of saints there would be no exhortations against sinning.

The 'myths' of modern enchantment

We are dealing, necessarily, since the purpose is such a serious one, in broad generalities. To emphasize this I shall introduce the word 'myth'. As with 'reality' and 'legitimation', 'myth' will be in quotation marks. What is meant by it here is one of the familiar uses given to the word by culture critics, but to other readers 'myth' is likely to mean simply 'story'. Like Edelman in *Politics as Symbolic Action*, I take 'myth' to mean a belief held in common by a large group of people that gives events and actions a particular meaning. It is a particularly sharp form of 'reality'-making. It covers a lot of ground, as it were, in a short space. And it is particularly effective in 'legitimations' of power because a 'myth' can appear to explain and justify power with high voltage clarity. I don't want to use some flat term such as 'common belief' because this would miss the element of magic suggested by 'myth'. 'Myths' have the magic quality of transforming complex affairs into simple but crystal-clear 'realities' that explain and justify how things are now, or how we would like them to be. Whether altogether false, or partly true, they have the transforming effect of hiding actual contradictions, confusions and inadequacies. When we speak of 'myths' we are not dealing with little things, but with the ways in which we simplify or deny the great contradictions of society. Studying its 'myths' can in fact make a good introduction to the study of a society, because the further removed 'myths' are from what happens the more they may tell us about a society's tensions. One can ask: If humans can delude themselves to this extent, what has gone wrong? What is, in effect, being covered up? To say that a belief is a myth is not to finish but to commence a discussion.

Examples of some of these great myths (present and past) are obvious enough: the free enterprise 'myth', the 'myth' of world revolution, the 'myth' of economic growth, the 'myth' of equality, the 'myth' of meritocracy, the 'myth' of divine right, the 'myth' of democracy, the 'myth' of the rule of law, the 'myth' of white superiority, the 'myth' of male superiority. I have tried to make the range of examples wide to emphasize that when we describe a collective belief as a 'myth' we are not expressing any views as to its moral worth or as to its refutability; we are, instead, speaking of its effectiveness in providing sharp, clear 'realities' that seem to explain a lot. In saying that a belief is a 'myth' we are not concerned with its truth, or its morality, but with its magic, that is, with its *power*.

In *Pyramids of Sacrifice* Peter Berger, after recalling how the French culture critic and revolutionary Georges Sorel helped to give myth its modern meaning, goes on to say:

> In ancient times, of course, the term had a religious
> connotation . . . however the concept of myth has attained
> a more general and at the same time secularized usage
> within social thought. For Sorel, a myth is any set of ideas
> that infuses transcendent meaning into the lives of men –
> transcendent with regard to the routine and selfish
> concerns of ordinary life. It is through myths that men are
> lifted above their capacity in the ordinary, attain powerful

visions of the future, and become capable of collective
actions to realize such visions. In this understanding of
myth, therefore, specifically religious contents are
discarded. Then as now, the figures of myth touch the lives
of individuals with transforming power . . . By definition,
myth transcends both pragmatic and theoretical
rationality, while at the same time it strongly affects them.

We must go further. The magic of 'myth' gives a trans-
cendancy even to pragmatism and rationality. There can be no
greater transcendent idealist than a pragmatist in a situation
where pragmatism no longer works. In Britain, the Chamberlain
family had produced generations of hard-headed, shrewd
Birmingham pragmatists with such transcendency that when
the most famous of all Chamberlains was removed from the
'realities' of Birmingham pragmatism to the 'realities' of his
meeting with Hitler in Munich he was transformed into a kind
of idiot. 'Myths' do not simply lift people out of their ordinary
lives: it is precisely to 'the routine and selfish concerns of
ordinary life' that myths also give meaning. There is no part of
our lives that can necessarily escape their magic.

In this sense, our life in modern industrial societies is still
'enchanted', even though we now prefer secular to supernatural
explanations of what is happening.

A public culture might be seen as the 'language' used to enact
the dominant 'myths' of a society. And, continuing the ideas of
the part-enchantment of even secular societies, to the word
'myth' we might add 'legend', 'icon', 'ritual' and 'festival', also
giving these words meanings that seem relevant to modern
industrial societies.

I will take 'legend' to mean a simple story (whether based on
fact or fiction does not matter) that illustrates a 'myth'. It is
part of the magic of narrative, without which the world would
not be imaginable. As one example of a legend: the story of
Neville Chamberlain's Munich adventure became an admoni-
tory legend in Western Cold War mythology: in his Vietnam

policy President Johnson was showing that 'he had learned the lessons of Munich'. The whole from-log-cabin-to-White-House aspect of the Abraham Lincoln story is a legend of the myth of individualism. The legend of the October Revolution is essential to the Leninist myth of the vanguard party. The legends of the French Revolution play their part in myths both of reform and of reaction. One of the important legends in the myth of Swiss democracy is the story of how people from three small states came together in the thirteenth century at a beautiful meadow at Rütli, and swore a 'perpetual pact' of confederation. In the mountain holiday centre of Koprivshtitsa in Bulgaria, there is a 'Monument to the First Rifle Shot' that recalls a notable uprising against the Turks that is one of the legends of the myth of Bulgarian nationalism; the nearly 200 monuments to the Russo-Turkish War of 1877–78 that are to be found throughout Bulgaria recall legends from a war that, because Bulgarians and Russians fought side by side, is vital to the myth of a history of Russo-Bulgarian community of interests. One of the greatest secular tale-spinnings the world has known has come from the legends of the 'discovery' of the Americas, Asia, Africa and Oceania by European explorers, the settlement of the 'wilderness' (namely land belonging to other people) by European pioneers and the general bringing of civilization to benighted lands; these legends have been the most powerful illustrations of the 'myths' of European racism because they have shown Europeans filling a role determined by destiny. The 'It's a Small World' river ride in Disneyland is devoted to the concept of the community of the world's children where, red and yellow, black and white, all the audio-animatronic dolls sing, 'There's so much that we share/That it's time we're aware/It's a small world after all': but its guidebook warns that the audio-animatronic models of 'fur-capped Cossacks . . . mark our departure from East Europe into mysterious Asia. Here is the exotic world of the Orient, once remote, strange, little known except to a few of the hardiest adventurers.'

Interwoven with the appeal of the simple tales the legends tell are the simple appeals of legendary personalities. Once again, whether or not they existed does not matter: the non-existent William Tell has been the single most effective personality in the Swiss imagination, and his legends are infinitely recyclable, so that he can be taken to mean *anything*. Soviet schoolchildren learn off stories about Lenin as children used to learn off stories of the lives of the saints; United States schoolchildren learn off equally sacred stories about Lincoln and the heroes of 'the American Revolution'. In Hungary children learn stories of the nineteenth-century rebel, Louis Kossuth, seen as a great nationalist and now also seen as a great proto-revolutionary, a precursor of Socialist Hungary; in Sweden schoolchildren learn stories of the sixteenth-century rebel Engelbrekt, seen as a great nationalist and now also seen as a great proto-democrat, a precursor of social-democratic Sweden. In Wales, in the 'marble hall', the ceremonial area of the City Hall in Cardiff, statues in white Serraveza marble portray 'the heroes of Wales'. Throughout the Americas and in Australia and, for that matter, still in some parts of Europe (Portugal, for example) some of the greatest heroes are still 'the discoverers'. The Columbus legend becomes, in the United States, a tribute to 'ethnics'; in Italy and Spain (which both claim Columbus) it is a tribute to the imagination and enterprise of Italian and Spanish predecessors.

Villains are needed as well as heroes: 'Bad King John' has been a useful villain in building mythic views of political freedom for schoolchildren in Britain, the United States, Canada, Australia and New Zealand. Centuries of legendary self-definition lie behind the continuing hatreds between Greeks and Turks. In the Soviet Union, Poland and Yugoslavia, films and television series still roll on, recalling the villainies of the Nazis and, in Yugoslavia (where, in Tito, there is also an heroic leader), they can recall the villainies of the Ustasha, the Chetniks and the occupying Bulgarians, with the Ustasha as reminders of the dangers of Croatian separatism, the Chetniks as reminders of Serbian chauvinism and the Bulgarians as reminders of the Bulgarian irredentism towards Macedonia that is part of the unfinished business of the Second Balkan

War. And there are the comforts of the great morality cycles, varying from one period to the next, and from one country to the other – the western, the gangster movie, the samurai movie, the spy movie, the star wars movie – always assuring us that evil is ever-threatening.

What we are speaking of are examples of mega-legends that bring a sense of anecdote and personality to some of the mega-'myths' of a public culture. But, as suggested in Chapter 1, out of 'the news' there comes, from morning paper to late night bulletin, daily material that, in personality and story, we render legendary. Some of it comes in the obvious form of great, confirming ceremonies – funerals, inaugurations, processions and so forth – that by their very predictability can come through as strongly in telling familiar stories as frescoes and carvings and stained glass did in medieval cathedrals. Some of it comes from old re-enactments. To the Irish Republican Army the British remain useful villains; the sense of legendary romance and adventure the IRA can gain from plotting to kill Britons or blow up their property can save them from contemplating the dullness of routine Irish existence and most of the social conflicts of Ireland; and to those who dominate Britain these re-enactments can confirm their fundamental contempt for the Irish (still a significant ethnic minority in many British cities) and their love of the existing British social order. No sooner was it known that the IRA had tried to kill Mrs Thatcher at Brighton in 1984 than law-and-order rhetoric was extended to the striking British coal miners, as if they also wanted to kill Mrs Thatcher, and even to the whole of the British left. 'Terrorism' itself (whether of the IRA, or Basques, or Corsicans or whatever) has become one of those random television threats that, along with road, rail and air smashes, city fires, floods, forest fires, volcanic eruptions, tornadoes, earthquakes, unusual murders, rapes, robberies, and hijackings can remind us daily of the frailty of human wishes and the uncertain nature of human existence. (Those who fight on 'our side' are not 'terrorists'. They are 'freedom-fighters'.)

Sometimes individual 'news stories' can touch on 'myth' so

strongly that they create new, instant legends. 'Watergate' was a legend that confirmed, for example, the 'myth' of freedom of the press and the 'myth' of checks and balances. In Australia one legend is called, simply, '1975' – recalling the year of the unprecedented dismissal of a prime minister by a governor-general, an action that confirmed, for both sides, the 'myth' of the rule of law (with each side arguing that *it* was the only true interpreter of the Constitution) and the 'myth' of representative democracy (with each side arguing that it alone was representative democracy's true upholder). Paris, along with the revolutionary legends of '1789', '1793', '1830', '1848' and '1871', now has the legend '1968'. Prague also has its '1968', in a legend of reaction. In 1956 there was both the legend of 'Suez' and the legend of 'Hungary'. The changes in the Catholic Church were encapsulated in the two words 'Vatican Two' that seemed to open up whole new styles for being a Catholic. Even where an event is in itself trivial, and will be forgotten in a few weeks, it may be given a legendary presentation. On 23 October 1984 one Israeli cabinet minister tried to raise the price of frozen chickens by 90 per cent. There was a rush on frozen chickens, disarray within the government and, after a night's argument, the increase in the price of frozen chickens was reduced to 24 per cent. This at once 'went down in history' (which is to say about two and a half weeks) as 'the night of the chicken'.

When, in the early 1970s, a blight affected the capitalist 'mixed economies' of a kind that, in the period of 'fine economic tuning', had seemed impossible, there was a 'reality'-maintenance crisis in the 'myth' of free enterprise, as it had stood in the period when the writings of John Maynard Keynes seemed to explain everything: the indicators in most of the prosperous capitalist societies were flashing both unemployment and inflation. How could that be? Just as white blood cells rush to a scene of infection in the body when it is invaded, 'myth'-makers rushed to this scene of infected 'reality'. These 'myth'-makers were not just professional manipulators, however, but were also to be found among the people themselves and, in an act of folk creation, it was among the people that there was provided the necessary 'myth' maintenance as many tens of thousands of ordinary people in the capitalist societies, with some promptings from above, spread the rumour, as it were, that this new crisis was no fault of the system. The rumour went out – the work ethic was still sound: unemployment was not the fault of the system, it was the fault of the unemployed. A new, mythic stereotype was invented by these people out of their own common sense – the stereotype of the dole cheat, the welfare loafer. People would then provide many telling anecdotes from their own experience of such-and-such a long-haired layabout who had made no effort to get a job, or of such-and-such an occasion when so-and-so advertised a staff vacancy and nobody turned up. ('There are plenty of jobs if you take the trouble to look for them.') On top of these acts of folk creation the professional manipulators then arose, preaching that it was not capitalism that was at fault but government interference: all that was needed was a 'return' to free enterprise fundamentalism. Only give capitalism a fair go, and it would work.

More regular than the great folk productions are the small daily transformations of 'the news' in which, in continuing morality plays, we constantly reinforce mythic stereotypes. Sport provides one of the best examples. In sport there are endless morality plays, telling stories of collectivism or individualism; of the virtues of hard work, ambition, sacrifice, technique, loyalty; of class, gender, ethnic, race and national division; and the ambiguities and tensions of 'the rules'. Sport provides a serial morality play of much of the public culture of modern industrial societies. 'The news' also constantly re-enacts morality plays that remind us of the roles expected of men and women. There may be an occasional prominent female politician, but the 'the news' is still very largely the world of men. They are all men who stand above the Lenin Mausoleum on the great national days of the Red Square marches, and even if a woman were to become President of the United States it would be mainly male officials who would stand on the Capitol steps surrounding her on Inauguration

Day. In both capitalist and Communist countries, women do not play the top roles in 'the news'. Indeed, only very recently have women been 'allowed' to *present* 'serious' news, that is, to give the appearance of 'interpreting' news. In the capitalist societies women are mothers, entertainers, victims, beauties; the 'new Soviet woman' is presented as 'a good mother and a good production worker'.

As another example of the daily reinforcement of mythic stereotypes there are, in the capitalist societies, the 'myths' of individualism and mythic stereotypes of individualists which allow us to construct further morality plays from 'the news', reaffirming the virtues of individualism. French farmers seen on the television news dumping their produce on the roads in protest against EEC policies can be seen by French viewers as epitomes of French individualism (the family farm being one of the most emotive of all symbols of economic freedom), even if what they are protesting about is a threat to some of the protection given to them by the EEC and their own government. In Australia, one of the stereotypes of individualism is that of 'the little Aussie battler', the little person, gamely surviving in a tough world, and Australians in following the news can push this stereotype so far that Alan Bond, the millionaire backer of the million-dollar yacht that won the America's Cup in 1983, could be seen as a 'little Aussie battler'.

There are also the great stereotypes of region, through which we can translate 'the news' into morality plays of mythic experience. In Italy, the north and the south suggest two different types of civilization; in the United States, 'East Coast', 'Midwest', 'the South', 'the West' and 'West Coast' are words filled with dramas of human difference; in Norway there are two different versions of the Norwegian language and they can summon up stereotypes of two different ways of being Norwegian – one folkish and environmentalist; one elitist and developmentalist; in Czechoslovakia Slovaks can see the Czechs as a Germanized people, beer-drinkers, tunnel-visioned, and they can see themselves as a Mediterranean people, wine-drinkers, light-hearted, shrewd; but the Czechs can see themselves as forward-looking sophisticates while the Slovaks can be seen as traditional-minded peasants. Such stereotypes of difference in the perceived national texture can be maintained in 'the news', if this is, as it were, permissible – or they can be suppressed. In Great Britain, where many people have maintained elaborate social antennae that can scan another person's attire, posture and accent and produce an instant class image, for many years the British Broadcasting Corporation spoke only with one voice, the educated southern English voice of the rulers: ethnic variants in accent were merely comic, or romantic; class variants could be deviant. Unless it is at some time of extraordinary conflict, a nation's soldiery can fall into comforting stereotypes, so that they are not only brave warriors – with their nicknames they are also affectionate puppies. Farmers also have their comforting names, so do city types. Whole peoples can see themselves as stereotypes in their behaviour, as the Dutch do, amusing themselves that their concept of *Gesellig* is untranslatable.

One of the great 'reality' creations of the nineteenth century was to create the rival stereotypes of *owner* and *worker* as a fundamental division of human society. One of the great 'reality' creations of twentieth-century liberal-democratic capitalist societies (above all, the United States) has been the stereotype of 'middle class'. Much of 'the news' can be seen in terms of this stereotype. 'The news' can become, partly, a mythic story of challenges to, and the survival of, the values of 'the middle class'. On the other hand, one of the great 'reality' maintenances of the Communist states has been to use the stereotype of 'the worker' so that the societies of those states can be seen as societies almost entirely consisting of workers (apart from surviving class enemies), presided over by 'worker-presidents'.

Hanging over everything else except the stereotypes of gender and race are the great mythic shapes associated with capitalism and socialism. In the capitalist societies this battle can be seen as going on at home as well as abroad but in both

capitalist and Communist societies it is above all an international battle, or, at times, Armageddon. What, on one side,
can seem perfectly natural seems the crassest propaganda on
the other side. In the 1980 Olympic Games in Moscow the big
show the Soviets made was of Soviet multiculturalism. No
doubt all this swinging of skirts in folk dances was inspired by
propagandist considerations – an Olympic Games opening *is* a
staged show – but as such things go it could seem unexcep-
tionable, and even related to what is left of the Olympic rhetoric
of internationalism. But in the United States this was seen (in so
far as it *was* seen) as pure political propaganda. Yet when the
1984 Games opened at Los Angeles a show was put on that
displayed 'the settlement' of the United States in terms of
unadulterated national chauvinism: dancers formed an outline
of what is now the United States; other dancers danced in with
their wagon trains, then set up towns. A travesty of United
States history continued. The whole show ended in patriotic
song. Even to people from other capitalist societies this could
seem an extraordinary excess of United States chauvinist zeal,
and it was the opposite of Olympic international rhetoric. To
most people in the United States (where it was a particularly
patriotic year) all this seemed 'perfectly natural', yet imagine
their uproar if in 1980 the Soviets had put on a song and dance
show commemorating the spread of world Communism.

In attempting to bring to life the enchantment of the public
culture by 'myths' I will introduce two other words to add to
'legend': 'icon' and 'ritual'. Others could be introduced; I am
not trying to be definitive but rather to illustrate the continuing
'tribal' nature, as it were, of the cultural forms of a modern
public culture.

'Icon' is a simple idea: secularized, like the other words, and
extracted from its religious origin, it is taken here to mean an
image that both records and carries a particularly heavy
conceptual and emotional weight. The examples are obvious. If
they are not obvious, they are not icons. A representation, for
example, of a hammer and sickle, or the Statue of Liberty, or a

crown are, in effect, sacred political images, as can be the image
of a great national hero. A representation of a monument can
also have this political magic – the Spassky Tower in the
Kremlin; the dome of the United States Capitol; Big Ben, the
clock on the British parliament building; Eidsvoll Hall in
Norway, scene of the making of the first Norwegian Constitution. A representation of a building can have other complexes
of connotations – Chartres Cathedral, for example; or the
Royal Castle in Warsaw; or the Parthenon; or the Yasukuni
Shrine in Tokyo; St Peter's in Rome; the Sydney Opera House.
Images of animals can be iconic and not only those heraldic
lions and eagles. At the 1980 Olympic Games the Soviets used a
bear to show how warm-hearted and cuddly they were; at the
time when Australia was seen as 'riding on the sheep's back'
because of its prominence in the world wool market, one of the
most revered national icons, reassuring Australians of both
economic stability and moral virtue, was the head of a merino
ram; in its tourist literature, South Africa is represented by a
young springbok, light-footed and graceful. Granite can be one
of the icons of the Finnish imagination; oil rigs can be icons of
national prosperity; so can sheafs of wheat (one of the oldest of
all signs of material goodness), or container ships (as symbols
of exports), or graphs with rising curves, or computers, or
automation consoles. In Idaho one of the symbols of material
well-being is the potato. Once the greatest of all icons of
prosperity, factory smokestacks, have, to some, now become
signs of technological decrepitude. There is no point in
extending this list, except to note that in the societies overtly
dominated by political parties some of the most profound
iconography is to be found in posters and that in the liberal-
democratic capitalist societies it is to be found in the logos of
brand goods. This is the new heraldry: in the motel strips that
lie outside United States towns, and sometimes run beside a
four-lane highway right through them so that no town is left,
the logos are suspended high above the traffic, like the
glittering shields of medieval nobility. In these societies the
most complex iconography is, above all, to be found in

advertising. Unless a television commercial or a display ad in a magazine or a billboard is iconic, it has failed. In most of President Reagan's commercials in the 1984 elections there was no concern with politics: most of the advertisements were made up of familiar advertising icons of wholesomeness, as if the President were as good for you as homogenized milk, or old-fashioned bread made with 'natural' bran fibre.

Ritual is *instrumental*, in the sense that it is trying to get something done (as in praying for rain, or voting, or putting on a protest demonstration); and it is *expressive*, in the sense that it symbolizes ways in which people come together. It involves the participants symbolically in a common enterprise, calling attention to their relatedness and joint interests in a compelling way, promoting conformity and satisfaction in conformity. A rain dance is not only concerned with getting rain, it is also an expression of community values. Putting on a protest demonstration is not only seen as a way of achieving some change; it can also be a demonstration of political style (the belief that it is through demonstrations and other forms of protest that change should occur) and of literary style (the placards), musical style (the songs), personal style (the clothes), all proclaiming the special 'reality' of 'protest'. And by using a 'them' against whom to protest, the solidarity of 'us' can be confirmed. Edelman, in *The Symbolic Uses of Politics*, is concerned with a polling day as ritual. A polling day is instrumental in the sense that voters can see themselves as electing the government; it is 'expressive' in the sense that elections draw attention to common social ties and a common type of political 'reality' and to the 'legitimation' of the government that comes out of the election. Yet even in a liberal democracy with a two-party or two-coalition system, all the voters are doing is making a choice offered by the party structure, and in a liberal democracy with a complex multi-party system – Israel, for instance, or the Netherlands – government-choosing will be settled later, in private dealing between the parties. In any case, scarcely anything of how the new government will act will necessarily have been determined by the election. The 'real' function of polling day might be seen to lie in the proclamations of social values, just as the 'real' significance of the preceding election campaign (with its many icons) might be seen as an act of public theatre emphasizing certain views of 'reality'.

There are other types of voting rituals in which by actions with their bodies (making marks on paper or putting up their hands) people can demonstrate their belief that they are about to be 'represented', and by their acts also give legitimacy to those who are about to 'represent' them – whether the executives of a trade union, or the board of directors of a business corporation, or the committee of some voluntary organization. And in the Communist societies a polling day is a simple declaration by the voters that they will be 'represented' by candidates who have already been decided for them, and where all kinds of other decisions that have been made privately, whether in the supreme Soviet or in a local works collective, are then voted on publicly, to show, by all those raised hands or markings on paper or castings of ballots, that there is absolute unanimity about everything.

In capitalist societies, Christmas shopping is a ritual exemplifying how, although doing things with special purposes in mind (instrumentally), what we are doing can also be expressive, upholding mythic 'realities'. People buy Christmas presents with special purposes in mind, yet the very means by which they do this – shopping – gives a special significance to the bought gift. As well as a celebration of the family and, for some, of Christian belief, Christmas becomes a celebration of the values of shopping – and of the general consumer ethic of the capitalist world.

Dominance in a public culture

Other illustrations could be given of the 'tribal' nature of cultural forms in modern societies that aid the enchantment of the public culture with 'myth'. The 'festival' is one, a ritualized break from routine that defines certain values in an atmosphere of joy in fellowship – to be found, for example, in annual holidays or in the sightseeing tour, or in the great occasions of sport, or in the office party, or in many other special events – and in the enormous bodies of stored 'learning' that support modern 'realities'. These may require vast libraries to contain them, but they can have the same functions in 'reality' maintenance as tribal oral lore, memorized by elders. But it is time to recall that we are *not* dealing with tribes. Words such as 'myth', 'legend', 'icon', 'ritual' and 'festival' are useful in pointing to what cultural forms in the public culture of a modern society are similar to those in all cultures: but a public culture, although it has similarities to a tribal culture, is not part of a tribal society. To describe a tribal culture is (virtually) to describe how everyone in a tribe usually behaves. A modern public culture is not a signifier of commonality. It is merely (in part) a pretence at one. A weakness in much of the use made of Gramsci is a lack of distinction between those parts of a public culture that are truly normative (hegemonic in Gramsci's sense), permeating the whole society or most of it, and providing it with ingrained movements of body and mind ('common sense'), and those parts that are merely pseudo-dominant, pretending to universality, but not fully permeating the society at all.

To say this is not to question the significance of a modern public culture, but to point to how its significance takes two different forms – those that provide the 'common sense' of most, or much, of the society, so that people know how to behave; and those that, although not universally or even widely normative, are nevertheless *dominant* within the public culture itself. Such dominance may be limited, but it can lead to a coercive monopoly of what purports to be public opinion. People often think of propaganda primarily in terms of persuasion but, as Jacques Ellul suggests in his book *Propaganda*, it can be thought of not as orthodoxy (common belief) but as orthopraxy (common practice): propaganda, he suggests, might be thought of as not dealing primarily with modifying beliefs and ideas but with provoking (or, one might add, suppressing) action. A coercive monopoly of public opinion can force participation, either actively or at least passively. There can seem no other possible behaviour. The way in which I would put it is that there can be a bullying (or sometimes a seductive) monopolization of public culture – not necessarily persuading everybody or even most people, but scaring off dissidence by breaking it up into hidden fragments or discouraging dissidence by making it seem un-'real' or 'immature'. The public culture can be seen not only as showing people how to act but also as terrorizing them (or, more gently, discouraging them) into not acting. The application of this to the overtly propagandized societies is obvious: but one can look at the liberal-democratic societies in the same way. In a liberal-democratic society, to imagine the dominance of a public culture one does not have to imagine, for example, that everyone is persuaded by everything that appears in 'the news'; it can be enough to understand merely that 'the news' is dominated by certain 'realities' and 'myths' and that this can lead to a fragmentation of contrary 'realities' and strategies. This can happen in something of the same way as can happen in the more overtly propagandized societies. There is not necessarily a terror (McCarthyism was unusual), except in the continuing fears of the sack or of other job failures, but there can be a weakening and a sense of powerlessness and loneliness. (It is also true that there can be an opposite effect: the public culture can seem so remote or antipathetic to groups of people, or even to most people, that its continued public dominance helps to make it seem tyrannical or even ridiculous: its very monopoly might help strengthen the opposition to it.)

Whether or not the public culture is pervasive, it can be of enormous importance to know what is dominant in it. And this is something one can discover by looking and thinking. What is prominent in a public culture? What 'realities' dominate it? How does it suggest society is organized? What promises does it make? What kinds of people seem to be the principal actors? What are the principal actions? In what ways does it enact its principal 'myths'?

Part Two:

'Myths' of the
Public Culture

4. 'Myths' of Industrialism and Modernity

Ingredients

Like any other attempt to analyse complex social habits, this attempt at discussing the main 'myths' in the public cultures of modern industrial societies will present as if they were separate ingredients habits that in fact don't occur separately, but are always found together – sometimes in mixtures, sometimes as compounds. Since one can't say everything at once, they will also have to be presented in some chronological order but it will be understood, I hope, that just because one 'ingredient' is presented before another does not mean that it is, somehow, more basic. There is one distinction. I shall begin with those 'myths' that are most common to all the 'modern', 'industrial' societies (and, in fact, define them). These are the kinds of 'myths' that in overall shape are much the same, from one country to another, whatever the political complexions of those countries.

So the first 'myths' to be discussed will be those elements in their public cultures that define these societies as 'industrial' and as 'modern'. Then will come two 'myths' in their public cultures – those of gender chauvinism and race chauvinism – that are pre-modern, but that have taken new forms in the industrial era. Then the 'myths' of national character, national identity and strategic imagination by which modern nation-states can be defined in their public cultures. After this, two interwoven sets of questions – the forms of what we think of as 'political' and 'economic' control in modern states and the varying mythic 'legitimations' by which 'political' and 'economic' power are explained and justified.

To these, in terms of rhetoric, might be added selections from the traditional virtues. In European societies these are selections from Judaeo-Christian and/or Graeco-Roman and/or humanist-enlightened rhetoric. But these are merely the spices in public cultures. The same words can be used in different contexts to bring out quite different flavours. I was so struck by the wording of the following sign in one country I was visiting that I wrote it down. It said: 'There is one road to freedom. Its milestones are obedience, diligence, honesty, order, cleanliness, temperance, truth, sacrifice, and love of country.' The place I saw this was in the administration block of the concentration camp at Dachau.

The 'myths' so far listed – industrialism and modernity; gender and race chauvinism; national character, national identity and national strategic imagination; and the forms of economic and political control and their varying 'legitimations' – are what might be thought of as the universal strands in the public cultures of modern industrial societies. They are to be found in all of these societies. There are five other elements which should be added, but all five are not found in all public cultures. These are what I shall describe as the 'myths' of 'the critics' culture', 'the labour culture', 'the neo-traditional culture', 'the religious culture' and 'the ethnic compromise'. In some public cultures one or more of these can occur as part of the central, directive elements of the public culture – those elements of the public culture that are least challenged and/or most dominant – but some or all of them can also appear in a public culture not as directive, but in conflict. If this happens, their presence indicates the limits of the areas of conflict that are, as it were, permissible in the public culture. In other public cultures, however, some or all of these may be so efficiently suppressed that they may not appear as part of the public face of the society, although they may still exist, submerged.

The accumulation of capital

First, the 'industrial' 'myths'. As to what these might mean,

Foucault provides the neatest answer in *Discipline and Punish* when he speaks of 'the accumulation of capital' and 'the accumulation of men'. In this respect, the Soviet Union and the United States, Japan and France, Bulgaria and Australia can be seen, in overall outline, as the same: in all of them, capital surpluses are accumulated centrally for investment and, in all of them, humans are 'normalized' to fit into 'working life'.

Whether a society is seen as socialist or capitalist, an overriding concern can be a belief in investment as a prime mover in that society. In fact one of the perceived distinctions between 'socialist' and 'capitalist' can be on strategies for centralized investment. They both do it. It's a question of how they do it. With this distinction, socialism can be seen by capitalists as a strategy for centralizing investment in the bureaucracies of the state, and capitalism can be seen by socialists as a strategy for centralizing investment in the dominating transnational business corporations. Before the modern era it would have been quite unimaginable that one of the prime ways in which humans might see divisions between themselves would be based on attitudes to investment.

In that period, if the rulers had anything left over they were likely to spend it on display, or entertainment, or on wars (that were themselves, amongst other things, part display and part 'entertainment'); the ordinary people, if they were able to save anything at all, might save it for feasting. If people did 'invest', it would usually mean simply buying more of the same kind of property, rather than 'improving' existing properties with what we now call 'greater capitalization'.

There were, however, primitive precursors – such as Venice. Number Five of Venice's sea buses, the *circolare*, at one stage of its route enters a wide canal through two tall brown and white crenellated towers and then passes a set of large, brick buildings, brown, with marble facings. This whole complex, walled inside crenellated high battlements, is what is left of the *arsenale* ('the house of industry') which for centuries was the productive base of Venice's empire of commerce and conquest, dominating in its heyday all the sea trade between the Black Sea and the Mediterranean and between the Mediterranean and Flanders. It is a very quiet place now, but, when it was the centre of Venice's ship building, repairing and outfitting, its 15,000 workmen, employed in something approaching production-line techniques, worked at such a multiplicity of tasks that it gave Dante some of his images of the Inferno. In the Correr Museum a room is devoted to explaining the *arsenale*, but what explains it even more are the two other rooms in the Correr that display the coins of imperial Venice and, much more important, the book-keeping systems of revenue and expenditure and investment of a commercial oligarchy that, above all others, was devoted to perfecting the use of money as a sharp, precise measurement of action. When tourists pass through the Ducal Palace, with its opulence of marble and gilt and vast allegorical frescoes, they are passing through the committee rooms of rich oligarchs who were concerned not only with profits but also with central investment.

Other precursors can be found elsewhere in Italy, and in Flanders, and in the Hanseatic League towns. What is entirely novel now is the widespread practice of capital accumulation and investment, its huge scale and extreme centralization – and the 'myths' that explain and justify it with their 'realities'. 'Reality' is seen as economic and material, just as in other societies it was seen as religious and supernatural. Both for Communists and capitalists 'the economic' can be used to explain everything, and to justify almost anything. The economic can seem the principal basis of policy – the only sensible way to get things done. The only practical programmes are economic programmes. Even programmes for intellectual betterment (educational programmes, for example) or social reform (equality programmes, for example) can be seen primarily and sometimes, in effect, almost exclusively as economic programmes. Politicians express their moral preferences in the size of budget appropriations. In fact, 'the economic' becomes a principal form of human expression. It is through 'the economic' that individuals can express themselves, in conspicuous spending on consumer goods, knowing the value of things by their price; and governments or industrial corporations can express themselves in conspicuous spending on costly capital investment programmes. Once, a community might have acquired prestige from putting up a cathedral: now it can express its importance in an expensive hydro-electricity programme.

'Realities' are sometimes most tellingly expressed in the precise measurements contained in graphs and statistical tables and, although all that these measure are goods and services on which a price has been put, it can be on these figures that most social policy is formed. A person works in a cake factory. That is 'economic'. It gets into the GDP figures. A person bakes a cake at home. That is not 'economic'. It does not get into the GDP figures. Someone works as a gardener in a public park. That is 'economic'. The same person does some gardening at home. That is not 'economic'; it does not get into the GDP figures. For much of the industrial era, conceptions of what was truly economic could become even more limited, so that the prime economic realities could be seen as in the production of things rather than services. Manufacturing could be seen as a central dynamic, but even manufacturing itself could take second place to 'heavy' industry and the production of machines. This could seem the real capital investment. This was 'industrialization'. Even more basic could seem vast schemes for the 'industrialization' of farming, vast mining schemes, gas and oil pipelines, schemes for dams and irrigation and, perhaps above all, schemes for generating electricity ('Communism,' said Lenin, 'equals Soviet power plus electrification').

No human policy could seem realistic that did not begin with plans for industrialization. In Stalin's Soviet Union the principal propaganda themes were those of capital accumulation; production statistics were the principal test of human striving; the virtues of socialism were epitomized in the construction of the Dnepropetrovsk Dam. After the Second World War, industrialization was seen as the precondition for prosperity and happiness in 'the Third World', even though if all the Third World countries had been able to 'industrialize' up to the level of the front runners it was doubtful if the world could continue to supply the necessary raw materials.

Now, in the most technologically advanced capitalist societies, these emphases no longer seem to work as well as they did in the period of the long post-war boom, with its miracle of low unemployment and low inflation appearing side by side in statistical tables: but people go on believing in them. In the United States, one school of thought saw an answer to this problem by 're-definition upwards of the level of natural unemployment' (a superb example of defining social conflict away by inventing a new 'reality'). The more usual answer, especially in countries other than the United States, is simply to try harder at doing better what has been demonstrated no longer to work. This was the basis of 'Thatcherism'. But to the magic of these old beliefs there can be added, if in contradiction, beliefs that what is now basic to human happiness are silicon chips, computers, automation, 'high technology'. This can allow an almost pure concentration on the abstract beauties of capital investment, since in automation programmes few diversions come from a distracting concern with human beings.

In the ideal images of its enthusiasts, the industrial society can be seen as itself a factory, rationally organized, with 'communications' (freeways, railways, natural gas pipelines, aircraft routes, electricity grids, teleprinters) linking its productive centres, with a constant concern with increasing rationality and efficiency, and with a constant pride in increasing figures of 'economic growth'. The factory-nation is seen as an 'economy' that can be 'managed'. The tests of 'economic management' are to be found in the figures of 'growth'. Gross Domestic Product should increase, or, more exactly, 'GDP' divided by the number of the population should show a 'per capita increase'. If this happens, there has been 'growth'. This shows an increase in 'productivity' and no human progress is imaginable without constant increases in 'productivity'. (If the figures do not show 'growth', then the society is 'stagnating'.) Yet as a basis for policy, 'growth' statistics have two remarkable characteristics. One is that a concentration on them enormously emphasizes the importance of the organizations that sell goods and services, as if these organizations were the prime springs of the society, but it does not emphasize human inventiveness and social organization. The other is that they are not a measure of how people live. 'GDP' statistics do not measure material well-being in a society (and they certainly do not measure overall human fulfilment) and even if they were a measure of material well-being they would not be a measure of its spread amongst the people. All that they measure are goods and services on which there is a money price. Yet on the simple indication of whether, according to certain statistical conventions, they have registered 'growth', whole nations are taken as successes or as failures. When the post-war boom ended in the capitalist societies and the crisis of combined unemployment and inflation began, the response of the autonomic nervous system of the rulers was not to consider the possibility of adopting different perspectives in policy-making. The concern remained and continues to remain with 'growth'.

The accumulation of labour

We pass now from the accumulation of capital to the other aspect of industrialism – 'the accumulation of men', as Foucault put it, so that 'the time of individuals is integrated into a production apparatus', turning them into 'labour power'. Foucault suggested that 'the disciplinarization of the workforce' may have been a precondition for industrialism (rather than the other way round). He suggested that (for reasons that don't matter here) the processes of 'normalization' began in the seventeenth and eighteenth centuries – in army barracks, police forces, factories, prisons, workhouses, lunatic asylums, schools, hospitals. It was then that there was an extension, beyond the monasteries, of such forms of discipline as the timetable, the exercise, hierarchical observation, the examination. In this he saw an emphasis on the control of the body itself. 'Power relations have an immediate hold upon it;

they invest it, mark it, train it, torture it, force it to carry out tasks, to perform ceremonies, to emit signs . . . the body becomes a useful force only if it is both a productive body and a subjected body.'

In the period when the factory was seen as the typical form of industrialism, the time and motion studies of 'Taylorism', the doctrines of F.W. Taylor, one of the pioneers of 'scientific management', seemed a perfect example of what Foucault would later describe as the 'sequestration' of individuals 'to the production apparatus by producing habits by means of a plan of compulsions, teachings and punishments'.

Modern industrial states could not survive without a 'labour force' of human bodies trained in logistical conformity (to play their part in the great transport systems of the cities), in punctuality (to arrive at work on time), and, when they are at work, in talents such as performing set, rostered tasks, obedience and marginal adaptability (learning new instructions). Among the potent symbols of industrial societies are the queue, the roster, the factory whistle. Schooling can be seen as a training for 'life' in that it drills us in punctuality and queuing; in working within a timetable at set tasks for set periods; in neatness, cleanliness and obedience; in skills in learning new techniques; in working when we are tired and bored; in learning to work within the rules of an institution and to accept its hierarchical structure. Given this, perhaps it is not so much the factory whistle that is a symbol of an industrial society, but the school bell. In an essay, 'The Secondary School: Administrative Wonder and Educational Absurdity', the Australian educationalist Kevin Harris recalls that in a schoolroom there can sometimes be that enervating moment when the time has come for the ringing of the school bell but it doesn't ring. People don't know what to do. They ask each other: 'What's happened to the bell?'

Foucault is right to concentrate more on human bodies than on human belief. There is no greater example of the power of habit than that it should have become part of the 'common sense' of our bodies. In a sense, it is with our bodies that we can demonstrate a 'myth'. But articulated belief does also come into it – most notably in the 'work ethic', a myth as strong in the public cultures of Communist societies as it is in capitalist societies. (One of the slogans displayed in Soviet streets is 'Glory to Work'. One of the aims of the educational reforms introduced into the Soviet Union in the 1980s was to 'help gear education and character development at school to the economic activities of the nation and to make vocation-related studies a major component of school life'.) In the work ethic, the only proper avenue to human dignity and welfare is seen as through income-producing labour. Those who engage in paid labour are useful. The others are (in effect) useless. (However, with varying degrees of graciousness and generosity, both the Communist societies and the 'welfare state' apparatus of the capitalist societies sustain the 'useless' by pushing some of the surplus in their direction.) The 'myth' of the work ethic is one of the most magically glowing cults of industrialism (not in the sense of creative production, but in the sense of putting your nose to the grindstone in paid labour). Paid work can be seen as giving a central meaning to life: it becomes a moral good in itself. In the capitalist societies links between work and reward are stressed. Success continues to be seen as something that can be earned by hard work and initiative. (In actuality, for most wage earners, working overtime provides the only available relation between hard work and reward; other than this, their reward depends not on individual effort but on the state of the labour market, and in most countries that is a result of union-management bargaining. So far as initiative is concerned, the very success of industrialism depends on most people doing what they are told to do. If they all displayed 'initiative', society as it exists would disintegrate.) Even in the Communist societies there is much boosting (called 'socialist competition') of hard work and its rewards. One of life's rewards is to be honoured by the title 'Hero of Labour'.

The way in which, when unemployment again returned to the capitalist societies, many of the ordinary people blamed unemployment on the unemployed themselves was a mark of the continuing intensity of the 'myth' of the work ethic: it remains to be seen what happens if there *is* 'an upward adjustment of the natural rate of unemployment'. If the 'myths' of the work ethic continue to shine their light in societies in which there is no longer official belief in full employment and no alternative to it as a legitimate means to dignity and welfare within those societies, there will be, on the one hand, the pure and the whole and, on the other hand, outside the walls of the shining city, the lepers. Already there is a crucial shift from the differences between working- and middle-class people, to those between the employed and unemployed.

One of the paradoxes of the industrial societies is that while there is an enormous emphasis on production so that production becomes, in a sense, a god, most people are remarkably 'unproductive'. They are engaged in routine tasks in which they would get the sack if they displayed any creativity. Their main reward is to be found in their pay packets; their main consolation can come not from work itself but from the companionship of workmates, and from the bulwarks of 'us' and 'them'. Among the 'myths' by which many live is that work is, of necessity, an unpleasant obligation carried on out there, 'in the real world'. It is commonplace among observers of industrialism that, when most production moved from the home and the extended family, there was a split between 'work' and 'the economy' on the one hand and private life and the family on the other and that any productive labour in which people may be engaged at home was seen as merely a 'hobby' or a 'leisure activity'. Thus it is seen as self-indulgent (if harmlessly so) when people enjoy themselves in some activity that, if they were paid for it, might seem creative or productive.

Perhaps as important as 'the work ethic' is the 'myth' of 'the home ethic', built up out of one of the most significant transformations of industrialism in which ordinary people developed an aspiration for, and, for the most part, achieved in varying degrees, what were seen as some of the consolations of bourgeois family life. Amongst many (including many of the activists in what became, after heroic struggles, the labour movement) there was an initial puritanism, in the disciplines and 'myths' of self-reliance, manifesting itself in thrift and moderation in bodily indulgences, in cleanliness, and in decorum in dress and manner. This was one way in which, faced with the insults of working life, industrial proletarian families could obtain self-regard. This type of restraint would now wreck the capitalist societies with their utter need to keep consumer spending high, but it still has its place in the Communist societies and in fact provides one of the bases of attacks on the moral degeneracy of the West. This 'mythic' belief in the improving values of self-restraint also provided much of the moral tone in another transformation that began in the nineteenth century – when it began to seem possible that every 'deserving' family had a right to a 'home of its own' (although whether or not the dwelling place should also be 'owned' varied from society to society) and that it was only in home life that there could be autonomy. (That this autonomy might be mainly for the patriarchs among the workers was nicely brought out in the way in which a common nineteenth-century phrase used to describe the new style was that it was one of 'manly independence', yet, for women, home was not a retreat, but a workplace.)

Obviously, this 'home ethic' provided a useful form of social control (and in the 1930s both Hitler and Stalin were also to proclaim their faith in the family), but this does not necessarily mean that the 'myths' of home life came from a conspiracy by the early bourgeois masters. These 'myths' might also be seen, at least initially, as a creation from among the people themselves. It is worth remembering that for the new industrial proletariat of the nineteenth century the alternatives to 'respectability' were the slums in the industrializing cities. In some ways these were not unlike the Nazi concentration camps or the black 'townships' in South Africa: they were a way of cheaply containing the desperate, for whom there were no remedies.

In the industrialized cities, the 'myths' of the home ethic continue to provide puzzles for those who seek social change.

One line of criticism runs that the 'privatization' of family life can be seen as a form of social discipline: it helps accommodate people to the monotony and lack of autonomy of paid labour by making 'work' seem necessarily detached from the rest of their lives. And it is also anti-communal. What appears to be the comparative autonomy of family life can be seen as a kind of sop, diminishing the possibility of collective action in the workplace. But this attitude may be based on a romantic view of the workplace as a centre of crafts. What happens in many modern workplaces can lead not to collective action, but to *collectivized* action, action collectivized by the authorities. Here there is a contrast with 'private life'. The autonomy of private life allows for most people at least the physical opportunity for creative productive activity, even if the public culture obscures realization of this. In 'industrialized' work this opportunity becomes less and less. For most wage earners, there is no hope for creative work in 'the real world' of paid labour. But there occur many examples, in some societies more than others, of forms of neighbourhood collective action (and it's worth remembering that in some societies where there still seems to be 'traditional' communalism there is nevertheless anomic behaviour).

With the ideals of 'the home' and 'family life' so generally spread among the industrial societies, it might be a more prudent strategy for collectivist reformers to begin by accepting some of the 'home ethic' (without its patriarchalism) and, as it were, looking for the good in it, especially the vestigial possibilities for creativity or even self-creation, and exploring it as a basis for social change. In that sense, it could be the Soviet Union where the greatest potential exists for democratic communalism – although it is not at present imaginable how the opportunity would come in such a police society, or, indeed, in *any* modern industrial state. There is the continuous manoeuvring by the Soviet authorities – in, for example, all those meetings at which people put their hands up in a ritual of unanimity about decisions that have already been made elsewhere – and there is the system of informers, but there is also a genuine communal feeling: the 'myth' of the *kollektiv* is characteristic of Soviet society to an extent that can alarm individualists from capitalist societies and, to United States individualists, can seem one of the characteristics most wrong with the Soviet peoples and the Chinese.

'Myths' of modernity

What we are discussing when we discuss questions of social change like these is one aspect of how humans might improve their general condition – not by religious practice, with a view to an afterlife, but here and now. This is an appropriate point to move from the 'myths' of industrialism to the 'myths' of modernity. It is 'modern' to consider that human improvement might be obtained not by supernatural action but by rational human decision and by rational human action, in the assumption that happiness is not a state achievable only after death, but can be obtained here on earth. In this regard, as with the 'myths' of industrialism, we find that the 'myths' of the modern are common to both capitalism and Communism – the possibility of rationality, of progress, of human happiness and perfectability and of human control over destiny.

Just as Foucault suggested that the developing disciplining of human bodies in the seventeenth and eighteenth centuries in at least parts of Europe may have been a precondition for the development of industrialism (rather than the other way round), one might also argue that the developing intellectual optimism of the seventeenth and eighteenth centuries may also have been a precondition for modern industrialism. This is not to say that it was not related to material changes. It seems to be part of the same story as the successes of the new merchants and traders and 'discoverers'. But there had already begun to develop the growth of science, with its seeking for secular explanations of earthly events and for 'laws' that would explain the universe so convincingly that humans, by taking thought and engaging in rational action, could see themselves as having control over nature and over their own destiny. And these faiths of the eighteenth century have continued.

Rationality, for example, is still a basic 'myth'. In the capitalist societies it can take the form of that belief in the rationality of the market, associated with the name of Adam Smith, in which it is believed that out of all the individual selfish decisions in buying and selling there will come, as if by an 'invisible hand', a 'centre of repose and continuance'; or it can take the form of that belief in the rationality of economists associated with John Maynard Keynes, in which the irrationalities of the market are seen as being offset by rational interventions by governments. In either case it can be expressed in the most rational of all languages – mathematics – in the precise measurement of human affairs by money. In socialist societies there can be a turning away from what are seen as the irrationalities, imprecisions and inhumanities of the market and a preference for a 'plan', a rational device also adopted, in practice, in capitalist societies, by their governments and by all of their business corporations who, although they may attack government planning as 'socialist', themselves attempt to plan their affairs with the precision of a battle, sometimes using military-style language ('targets', 'sales drive', 'strategic objectives', etc.) and often producing military-style fiascos.

Just as rationality produced 'laws' in science, for social organizations it produced 'rules'. It was in the eighteenth century that the first modern 'constitutions' were composed setting out the rules for political life – in the United States, in France and by now in almost every country in the world. As Max Weber pointed out, 'the rules', ever more detailed, become one of the principal 'legitimations' of power, acquiring their magic partly from their very remoteness, so that we obey not the office holder but the office he holds. At school, we learn how to obey 'the rules' and as we move from one place to the next we know we must read, and obey, the instructions. One of the great dramas of sport is the tension it constantly demonstrates between action and 'the rules'.

And, as Weber also pointed out, there is an increasing demand for expertness, and for the 'credentialling', according to 'the rules', of those (and only those) who are judged fit to do this or that. Such a class of people is essential to the strategies of modernity, as part of the general process of specialization. With the 'myth' of expertness there has developed the prospect (once provided only by the Church) of a *career* movement upwards, in what Burton Bledstein in *The Culture of Profes-sionalism* describes as 'a pre-established total pattern of organized professional activity, with upward movement through recognized preparatory stages and advancement based on merit and bearing honour'. As Bledstein says, this gives people a 'vertical vision'. It compels them 'to look upward, forever reaching towards their potential . . . upward, towards the future'. A survey was carried out in the Soviet Union in 1977 because of the difficulty in recruiting staff for blue-collar jobs; it showed that a majority of the young people surveyed preferred a *career* to blue-collar work. There are strong connections between the idea of a career – with its images of 'stages' and 'progress' – and the ideas of modernity.

The 'myth' of progress, of what used to be called 'improve-ment' in industrializing Britain, is still thoroughly embedded in the public culture. One can see this, however, only if one recognizes that what is meant by 'progress' and 'improvement' is decided in the mind of the improver. 'Improvement' is a technique for making things better, but 'better' only according to a point of view. The essence of 'improvement' is faith in a rational expertness, belief in human control over nature and destiny. The 'discoverers' were in this sense 'improvers'. They brought 'civilization' to 'the wilderness'. Hitler was, in this sense, an 'improver' – his mind was filled with the dreams of a would-be engineer and architect. Science and technology are constantly 'improving': the reputation of their 'researchers' lives on novelties in discovery and invention. Economists see 'improvement' in ever-continuing 'economic growth'. Even the crassest producer of consumer goods is an 'improver', committed to building the constantly 'improved' mouse trap. The advertising industry, like scientific and technological research, lives on novelty. Fashions in taste sweep through societies like a speeded-up movie. In 'high art', novelty, the principle of making it new, became a defining characteristic of modernity.

The scientists and the engineers are the prototype 'improvers' (although, as will be suggested later, they do not necessarily get the greatest honour in their own countries). The scientists can devise how to make two blades of grass grow where one grew before, and how to ensure that no blade of grass will ever grow again. The engineers can build dams that make the desert bloom. (Scientists and engineers can also devise the latest nuclear weapons, the latest electronic surveillance devices and, in capitalist countries, casings that will make this year's video recorder seem more progressive than last year's.) But, right from the eighteenth century, 'improvement' extended beyond the production of material objects. Humans could devise more efficient factories; they could also devise more efficient social organizations. They could improve the production of wool; they could also improve the nature of human existence. The possibility of human betterment is essential to the public cultures of all 'modern' societies (although, in this, some humans are more human than others: betterment is not necessarily for all). And the critics of those societies are also likely to be looking for something better. The 'myths' of modernity explain and justify the industrial state: but they also sustain those who would like to modify the industrial state, or even destroy it.

Which *are* the 'modern' 'industrial' societies? I would exclude India and China, which are better thought of at present as *sui generis*, and indeed most of Asia, apart from Japan and a few small places; all of Africa would be excluded, apart from South Africa (which is itself a special case); the Latin American nations are in an ambiguous position. Singapore, however, is a paradigm modern industrial state. While in both capitalist and Communist industrial societies the growth of bureaucracy can seem to endanger the founding political ideas, it is the political idea of efficient bureaucracy and technology that is the founding political idea of Singaporean nationality. In Singapore, to quote one of its critics, a bureaucracy has efficiently taken over the day-to-day-running of the state so completely that 'the result is neither a democratic nor an authoritarian state, but rather an administrative state run by trusted managers'. With politics something enacted in the speeches of the Prime Minister, Singapore became 'a vast lecture theatre, arid and dry'.

5. 'Myths' of Race, Sex, Nation

The logic of race and gender chauvinism

In his book *The Dialectic of Ideology and Technology* Alvin Gouldner, discussing the kind of 'reality' presented in 1789 in the Declaration of the Rights of Man, saw it as a 'model charter of bourgeois society'. (In our terms it was a basic statement of 'myth'.) Towards the end of the chapter he says:

> The middle class sought to remove limitations in the political and public sphere that prevented it from achieving political influence and public distinction commensurate with its wealth, and which it could in turn use to augment its class position. The Declaration of Rights took no notice of other, non-feudal but still traditional social distinctions, insofar as these entailed social inequities. While it acknowledged and sought to remove impediments to freedom of religion . . . it undertook no responsibility to restrain religious prejudices or discrimination . . . Hence while the Declaration enlarged religious tolerance, it also countenanced anti-Semitism and, for that matter, other forms of ethnic discrimination. Although speaking for a generalized equality, it left ancient distinctions of race intact as well as many traditional restrictions on women. The new bourgeois society, then, entailed an accommodation to 'racism' and 'sexism'.

This statement of Gouldner's serves as a relevant introduction to the second set of 'ingredients' of the public cultures of modern industrial societies that are, one way or the other, still common to all of those societies – the 'myths' associated with 'sexism' and 'racism' which, when so much else was discarded from the old order, remained strong and entered into complex relationships with industrialism.

To provide a uniform approach, I will introduce the word 'chauvinism'. 'Chauvinism', as every French schoolchild used to know, began life as an expression for exaggerated patriotism. Nicolas Chauvin was a patriot of the Napoleonic era, but by the 1830s his name had become that of a vaudeville stereotype for what the English were later to call jingoism. The word was given a new and more general life when it was extended by feminists in the 1960s to describe prevailing male attitudes to females – quite an apt re-presentation of 'reality', drawing attention to a new perspective. I will use 'chauvinism' as having two levels of 'myth': that of *superiority* (we are better than you), which is universal to it, and that of *dominance* (since we are better than you we have the right to dominate you), which may sometimes apply in fact, sometimes in aspiration, and sometimes not at all, except perhaps in fantasy.

Supporting the 'mythic' chauvinisms of sex, race and ethnicity are strong 'legitimations' explaining why a particular sex or race is superior and, if it is dominant or wants to be, why this should be so. Each of these 'legitimations' presents its own 'reality' and, since we are speaking here of what are claimed to be primary divisions of humanity, *this 'reality' is likely to be a large part of the common sense of all art forms and all bodies of knowledge.* The appropriate views of males and females, for example, in any society are likely to be enacted in *all* drama, *all* fiction, *all* poetry, *all* history, *all* sculpture and painting and *all* stored knowledge – except that produced by 'deviants' – although some of it may seem so natural that it is not worth saying. (For example, for most of human history, government has been seen as naturally male and property has been seen as naturally male, although laws were also there to enforce it.) With race chauvinism, suppressed groups are sometimes presented as a primary threat ('The Jews are Germany's misfortune'); but on other occasions they are likely to be disposed of in the public culture, mainly in entertainment, in a few effective stereotypes, either with supposed good humour ('sambo', 'mammy') or as threat ('buck nigger'). But what can be most effective is that in most of the public culture for most of the time *they are simply not there at all.*

The divisions on which sexism and racism are based are divisions between people with different kinds of bodies. In the first case, the distinction is made on the physical attributes of sex, in the second on considerations of certain inherited physical attributes: degree of hairiness, the presence or absence of hair crinkliness, colour of hair, skin pigment, height and weight, shape of nose, the nature of the inner eyefold, the presence or absence of pads of fat over the cheekbones. Of course, to make these distinctions is not in itself chauvinist. The chauvinism comes into it when these physical attributes are seen as justifying claims of superiority and/or dominance.

For example, if you go to a museum presenting 'primitive man', unless some modernizer has cleaned it up, you are still likely to be presented with the image of the male as *hunter* and the female as *gatherer*, and probably also as cook. When people see this distinction demonstrated to them, it is likely to have several sets of meanings. One is that the distinction is explained simply by comparative strength. This distinction can seem 'perfectly obvious' – although, if you are talking about hunting and not simply the ability of males to act aggressively towards females, it can be shown that much hunting was done by women, if with some different techniques. But even if it were true that only males were physically able to hunt, this would not lead to the second set of meanings, in which *hunting* is seen as equalling intelligence, initiative and prestige, and *gathering* is seen as equalling the routine, the passive and the ordinary. From what we know, this is a mis-statement of how hunting and gathering groups saw their division of labour. There was mutual regard between these two fields of speciality. It could be useful to think of the males and females engaging in a division of labour, as if they were guilds, each storing and exercising its own skills. But the matter goes beyond rational modes of discourse. The legend of *man the hunter* is one of the most effective in the whole repertoire of the 'myths' of male gender chauvinism.

In the case of race differences, whole stores of knowledge were accumulated to display how, physically, subject races deserved to remain subject because they were dim-witted. For a period, phrenology was much in use. After one massacre of Aborigines in Australia, the heads of those slaughtered were boiled down to get the flesh off them and the skulls were sent to London for phrenologists to use in demonstrating the physical basis for the superiority of Europeans over Aborigines. Phrenology was later replaced by 'intelligence tests'.

Stores of knowledge used to indicate how it was God who had decided the differences of sex and race. Now the argument is more likely to be one of biological determinism – that our bodies produce fundamental and irrevocable distinctions between classes of humans. For example: you have black-pigmented skin, a flat nose and crinkly hair, therefore you are lazy. Put like that, the argument is obviously weak. But in its more obliquely presented forms, with hidden leaps in logic, it can sound important, at least in part because it is so familiar that even the disadvantaged group will internalize and accept it. There are, however, difficulties in arguments for biological determinism, even if they use the rational mode of discourse. Not, of course, if they are concerned with the absolute limitations of our bodies. We haven't got eyes in the backs of our heads, and that's that. (Except that we have invented mirrors.) But most of the questions of limitations in our bodies apply to us all – male or female, straight- or crinkly-haired. A few do divide us, particularly our sex attributes. But even if you assumed that the exclusive potential for females to bear children necessarily meant certain emotional or even perceptual differences dividing females from males, these would still have to be seen merely as genetic instructions built into our bodies. That raises difficulties. One is that we can disobey them. The second (and decisive) is: how could those bodily instructions produce, for example, those parts of 'the feminine mystique', described by Betty Friedan, of the woman necessarily being *housekeeper* and *shopper*? How did the body know about the *house* and the *shop*?

Chauvinism and industrialism

Argument about the relationship of sex and race chauvinisms with industrialism has no end to it. One can argue that pre-industrial race and sex chauvinisms partly shaped some of the forms of industrialism. Equally, one can argue the opposite – that industrialism exaggerated the forms of sexism and racism. Or one can argue both (which I would be inclined to do). For the purposes of this book it doesn't matter which of these perspectives one takes, or even if one takes the view (with which I thoroughly disagree) that industrialism 'caused' gender and race chauvinism. The main point is that there was, and still is, a complex relationship. A familiar example, as far as gender chauvinism is concerned, is the way in which industrialism accentuated forms of sexism as a social chasm opened between 'work' and 'home', between 'public' and 'private', with the one honoured by financial reward and the other not. The 'private' work that was seen as women's work supported and enabled the 'public' work that was seen as men's work, providing new – and crucial – aspects of male dominance.

The 'myths' of race chauvinism were a necessity of indus-trialism; it was the world expansion of the industrializing powers (imperialism) that gave the 'myths' of race chauvinism their vehemence. When Europeans pushed aside the native inhabitants in the Americas and Oceania and planted their own societies, and, in Africa and some Asian countries, took over the running of 'native' societies, there had to be some 'mythic' justification for this gross trespass. Equally, the black slave trade was an essential element of industrialism, both in providing cheap labour to produce raw materials and in providing from its profits a huge capital accumulation in Britain that helped finance the early stages of the Industrial

Revolution. Again there had to be some 'myth' of justification. As with Hitler's attempt to colonize Eastern Europe (even though the Slavs were not 'coloured', he saw them as the orthodox imperialists had seen the 'natives') the justification was in the essential inferiority of the colonized. It was from this need that the 'myths' of modern race chauvinism were constructed. Here also there is still unfinished business – with the displaced aboriginal societies in the Americas, Australia and New Zealand, with the spread of coloured immigrants in various Western European countries, with the unsettled business of the descendants of slaves in the United States and with the apartheid system in South Africa.

Anyone who doubts the continued vitality of the legends of imperialism might go on the two water rides in Disneyland that take the traveller beyond the 'frontier of civilization'. In the 'Adventureland Jungle Cruise', having queued for the *African Queen* beneath a grass-thatched roof decorated with spears, skulls and other reminders of savagery, while the tape plays the threatening sound of the tom-toms, the travellers are warned by the guide, 'Wave goodbye. This may be the last time we see civilization.' The *African Queen* passes giant poisonous spiders guarding red rubies, king cobras guarding stone idols. A Bengal tiger roars at the travellers and gorillas savage a European safari. When a 'dangerous hippopotomus' threatens, the brave guide shoots at it and it 'dies'. *The African Queen* then enters the country of the head-hunters: there are piles of skulls . . . talk of a war party . . . threats. Travellers who survive the 'Adventureland Jungle Cruise' can then go on the 'Frontierland Cruise'. Again they begin by saying goodbye to civilization, this time on the Mark Twain Steamboat, as it passes the Fort Wilderness Snack Bar on Tom Sawyer's Island. This time it is the redskins who threaten the travellers: the Mark Twain Steamboat passes a settler's cabin that the Indians have put to the torch; there are rumours, says the guide, that an Indian war party is on the move . . . An inferior and untrustworthy race again brings its threats.

As to the relations between sex chauvinism and industrialism, it is true that societies were patriarchal before the coming of industrialism, but with industrialism, although the dominance of fathers over sons could to some extent be 'legitimized' by much the same old 'myths' – at least until the sons went out to work – there were in the new conditions of mass wage labour new difficulties in explaining and justifying the old superiority and dominance of males over females. For a long and successful period, in the capitalist societies this was done by successfully pretending in the public culture that working women were not there – or, if they were there, that they really shouldn't be. Although in the first industrialized factories in Britain, the great majority of paid labourers were women and children (work in the new factories was seen as so demeaning that it could seem fit only for them), as the new habits of employment spread to males, by massive illusionism the 'reality' was created that work was male. The 'real world' of work was seen as a man's world. Even trade unions in areas of work in which women were the majority were dominated by men. Work became the capitalist society's equivalent of the museum presentation of *hunting*. The appropriate work for women remained *gathering* (now done by shopping). It also seemed 'appropriate' that women's work should be done not for money but for love. Work was becoming a central part of male honour: there was no place for women in it. In the fascist capitalist societies the leaders were very clear on that – in their rhetoric, if not their practice. In the liberal-democratic capitalist societies, when the existence of working women could not be avoided, except at times of particular need, it would be presented (especially if the women were married) as a 'problem'.

A superb example of how 'invisible' women could be made in the workforce was found in Australia early in the twentieth century at a time when Australia was something of a leader in social reform. A new concept was developed, that of 'the basic wage'. This was seen as one of the ways in which Australia would show the world a better way to live. A court would determine from time to time what the minimum wage should be, so as to sustain in 'a position of frugal comfort estimated by current human standards' a man, his wife and their three children. But women did not get this 'basic wage'. A male with no wife or children would get the basic wage. A female supporting her children would get less than the basic wage. To imagine the male as household head and breadwinner was so 'natural' that it took several generations before Australians began to see, behind the self-congratulation on the basic wage, the invisible woman.

The Soviet Union was the first industrial society to place the issue of women's rights firmly into the public culture. Lenin spoke about it and in Stalin's 1936 Constitution there was the equivalent of the United States' proposed 'equal rights amendment'. ('All rights on an equal footing with men in all spheres of economic, government, cultural, political and other social activity.') Not that this meant in practice what it said in theory (the 1936 Constitution also promised freedom of speech, freedom of assembly, freedom to demonstrate, inviolability of the person), but the point is that this *has*, for a long time, been a public issue in the Soviet Union, and then in the newer Communist countries, in a way that has only comparatively recently become the case in the liberal-democratic capitalist societies. It is true that there are no women in the Politbureau and only a handful on the Central Committee. But women are there in the statistics: 85 per cent of women of working age do paid work; the overall workforce is as much female as male; a third of the judges are women and almost three-quarters of the doctors; as many as one in ten plant managers are women. The problems of working women receive an honoured place in policy-making: day care and paid maternity leave, for instance, have been on the policy agenda for generations, although the system is too rigid to provide the part-time jobs that would solve many of the problems of women. And women are there symbolically: in all those neo-classical sculptures and socialist-realist paintings males and females are raising their clenched fists or working together on collective farms; and just as in the United States in this decade it became an issue to have more women at the party conventions, in the Communist countries they have for some time been making sure that in the honorific assemblies there is an 'adequate supply' of women's faces.

It is also true that in the Soviet Union the lowliest jobs tend to go to women. There seems to me no particular significance in women working as street cleaners (for long, a horror story in capitalist societies about the degradation of women in Communist countries), but it is significant that most of the street cleaners are women. In this sense, some Soviet women 'work like blacks', in that they have the worst jobs. And in the Soviet Union, although there is 'equal pay for equal work', the fine sense of equality is marred by three observations: rates of pay in the areas where women predominate (medicine and teaching, for example) tend to be among the lowest; throughout industry the top jobs tend to go to males; and, as in the liberal-democratic countries, women add to the burden of paid work that of the responsibility for unpaid domestic work.

Some of the accumulating of capital that was essential to industrialism was made easier by exploiting women wage earners. Despite legislative intervention women were paid less in capitalist societies, and in both capitalist and Communist societies the kind of work in which women predominate is likely to be paid at lower rates than other kinds of work. Capital accumulation has been made easier because women have been made cheaper. In this form, along with the fact that even in industries where there is genuine equal pay men tend to get the best jobs, industrialism introduced new ways of demeaning women, and it still does. Just as in the capitalist societies, until recently, women wage earners were conveniently invisible in the public culture, the inequalities for women in work are still kept relatively invisible in the public culture of Communist societies: otherwise they would provide a crisis in the overall 'myth' of 'the worker'. But the justifications for these inequalities became part of the public culture of the capitalist societies – and quite overtly. (It remained furtive, and inferential, in the public cultures of the Communist societies.) If it was deviant for women to work, it was obvious that they shouldn't be paid as much as men. The already existing patriarchal 'myths' were amended to explain and justify this new situation. This suited the interests of the capital accumulators whose work was made easier by the cheapness of women. And it suited men, and the myths of 'progress', that one can measure this by looking down on someone else worse off.

Lenin spoke of the 'domestic slavery' of women, but in the Soviet Union, although 'working women' have been more visible in the public culture for longer than in any other industrial society and, despite discriminations, have made many comparative gains, when they 'come home from work' they must then do more work, this time unpaid: it is they who do the shopping, the cooking and the house-cleaning. A Soviet survey showed that in three-quarters of families, women did all the shopping – in all the industrial societies it is 'common sense' that housework is women's work. Where a difference between capitalist and Communist societies lies is that in the capitalist societies it has been this that has been projected as the principal role of women in the public culture. In the Soviet view, it represents a 'vestige of past inequality'. The Nazi view of women as exclusively concerned with the realms of *Kinder, Küche und Kirche* is not much different from that which used to be projected in the ads in the women's magazines (and in the editorial pages of the magazines themselves). This has been the view of women as being defined in their relation to men – as objects to be possessed by men and whose very existence is defined by their relationship to men. In societies where there has been so much glorification of the modern 'myth' of the family, it has not really been families *as such* that have been glorified, but an idealized 'average family', with wife and children supported by a male breadwinner. This is not, in fact, the 'average family' in industrial societies. In the United States, for instance, most families do not depend solely on a male breadwinner; families with working wives have become more numerous than families with sole male breadwinners; there are many families with only one parent (more often than not a woman); there are families in which the parents are not married, families in which some or all of the children are from

divorced parents, families with no children, and households of
people who lead a common life without being a 'family'. Yet
even the concept of the normal living space continues to be
based on a family with a sole male breadwinner.

The process of defining women by their relationship to men
achieved particular excess in those societies where a woman not
only took her husband's last name but also, in losing her own
first name, lost public recognition of her autonomy. On the
very day when the Republicans put three women speakers on
their platform in evening prime time to show that they cared,
some of the women had a luncheon for daytime television in
which 'White House wives' and 'Capitol Hill wives' put on a
fashion show. The women were introduced as 'Mrs James
Baker, mother of eight children', 'Mrs John Block, mother of
three'.

When the feminist movement began re-asserting its strength
in the 1960s, one of the declared objectives was 'consciousness-
raising', or, as it would be put in this book, 'reality' reconstruction. The women's movement lives or dies according to
whether it constructs new 'realities' – ways of seeing a new
world, with women in it defined as equal human beings and not
merely by their relationship to men. But if women are to be
'liberated' this will only occur by a great cultural transformation
of industrial societies: to those who seek social change, the
women's movement, or the movement of women to a different
status within society, must remain a central consideration.

Icons of subjection

Modern societies are rich – or, as one might equally well put it,
rotten – with examples, in word and image, of the construction
of 'realities' which demonstrate the inferiority of women and of
unfavoured races. Of these countless examples I shall take only
one – the art museum nude. With prudery at present out of
fashion, in modern societies people can swim naked, they can
see naked forms on cinema and television screens, and in the
sex shops of the liberal-democratic societies men can stand

among the magazines and the gadgets and buy sexual fantasies, or peer into the eyepieces of coin-in-the slot machines or go to 'adult movies'. With the spread of the videotape industry hard porn can be watched on household television sets. But for most of the period of modernity the classical nudes and the nudes of the Old Masters were, apart from graffiti and filthy postcards, the only reproductions of human nudity most people were likely to see.

What did they see?

Most art museums in Europe have at least one nude from the Cranach workshop in Wittenberg, established by the painter Lucas Cranach and carried on by his son Lucas Cranach the Younger as part of more general business activities (wine shop, pharmacist, bookshop, printery, property ownership) that made Cranach the wealthiest man in the district. When Cranach painted Northern Europe's first nude goddess in 1509 (*Venus and Cupid*, now in the Hermitage Museum in Leningrad) he brought from across the Alps the idea of painting naked women that had begun in Italy a few years before. Botticelli's *The Birth of Venus*, in which Venus rises with her hands pointing to the parts most desired by lovers, was painted in 1485 and almost at once, and particularly in Venice, painting naked women took off. However, it was not until 20 years after his pioneering *Venus*, when Cranach was 60, that he and his workshop began producing most of the 31 *Eves*, 32 *Venuses*, 35 *Lucretias* and various *Dianas*, *Judgements of Paris*, *Nymphs* and other nudes now seen in European galleries in varying studies of yellow and gold and red. He had established an early factory in the pin-up industry.

With their long slender legs and slender waists, his women reveal their nudity with cool smiles and sidelong glances. With precise, delicate pleasure, they embellish nudity with a courtly elegance, standing naked but for jewelled waistbands or necklaces or rings or bracelets, or a pearl snood or even a large, floppy, fashionable hat. Sometimes with cool sensuality, hands are placed with a calculated negligence on or near pleasurable parts; or they may hold diaphanous scarves over swelling mounds revealing the faintest of pubic fuzz. Occasionally fabrics or soft, lustrous fur add sensuality to skin. These women know they are arousing the erotic curiosity of men – that is why they have been painted.

In producing standard *Venuses*, *Eves* and *Lucretias*, Cranach took three of the most popular of the 20 or so characters in Christian and classical stories that, along with the Three Graces and various other allegorical figures, were used to 'excuse' painting female nudity. Venus and Eve were the prototype nudes of pagan and Christian myth, and the legend of Lucretia was useful because this faithful Roman matron, after being raped, stabbed herself to death, and, while for some painters this allowed a concentration on Roman virtue, for others, and notably Cranach, the concentration was on how the flesh of a woman's breast could be given extra tension by being pressed with the point of a knife.

Saints Agatha, Agnes, Mary of Egypt and Mary Magdalene were also available for the exploitation of nakedness: Agatha and Agnes because one of the torments preceding their martyrdom was that they were forced into brothels, and the two Marys because before conversion they were prostitutes. In the London National Gallery Veronese has Mary Magdalene laying aside her jewels: the top of one breast is so luminous that it dominates the painting. In the Dresden Gallery Paolo Pagani shows her as *The Repentant Magdalene*: to do her repenting she has taken off all of her clothes, relying on shadows and hair to conceal breast and genitals. All around her are naked angels; the whole painting shimmers with flesh.

Three *Rapes* were 'useful' – *The Rape of Europa by Jupiter* – abducted by him in the form of a bull and then ravished by him in the form of an eagle, *The Rape of the Daughters of Leucippus*, abducted on their wedding day, and *The Rape of the Sabine Women*, which combined sexual with military ferocity. Three bathing scenes involved voyeurs – Bathsheba washing herself, privately lusted after by David, Susannah bathing, unknowingly titillating two elderly voyeur-blackmailers, and Diana and her

nymphs washing in a forest pool, observed by the unlucky
Actaeon. From Egypt there were Potiphar, the temptress of
Joseph, and Cleopatra, both as ruthless seducers and as one
who, like Lucretia, chose a method of suicide involving the
baring of a breast. Lot's daughters made him drunk and
seduced him and Amnon pretended illness and tried to seduce
his sister. Two favourite set pieces involved two more of the
disguises of Jupiter – the fable of Leda, to whom Jupiter made
love disguised as a swan, and the fable of Danae, to whom he
made love disguised as a shower of gold.

In some of these paintings the women are sexual persons. In
their soft smiles and steady gaze Cranach's nudes seem to enjoy
their own nudity. Rembrandt's Danae in the Hermitage is a
sexually developed woman, awaiting gratification; Titian's
Danae in Vienna's Kunsthistorisches Museum is leaning back
with relish, a hand between her legs; in the London National
Gallery Velazquez's Venus, lost in her own flesh, stretches into
the secret satisfactions of her body; in the Louvre, in a strange
painting from the Fontainebleau school, two naked women
aristocrats stand side by side in a bath, a lady holding the nipple
of a duchess; in the Kunsthistorisches Museum, Cagnacci's
dead Cleopatra lies in a chair, her dress fallen down to the
beginning of her pelvic curve, as if asleep after some pleasant
excess. In Hampton Court Palace, in a copy of Michelangelo's
lost *Venus and Cupid*, Venus arches with sexual pleasure; as
Cupid, her son, moves to kiss her mouth he caresses her thighs
and her mons veneris with his foot; in the church of Santa
Maria della Vittoria in Rome, in *The Ecstasy of St Theresa*,
Bernini shows the saint at the moment of orgasm.

But for women to show sensual pleasure is rare enough and it
is usually in anticipation, or recollection, conveyed mainly by
inference: or it is with a bull, an eagle, a swan or a shower of
gold, or by their own hands. In only a few European Old
Master paintings are women shown enjoying sexual pleasure
with men, and hardly ever guiltlessly. In *The Bedstead*, an
engraving in the Amsterdam Rijksmuseum, Rembrandt shows
a man and a woman together on a large bed. The scene is 'real':

their clothes are tousled, the bedclothes rumpled; the scene is down in one corner of the picture; it is off-balance, incidental. Yet there is no doubt of the importance of the act to those engaged in it. In allegorical paintings the leer of sexual pleasure is permitted: it symbolizes the price morality must pay in the portrayal of a woman's passion. In the Uffizi, in an *Allegory of Sexual Indulgence*, a woman uses her diaphanous cloth to make her nakedness more evident, and leers with an open self-regard and acceptance of delight. In paintings of the seduction of Lot by his daughters there is also an acceptance of women's pleasure – so long as it is presented as loose.

Women's naked bodies are usually part of the furniture of display, but, apart from the few women enjoying themselves, one must make another exception: some women are naked in paintings to express character interest, or for some serious expression of an artist's experience. Rubens could spread women's flesh across canvas as if it were pâté, but there is tenderness and love in what he is doing. At his most successful, as in *The Little Fur* in the Kunsthistorisches Museum – a full-length portrait of his young second wife – Rubens achieves a recognition of the non-ideal in the individual realities of a body, but at the same time imparts the overall glow of love that idealizes them into a unity. But usually women are painted nude so that they can be occupied by male eyes.

Voyeurism can become most obvious in the peepshows of the bathings of Bathsheba, Susannah and of Diana. In the Rijksmuseum, Cornelius van Haarlem arranges his Bathsheba to show frontal nudity and her servants to show rear nudity; he adds a statue of a naked woman spouting water from her nipples. Sometimes the preferred effect is of vanity observed: in the Kunsthistorisches Museum Tintoretto's *Susannah* admires herself in the mirror as she dries her feet; Massy's *Susannah* in the Old Masters Museum in Brussels is confident of the luminous beauty of her skin, enjoyably displaying it to her attendants, while the old men eye her from behind a pillar. The bodies of Diana and her nymphs are appropriated as symbols of chastity, with hints of the possibility of lesbian love.

The most sophisticated of all the peepshows – Fragonard's *The Swing* in the Wallace Collection in London – is presented to schoolchildren by the guides as an epitome of French charm and elegance. A gentleman reclines on the grass. A lady is pushed on a swing. In fact the painting was done to place the gentleman at exactly the position where he could see up past his mistress's skirts to her genitals.

The most typical display setting for woman's flesh, as conventional as display methods in a butcher's window, is that first worked out in the Venetian Giorgione's *Venus Asleep*, painted about the same time as Cranach's first *Venus*, and now known as *The Dresden Venus* because it has been there since 1699. In painting a naked woman lying down, the fingers of one hand curled between her legs, Giorgione invented a new cultural form – that of the reclining nude. Titian, a fellow Venetian, was the popularizer of this new form: Tintoretto, also from Venice, turned her into Potiphar's wife and had her stretch her arm out to pluck at the young Joseph's clothes; Correggio, in *The Sleep of Antiope*, tilted her upwards, and Boucher turned her upside down to show off her bum and made her pink and rounded in a soft setting of velvet and silk. The reclining nude went on, stretched out on her couch for 350 years until Manet, in *Olympia*, in 1865, gave her an intelligent face and placed her hand over her genitals, not as a signpost, but as a sign that she owned them and would herself decide what she would do with them. The nude continues to recline in *Penthouse* and *Playboy* in the pose pioneered by Giorgione.

It would be wrong to see 'the nude' mainly or simply from the viewpoint of women undervalued as sex objects. Most female nudes are not sex objects – but simply *objects*. If they were sex objects, even if the function of their sexuality was to please men, they would be presented as sexual women. Unlike the women photographed for *Penthouse*, they don't even have pubic hair. The non-sexual Old Master nudes make women non-human – mere exhibits, framed collector's items, something of financial value, finely finished, like rare porcelain. Some even look like rare porcelain. Of all the hectares of paint representing exposed women's flesh, there is a painting from the Fontainebleau School in the Fine Arts Museum at Basle that might be taken to epitomize the presentation of woman as collector's item: it shows a naked woman; she has jewels in her hair, around her neck, on her wrists, on the table; she holds a ring between her fingers; her nipples are painted as if they were also jewels. With the neo-classical degenerations of the nineteenth century marble nudes of women had become a form of insipid decoration; women were lustrous bric-à-brac. This is the 'myth' which high art, and eventually popular culture, reinforced.

In *Ways of Seeing* the English art and social critic John Berger makes an essential point: imagine men in the poses traditional to the female nudes. Imagine in the galleries of a great art museum: a naked man stretched out frontally across a canvas, pearly white, with pink-tipped nipples, offering himself to the spectator; three naked men lined up, pointing to the most desirable parts of their bodies while two women judge which man is the most beautiful; a naked man bathing and admiring himself in a mirror while two old women secretly lech on him; two beautiful naked young men seducing their aged mother; a naked man, bejewelled, with his genitals painted as if they were jewels; a naked man coyly holding a diaphanous cloth over his genitals; another in a soft setting of silk and velvet, lying on a couch, turned upside down, the better to show off his bum.

'Myths' of nation

All of the modern industrial societies are also nation-states, a form of state that in some cases preceded industrialism, but that, with industrialism, became the universal form of organization of industrial societies. Since these nation-states exist, their 'reality' must be 'invented', in the sense already discussed in the first chapter: a 'reality' must be created for them. We cannot have a nation-state without imagining what it is – and once it is imagined, that is what it becomes, as a basis for thought and action. This particular 'reality' can be thought of as a 'national identity' – a claim about what 'the nation' really is. There can be many and conflicting claims to national identity – making claims about the true nature of one's nation can be part of the rhetoric of social conflict – but of those, certain claims to national identity (which for our purposes might be thought of as 'myths') came to dominate the public culture. Could one get a better example of this than in a walk around Dublin?

Between the two grandest porticoes in Dublin, those of the Bank of Ireland and Trinity College, are reminders of the time when Dublin was the second city of the British Isles. On a traffic island there is a statue of an eighteenth-century orator in classic pose, hand uplifted. The statue maintains a style of its own – just as Henry Grattan, the great Irish orator whom the statue represents, maintained a stylish eloquence in the successful agitation (backed by hints of force) for the right for an Irish parliament to legislate for Ireland. What became known as 'Grattan's Parliament' met, as every Dubliner will tell you, in what is now the Bank of Ireland, for 18 years, until it was destroyed in British reaction to an Irish uprising. Two street lengths from Grattan's statue, in St Stephen's Green, there is a statue in modern style, put up in the 1960s. A young, determined face emerges from a strong body, finished in a tough, brutal style, in rugged clothes. The statue represents Wolfe Tone, symbol of the 1798 uprising of 'the United Irishmen' and also of the modern tradition of rebellion, betrayal and disaster in Irish history. Reminders of fiasco become even more melancholy with the statue of Robert Emmett, across the green, put there by the Robert Emmett Statue Committee of the United States, as a reminder of Emmett's plan for an uprising, his betrayal, capture, hanging and beheading. No monuments remain to commemorate the Act of Union by which the English in 1800 destroyed all pretence at independence in Ireland. The Irish have blown them up. But everyone in Dublin can tell you where they were.

Dublin's largest and most heroically generous group of statues commemorates the man who first had any success in giving shape to Irish Catholic peasants' hopes for overthrowing the landlords and the ascendancy of the Protestant British. Between the bridge named after him and the street named after him, the statue to Daniel O'Connell rises in three tiers, with bullet holes in the allegorical statues of Patriotism, Fidelity, Eloquence and Courage as reminders of later, patriotic street-fighting. At the other end of the street from the O'Connell monument, a monolith commemorates Charles Stewart Parnell. A sculptured torch is on top and, in letters of gold, supported by a golden Irish harp, is one of those sets of words that any Irish schoolchild knows: 'No man has a right to fix the boundary to the march of a nation.'

In St Stephens's Green a plaque on a block of granite brought from the Wicklow Hills commemorates O'Donovan Rossa, one of the first of 'the bold Fenian men' whose Irish Revolutionary Brotherhood began the long tradition that is still alive in Dublin, as base for the IRA activities in Northern Ireland, and whose sense of a living tradition is commemorated in the gold-on-black plaque marking the headquarters of the 1916 Easter Uprising; in the bright lettering of nationalist-martyrs' names in the flaking stone of Kilmainham Gaol; in the 'Garden of Remembrance'('for those who gave their lives in the cause of Irish freedom'); and, in the National Museum, in hats with bullet holes, pistols, tattered flags, minute books, handbills, old uniforms.

The very street signs – in Gaelic as well as English – are a reminder of the 'Irishification' of Ireland that began in the 1880s. In the National Museum is the first typewriter with Gaelic letters, along with other relics of the Gaelic League – and relics also of the Gaelic Athletic Association, a mass movement that fought a long guerrilla action against the corruptions of English sport. In the central part of St Stephen's Green, a Henry Moore sculpture commemorates W.B. Yeats; and the Abbey Theatre, once the centre of the literary revival, is now also one of the centres of the tourist trade. In the main hall of the National Museum are relics of the golden age of the Celtic past – gold discs, bronze trumpets, amber necklaces; in the Trinity College library is the illuminated Book of Kells, seen, along with the high crosses, as a reminder of a uniquely Irish Christian tradition. If Dubliners want any further reminder of what it is to be Irish, they can go to one of the ballad clubs, where in a hotel bar people can sip Guinness and preserve traditional sentiment in the most traditional way – singing songs about who they are and what their ancestors have been.

Dublin remains a city enchanted by the magic of the 'myths' of the revolutionary origin of the Irish nation-state. There are, of course, other 'Dublins' and other claims to 'mythic' Irish national identity. But there still survive interpretations of Ireland based on its past that have meanings for the present and the future, even if partly as distractions in the making of new 'realities' that would provide fresh bases for action. In this, it is worthwhile comparing Ireland with the United States and the Soviet Union, two other nation-states whose 'myths' of origin are connected with a perceived revolution. For both those nations their revolutions are projected as events of unique *world* significance, but the 'myths' of their revolutions are reinterpretable: their revolutions are, as it were, a 'mythic' resource that can be drawn on to give any meaning that modern circumstances may demand. The 'myths' of the Irish revolution remain, historically, pure – to such an extent that the two principal political parties are based on a division as to how that revolution should have occurred.

Foundation 'myths' are only one of many possible elements in the 'myths' of national identity that can prevail in a public culture. Political concepts may also be part of a national identity: in the Soviet Union and the United States they are the main part. Norwegians can lay claim to defining themselves by their equality, the Swiss by their sense of practicality (*Sachlichkeit*), the Swedes by their seeking for harmony, the Finns by their *yksimielisyys* – a unanimity on matters of national security; for the Dutch it was their institutionalization of conflict (*verzuiling*) that led to politically based claims of national uniqueness.

The kinds of statistics used in a public culture can also help to define the matters on which the nation displays its successes and failures. Some nations seek pride in population growth. Others see the test of success in export statistics. In an early stage of nation-'creating', literacy rates can be important. There are occasions for hope or fear in figures of economic growth. A nation's strategic imagination (its habits of policy and style in diplomacy, trade, immigration and military policy) can help define it: the different concepts of neutrality of Sweden and Switzerland, for example; the Dutch concept of the Netherlands as 'an island of sanity'; the French thirst for their own independence; the Norwegian thirst for influence; the British thirst for glory. 'Britain has found herself again in the South Atlantic,' said Mrs Thatcher, after the Malvinas expedition.

Conflicts over 'national identity' are symptoms of wider social conflicts. For instance in Australia in the late 1960s and early 1970s there was a period of 'new nationalism' that reflected contradictory views of what Australia should be. Disputes as to whether Australia should have its own national anthem and take the union jack out of the top left hand corner of its flag were disputes about Australia's position in the world: they were reactions against the prevailing Anglocentrism (also dramatized by use of the new word 'multiculturalism') and, to some extent, reactions against the traditional 'vassalage' of Australia in which both national honour and national self-interest were defined in terms of Australian fealty to a world power ('a great and powerful friend'). A stripping away of old images of 'the bush' as the true Australia and an emphasis in sociology, history and novel-writing on Australia as one of the most urban societies in the world was, amongst other things, a denial of a colonial and dependent past with an emphasis on the loyal export of primary products and an assertion of a more independent and 'sophisticated' Australia; it could also be seen as an assertion of the interests of an educated, city-dwelling, 'new middle class'. Recognition of the collapse in South-east Asia of what had been seen as the protection of the European empires was accompanied, for a season, by speculation as to whether Australians were 'white Asians'. That Australia lay between two oceans – the Indian and the Pacific Ocean – could also lead to speculation about Australian identity that was connected with changes in strategic imagination: the idea of Australia as a 'Pacific power' was comforting, with reassurances of friendship with the United States and Japan, and dominance in the South-west Pacific; the idea of Australia as an Indian Ocean power was, however, filled with a sense of threat. In the strategic debate, one kind of politician looked up statistical tables that suggested a weak Australia that obviously needed foreign business firms and foreign military forces to support it; another kind of politician looked up statistical tables that showed a nation that was among the world's great exporters and whose GNP exceeded that of all South-east Asia – and was therefore capable of more independent policies.

'Myths' of national identity are not necessarily national-chauvinist. In themselves, they are simply theories about the nature of a particular nation-state. It is only when they claim superiority/dominance that they become chauvinist. In fact, many 'myths' about the identity of a nation can be anti-chauvinist. Revolutionaries, for example, *must* have an anti-chauvinist mythology, at least to the extent that they wish to overthrow the kind of 'nation' represented by the existing regime – although they may see a *pays real*, a true nation of the people themselves, essentially good at heart which will then take the place of the false nation presented by the regime. However the 'myths' of revolutionaries do not gain a place in the public culture except at a time of breakdown. In societies where there is operating what, in a later chapter, I will introduce as 'the critics' culture', there is likely to be a place for the presentation of unflattering 'realities' about the nation. In the United States, where shifts in the surface shapes of the public culture from one season to the next may be greater than in any other modern industrial society, seasons of extreme patriotism can be followed by seasons in which careers are made from national self-criticism. The celebrations of 'American-ism' of the late 1950s were followed by a long spell of commercially successful self-criticisms, building up from Tom Lehrer and books about Organization Men and Hidden Persuaders, to Woodstock and flag-burnings and 'Watergate'. Certain forms of self-criticism can even become institutionalized within the public culture, defining the boundaries of criticism. In the Soviet Union there is a continuing concern in the newspapers with providing 'critical materials'; in Britain techniques of self-criticism abound which allow the criticism of everything except what most matters. All public cultures display certain permissible stock figures of fun as national stereotypes. The good soldier Schweik can still be seen as necessary in understanding 'the Czech character'. As with Fassbinder and Günther Grass, there can also be continuing forms of acerbic scolding. In some societies there can run through the public culture themes of the essential second-ratedness of the country to such an extent that it can become a matter of pride. The Canadian historian and culture critic Arthur Lower would describe how the English Canadians of his time made a cult of being 'second best': being provincially derivative was the main way in which they sustained their honour.

But even 'myths' of national identity that are not national-chauvinist may be chauvinist in some other way. To detect these chauvinisms, one can ask questions such as: Who are the principal kinds of actors in the national legends? What roles are they given? What kinds of people provide the stereotypes of 'national character'? Here one is certain to find other types of chauvinism. Gender chauvinism, certainly. In all countries males are presented as the principal or motive actors in national legends. There is likely to be ethnic chauvinism, too – although in some nation-states there can be what I describe in a later chapter as 'the ethnic compromise', with various flavourings of multi-ethnicity in 'myths' of the nation. And, of course, there will be concentrations on certain perceptions of economic class. At the time of 'national landscape', even landscape paintings could seem to serve some interests rather than others (almost always conservative). Since all nation-states are organized so that some groups win and some lose, it is not surprising that there should be such a bias in 'myths' of national identity – although this can need some subtlety in reading. For much of the time the operative chauvinism of national 'myth' is not a claim to the superiority/dominance of the nation but to a superiority/dominance of gender and/or ethnicity.

Nevertheless there can also be a brute patriotism, a gut national chauvinism. It is clearly evident in sport and this can be one of the main social consequences of sport: it can provide exemplary displays of superiority/dominance, or at least the struggle to achieve them, the hopes and fears, and the morality plays. But gut patriotism is mobilizable for other purposes, some of them peaceful, if passionate, and some of them helping to legitimate, in suppression or war, the monopoly of 'honourable' violence held by the state.

In a 1976 bestseller, *The Russians*, the United States journalist Hedrick Smith gave an account of the mobilizable qualities of Soviet patriotism. He found the Soviets 'the world's most passionate patriots'; he commented on how they could still be bonded by recalling 'the shared ordeals and triumphs' of 'the Great Patriotic War' of 1942–5; how they shared 'a Victorian pride in the power and accomplishments of the Soviet Union', from exploits in space to victories in sport (and he then suggested that 'big time sports in the Soviet Union are not entertainment, as in the West, but politics'); he spoke of the Soviets' 'moral chauvinism', their liking for singing patriotic songs, their 'basic, unquestioning confidence in their own way of life', their simple faith that 'ours is best'. Then he spoke of their 'Victorian pride in national power and empire and conviction of moral superiority that echoes American's earlier age of innocence'. He was writing in 1976, when he thought that the age of innocence of 'America' had gone. But he had not recognized that, to many outsiders, what he was describing was not just Soviet patriotism, but United States patriotism as well – as a mobilizable potential, not always dominating the public culture (and it wasn't in 1976), but mobilizable when the time comes, as it certainly did, for example, in the Great Patriotic Year of 1984, with all the gold medals in the Olympic Games (no politics in sport!) and the election victory of Ronald Reagan, in which both campaign teams tried to outdo each other in flapping the stars and stripes and invoking 'America' (with that casualness with which United States citizens appropriate to the United States the name normally given to two continents). In some other parts of his chapter on the uniqueness of Soviet patriotism he gave the game way by taking all of his illustrative examples from the United States. The feeling for the Soviet homeland, he said, had the same compulsion as the United States patriotic song, 'My Country, 'Tis of Thee'; the Soviets' belief in their legends were like the United States belief in Davy Crockett. When he said, 'The war theme is more important than westerns are to Hollywood', he missed the point. It is the very belief in the 'myths' of 'the West' (although no longer westerns) that is so significant in the United States. And for sheer flag veneration there is nothing in the Soviet Union to equal a ceremony that occurs every hour in the National Museum of American History in Washington. After a roll of drums, a huge curtain slowly descends, revealing the floodlit remains of the colossal flag that inspired, in 1814, the writing of the United States national anthem. As the curtain unveils the flag, the national anthem is played as it was in the nineteenth century. The floodlit flag is displayed fully, briefly, then the curtain slowly rolls up again. The national anthem again plays, this time in a twentieth-century rendering. The national anthem itself is an ode of praise to the flag.

In the south-east of France, Bayonne has preserved an 'Old Town', grouped in two sections ('Great Bayonne' and 'Little Bayonne') on either side of the River Nive, with four small bridges connecting them. Its presentation of itself as a reminder of the past is credible except for two buildings – the new Municipal Market, which seems too modern, and the Musée Basque, which seems too old. It has been painted white with red shutters and these, the colours of the Basque separatist movement, have a traditional meaning greater than the antiquity of plain, grey stone and one that is a threat to the French state – an assertion of the need to take away the Basque provinces from France and Spain and to express an old culture by founding a new state. A shop nearby is devoted to books, records and tapes concerned with Basque culture and Basque struggle. A special Basque printing press is in a nearby street. Pamphlets in the museum itself speak of the French colonization of the Pays Basque. And in Spain, making it all seem more real, there are the bombings and the shootings. Inside, as in most folk museums, there are authentic commemorations of old ways, displaying sincerity through old cooking pots and carved chests. But there is also a concern with the Basques as a nation and as a force in European imperialism: 'The Room of Basque Expansion' shows the contributions of the Basques to the Crusades, to the European world 'discoveries' and to the world expansion of the Catholic missions. There is even a reminder of the Basque contribution to proto-history in the famous cave paintings at Lascaux.

In the museum bookshop is a pamphlet, *Histoire de la Colonisation Française au Pays Basque*, which shows 'the history of France' as a brutal imperialist occupation by the Capet kings of Paris of other territories and nations (Basques, Bretons, Flemings, Alsatians, Corsicans, Catalans, Occitans). The pamphlet gives the principal dates of this Parisian conquest, the dates of the principal examples of Parisian repression, then the story of the 'Francization' of the peoples of the conquered nations. Political 'reality' is given to the separatism of the fringes of France by the many bombings in Corsica, the occasional bombings in Britanny, or by graffiti, such as *Oc Libre* in the south of France or *Alsace aux Alsaciens* in the west.

As the nation-states began to form in Europe there were attempted impositions on their peoples of the metropolitan culture and the metropolitan language, just as, in each of the immigrant settler societies of European world colonization, including those of the Russian eastward expansion, a dominant ethnic group would attempt to make its language and its culture the language and the culture of the newly forming or expanding nation. These attempts at ethnic monopoly, whether in the old Europe or the new societies, would frequently leave the public culture entirely dominated by the winners. It was their 'reality' that made up the public face of the nation, defining a world that justified their dominance. It was from the needs of nation-making that the 'myths' of modern ethnic chauvinism were constructed. But now, in Europe, and in the new societies, the old dominance can be threatened, as some of the minority groups, such as the Basques, may wish to secede from the nation. In other nations, as with the *burakumin* in Japan – who in race and language are as Japanese as everyone else but are an hereditary underclass hated out of habit – they wish, as it were, to join the nation, both in the sense that they want to overcome material discrimination and also to share some of the space in the public culture.

6. 'Legitimations'

Capitalists and Communists

Within the public cultures of the industrial societies are vehement declarations of difference between the Communist and the capitalist societies, yet no matter what differences are proclaimed in the public cultures of these two societies, there are certain similarities in approach to their 'economies' – the emphasis on the accumulation of capital and the accumulation of labour, the belief in economic growth, the belief in 'work', by which is meant not, in fact, work in general but waged work.

There are two other similarities between these societies that, to some extent, belie what could seem their proudest differences.

Both are related to the belief that one of their fundamental divisions is on attitudes to the free market and to private ownership. Yet, to some limited extent, the Communist societies do have free markets and private ownership, and to some extent the capitalist societies do not. Even in the Soviet Union, the market and private ownership are important. Something like 10 per cent of shopping in the Soviet Union is conducted, legally, on a free market and up to a third of shopping is conducted on a free market that, being illegal, is a 'black' market. At the same time, something like a quarter of Soviet food supplies come from farmers operating privately (and, on the whole, legally). On the other hand, there have never really been fully free markets in the capitalist societies. All of the markets in these societies are dominated by big business and big government and, if they are also liberal-democratic societies, to varying extents by big unions. The small farm, or the small family firm, or the simple corner store (the mom and pop shop of United States 'myth') can be seen as paradigms of the free market, but although there are still many small firms, the conditions of their buying and selling are largely determined by the policies of governments and of giant corporations. Governments intervene in a myriad of ways to assist businesses to go on making profits – by providing transport, energy and communication systems, by education, by scientific and technological research, by protection of specific industries (in all manner of means, from providing cheap electricity to restricting import restrictions), by taking the poor off the streets, by attempted 'management' of the economy, by taking over essential but loss-making industries, and by contracts. This last occurs most notably in the United States where the military contracts are so huge that even a Republican president spoke of an 'industrial-military complex', and where threats of a real peace would, unless the government put out different kinds of contracts, produce the economic collapse of the United States. The attitude of business people towards government intervention in the capitalist societies is, as Kim Beazley, an Australian politician, once put it, to 'capitalize their profits and socialize their losses', or, as Gore Vidal writes, it is one of 'socialism for the rich and free enterprise for the poor'. And not only are markets less than free and governments more essential to profit-making than purists would admit: the question even of ownership has become vexed. A significant part of *large* ownership of productive resources is held not by individual impresarios of capital accumulation, but by the state and by great 'private' corporations in which the biggest shareholders are other corporations, so that, to describe what is happening, words such as 'interlocking corporate structure' are as necessary as words like 'competition'. Some of these great corporations are 'transnational' – great world business empires (more of them based on the United States than on any other single nation), each with annual budgets larger than those of a number of small nations and offering 'careers' to 'executives', as in the days of overt imperialism careers were offered by the various colonial services of the imperialist nations. One of these 'transnational' corporations might be interlocked with much the same companies – banks, advertising, transport, etc. – throughout the world, further increasing its mass, and these world companies might enter into relations with the large 'national' companies of individual states so that these smaller companies (themselves monopolies or oligopolies in their own states) become 'compradors', native accomplices of the great world companies. And among these great world companies and their national associates there can develop a kind of transnational culture, with its own myths, 'realities and styles, adopting itself with varying degrees of diplomacy to the public cultures of individual nation-states, but also at times colouring them.

Another similarity can be observed within the actual organization of the two kinds of societies. In terms of critical mass they might seem dominated by large, abstract bureaucracies of various kinds – in the Communist societies, some of them party, some government, some state industrial corporations: in the liberal-democratic capitalist societies, some government, some business corporations, some state industrial corporations. (In capitalist societies that are not liberal-democratic there can also be unstable agglomerations of party officials.) There can be differences of tone and style within these bureaucracies, but they all offer the 'vertical vision' of a career, and increasingly the entry to a career comes through some form of educational qualifications. A 1980s Soviet movie about a top executive with a career crisis (*Private Life*) needs only superficial changes to become a United States movie about a top executive with a career crisis.

So it could appear that one way of distinguishing between Communist and capitalist societies might be to compare their bureaucracies. Tests such as the degree of market choice, or the degree of police penetration, might determine the extent to which the bureaucrats tried directly to control one kind of society compared with another. The styles of bureaucrats might also be contrasted – their professed aims, their performance. But we have yet to find a president of the United States who says that what distinguishes 'the free world' from Communism lies in the differences between their bureaucracies. It would be equally unlikely for a Communist leader to boast of the superiority of the Communist bureaucracies over those of the West. In both nations it can be the bureaucracies that are seen as principal enemies of the great ideals professed in the public culture.

When we turn to the 'myths' in the public culture that explain and justify why economic power should be as it appears to be in these societies, we find (and this is not surprising) that one of the effects of the 'myths' is diversionary. It is not that they merely justify and explain a power situation that exists. To varying extents, they divert attention from the actualities of power by justifying and explaining a power situation that does *not* exist – except in the few countries where the social democratic parties have achieved some shift not only in power but in definition of what the 'myths' are, so that they speak fairly precisely the language of *managed* capitalism. But what can also be seen in these 'diversionary' myths (at least in those of Communism and liberal-democratic capitalism) is that they begin from much the same assumption – the principle that a certain type of control of economic resources could be justified if it is useful. As Alvin Gouldner argued in *The Coming Crisis of Western Sociology*, the enlightened eighteenth-century bour-geoisie and nobility which articulated the main 'myths' that were to explain and justify capitalism found grounds of sheer *utility* as a principled argument against the old aristocratic justifications of privilege (birth, God, etc.), thereby opening out for the first time in history a 'myth' of access to power by anyone who had earned it – through usefulness. In the capitalist societies, at their most capitalist, the principle of 'utility' can simply be that what is useful is what makes money. But it has extended in spectrum: in socialist 'myth' there is also a concern with usefulness, but in the principle not of individual but of social utility. In 'myth' in both cases utility prevails, but there is a 'mythic' contest between individualism and collectivism. (In fascist, corporatist and other types of capitalist societies that do not use laissez-faire 'myths', however, different kinds of 'legitimation' prevail.)

'Myths' of free enterprise

In its pure form (which we will assume, for the sake of argument) the 'myth' of individualism is founded in the 'myths' of free enterprise and of private ownership. In turn, the 'myth' of free enterprise has two sides to it. On one side, the profit motive is seen as the greatest force for innovation and expansion known to humankind: no one would bother to do anything unless they could make money out of it; give them the opportunity to make money and they can do anything. On the other side, the competition of 'market forces' provides a rational restraint (operated by Adam Smith's 'invisible hand') so that all of this dynamic profit-making is likely to work into a general equilibrium.

Justifications of private ownership come mainly from the illumination shed on them by this model of eighteenth-century rationality. This can take the particular form that it is essential for business (and therefore for overall human progress), that business should be free of government control, otherwise neither the profit motive nor the market will be able to perform their civilizing functions. There are two difficulties with this elision. One is that there is no necessary relation between private ownership and free markets: businesses can make more money with monopoly than with competition. The other is that there is always difficulty in providing arguments of utility to justify the riches of the rich if their wealth has not been 'earned', but inherited.

Since 'myths' *are* myths, the way out of these and other difficulties has been not rational, but associational. One of these associations has been the establishment in the capitalist societies of 'the consumer ethic', established with some contradiction to the 'work ethic' with its emphasis on effort, frugality and self-restraint, but established, nevertheless. Its establishment was not, in itself, a capitalist plot. As Stuart Ewen argues in *Captains of Consciousness*, the early capitalists saw their workers primarily as producers – consumption was mainly for the better off – and they were brought to the consumer ethic by something that had happened despite them: the higher wages the workers got for themselves. They produced a new demand, and business people, ready to match potential output, began to see that they needed 'a general strategy to consumerize the worker'. In the increased development of brand names, advertising and other marketing devices, growing themes became those of indulgence and the 'myth' that the meaning and satisfaction in life was to be found in acquisition. Capitalist societies are now organized around the consumer ethic. It is an economic need for them. Without it, they can't make profits. One critic, Joan Robinson, suggested that 'They must continue to use ever more deleterious means for ever more trivial ends.' For the purposes of the argument here we can distinguish between what ordinary people actually do and the types of values being endlessly propagandized all around them by the glitter of the shop displays and advertising; so that by titillating appeals to envies and anxieties progress becomes the need to buy the latest models of consumer goods, and competitiveness and material acquisition become central to life. These seductions of consumer marketing are one of the dominant aspects of the public culture and the common signals they send are that we live in a free society. What could be more free than a society in which one can choose between Brands 'A' and 'B'?

In varying degrees in different capitalist societies belief in home ownership can also elide into belief in the unquestioned utility of large business corporations: one of the greatest supports for the comparatively few large owners can be that there are many small owners who can feel a community of interest with large owners. This is the 'myth' of the property-owning democracy in which what is good for 'the average American' is good for General Motors, as if there were no difference between personal property, small, privately owned productive property and large, privately owned productive property (a distinction recognized by the Communist countries which all allow personal property and some of which also allow private ownership of small productive property). The large corporations of a capitalist society could be brought under social control without threatening either home ownership or small businesses. But it can be of great advantage to these corporations if home owners and the owners of small businesses see themselves as part of the same 'free enterprise system' as the business oligopolies.

Even more emotionally convincing can be the belief in the family firm, the family shop and the family farm as key symbols of 'free enterprise' and therefore the very centrepieces of capitalism. This belief can be quite convincing because, although they operate in a world dominated by the large bureaucracies of big business and big government, and sometimes of big labour, small businesses are those that people themselves run. The free enterprise 'myth' is about *them*. They live with risk: the world in which they operate may not be a free market, but it is at least a world of real dangers – threats from good and bad seasons or market changes, threats from big business itself, threats from the effects of personal ill health or personal misjudgement. Wage earners can also be sacrificed to uncertainties, but in capitalist societies the dangers of wage owners are not likely to be heroicized in the public culture in the same way as those of the small owners. The small owners can feel, and be seen as, the backbone of the nation, the salt of the earth, and so forth. This does not necessarily mean that 'society' is committed to their individual survival. Far from it. Individual by individual, they are too small to matter. A failed corner store is neither here nor there, but a failed transnational corporation can threaten the social order. Small businesses live out a 'myth', like soldiers who fall in battle. It is part of the honour of small businesses that they can go bankrupt, as they do each year in their tens of thousands. They are making their patriotic sacrifices to the 'myths' of free enterprise. They demonstrate the 'reality' of the free market.

The 'myths' justifying private ownership or control of productive property can reach their apotheosis (above all, in the United States) in the 'myth' of individualism when it becomes coloured by economic meanings. Historically, individualism can be seen emerging from the cultural revolution that preceded industrialism, in the separation of the individual from the world of the supernatural. If you walk through a large art museum looking at Crucifixions or Madonnas, you are supposed to find individualism commencing in the late pre-renaissance art that used to be praised for showing the beginnings of the signs of naturalness but which is now likely to be attacked by some critics as showing the beginning of modern individualism. I am not at all sure that the 'individualism' that becomes obvious in fifteenth- and sixteenth-century Christs and Madonnas is the same as the 'individualism' of the robber barons of late nineteenth-century business or of rich shoppers in late twentieth-century luxury boutiques, but the subject is too complex to argue here. The relevant point is that 'individualism' became associated with property rights, competitiveness, the measure of usefulness by money and the glorification of selfishness (profit-seeking) as the main dynamic of society. It received gross expression in the social Darwinism of the late nineteenth century, in which W.G. Sumner, one of the greatest United States prophets of Herbert Spencer's 'survival of the fittest', could say that in 'the competition of life millionaires are a product of natural selection'. Individualism continues to be a strong 'myth' in capitalist societies; 'freedom' can be seen primarily as the individual right to pursue money-making as one wishes.

Individualism is of course a 'myth' that can attract attention away from accumulations of wealth by telling simple stories. It is not workable. An entirely 'individualist' society would crumble. One token of this is the United States homicide rate. The smoking gun is one of the symbols of United States 'individualism'. In the regular tours of the FBI building in Washington most of the tour is given over to demonstrations of the technology of crime detection: 'hundreds of cases can now be solved that until a few short years ago would have remained a mystery'. (In fact, as the technology of crime-solving increases, so do the crime figures.) The tour ends with what is described as a 'demonstration of ballistics'. Tourists go down two escalators to a large hall in the basement, where they sit in front of a very wide curtain until the hall fills up. The curtain rolls back, showing a bullet-proof glass wall. On the other side of the wall is a shooting range. A man walks on to the range, introduces himself as an FBI agent, and explains that he is going to shoot at one of the dummies in the range, first with a revolver, at two different distances, and then with a tommy-gun, in single shots and then in bursts. That's what he does. He stands on the other side of the bullet-proof glass wall and silently pumps lead into the dummy with his revolver, at two different distances. Then he silently pumps lead into the dummy with a tommy-gun, at first in single shots and then in bursts. The dummy is backlit. It is riddled with a wide ring of bullet holes. The curtain slides back over the wall of bullet-proof glass.

Individualism does not usually receive such enthusiastic expression in the public cultures of other capitalist societies. But I am taking the liberal-democratic to be the typical form, at the present time, of modern, industrial societies that are capitalist: there are other possibilities for capitalist societies, ranging from the social-democratic to the fascist – these will be considered later – but the prevailing form for the moment, at least for fully modern and fully industrial capitalist societies, is the liberal-democratic, and individualism is part of the 'myth' of liberal democracy. However it should be noted that (however much individual capitalists may flourish) individualism as such can be denounced in capitalist societies that are fascist, or theocratic, or militarist, or patronalist, or highly national-statist in their public culture. Individualism goes against the tradition of dependence in Latin American societies, where the great national legends are not usually of success but of heroically sustained and exemplary disasters, reminders of the limits of human action, and where the state itself is seen as the prime mover, creating capitalists as one of its concessions. But it seems likely (and partly for this reason) that these societies are not really industrial in their public cultures. The relevant exception is Japan. Japan is highly modern and highly industrial, but, whatever private practice might be, it is considered impolite to speak the language of individualism in the public culture in Japan: what is proclaimed in the public culture are the 'myths' of group loyalty and group harmony, with a declared dedication not so much to profits as to 'Japan'.

What I am suggesting is that the 'myth' of individualism is common to all the public cultures of the modern, industrial, liberal-democratic societies other than Japan – but in varying degrees (and with no necessary relationship to what actually happens). In the United States it can seem so strong (not even in contradiction with patriotism to 'America', because to be individualist is to be 'American') that while the first Reagan administration in fact practised the despised 'demand-management' economics of Keynesianism – creating a 'recovery' with deficits of previously unimaginable grandeur – most people did not notice, since the government still spoke the language of individualism with its appeal to the rationality and utility of individual selfishness. 'Myths' of individualism can be softened in other capitalist societies by modified appeals to traditional values. The English monarch, for instance, does not make speeches praising cut-throat competition. But the most democratically interesting modifications occur if, in the type of political debate permitted in the public culture, it is accepted that government economic planning and government welfare policies do and should exist. I say 'democratically interesting' because it is part of the 'myth' of liberal democracy that it is not only democratic but *useful* (efficient) that there should be informed debate in a free marketplace of ideas about what is supposed to be happening. What *is* happening in all of the capitalist societies is that in the interests of preserving a modern, industrial state governments permanently concern themselves with the forms of the accumulation of capital and labour and with the 'management' of the economy. They dispose of the socially 'useless' through welfare policies. However, in most of the liberal-democratic capitalist societies, the parties of the right, especially when they are self-consciously parties of capital (which is to say most of them), simply do not take this as given. Election after election can still appear to be partly about 'free enterprise' versus 'socialism' (government economic planning and welfarism) – matters that were settled long ago, at least by the time of Bismarck, one of the great exponents of state welfare and state economic intervention.

What else is common to the 'myths' of the public culture of liberal-democratic societies other than the 'myth' of individualism? Well, there *is* the 'myth' of the free marketplace of ideas – an extension of the 'myth' of the rationality of the economic market: if all the citizens have the necessary information, they can argue it out, freely, among themselves; then, from these competing opinions will emerge the most efficient 'answer'. With this are associated the 'myth' of free speech and a free press (by which is usually meant that the content of the news media should not be controlled by the government), and also the 'myth' of freedom of organization (extended, sometimes reluctantly, but necessarily to trade unions). Then there are the special 'myths' of government: the 'myth' of a free choice between political parties (itself another extension of the 'myth' of the free market), and the 'myth' of representative government – that the government has the right to govern because it represents the people (although with this can be combined the 'myth' of checks on the government, so that the government doesn't do too much governing, or, perhaps more exactly, so that the government doesn't govern in the interests of the wrong kinds of people). There is also the 'myth' of the rule of law – both that all citizens are equal under the law and that the law (decided on by the voters through their representatives) is the ultimate guarantor of freedom. (The idea of 'equality before the law' not only conceals inequalities of access; what can be even more important is that it can conceal the inequalities of the law itself, with its declarations of what is legal and what is not.)

It is easy to dismiss all this as a set of 'myths' peculiarly suited to the advantage of the privileged in capitalist societies and uniquely related to the market economy – not only because they provide an inherent defence of private property but also because they provide a distraction from what is actually going on. Thus the right to organize is always restricted, and the right for organizations to act is always limited: the most telling example is that trade unions gained, through their own struggles, the right to organize, but their right to *act*, in strikes, is always limited. In any perceived crisis in industrial action, a liberal-democratic government will always act against the strikers. And there is *not* a free marketplace of ideas: there is a public culture dominated by a restricted range of ideas. Sometimes in liberal-democratic societies people can say almost anything they like and not be arrested. At other times the likelihood of arrest might be quite great. Sometimes censorship of published material is light; sometimes it is heavy. But even at the most demonstrably liberal times there is only a restricted range of public debate, and access to the amplifiers of opinion is limited by certain rules.

Nevertheless, if all these particular 'myths' of liberalism are to be dismissed as suited only to the advantage of the privileged in capitalist societies, there is, to put it mildly, a problem for those who want a better world. I will come back to this.

The 'myth' of free choice between political parties, and the 'myth' of representative government, can also be seen as being to the advantage of the privileged in capitalist societies as (even more definitely) a distraction from the facts of power. In the first place, the choice between political parties is *not* a free market. The market is necessarily rigged – by the existing party system. What voters are given, as Joseph Schumpeter definitively argued in *Capitalism, Socialism and Democracy*, is not a free choice, but a choice between what is offered to them by the party system. And this will be a choice only within a restricted range. (A more positive way to look at it might not be from the shopping list perspective of 'choice' but from the perspective that in a state with more than one party, even if the range offered by the parties is narrow, there is the constitutional possibility that a government can be dismissed.) It has already been indicated how misleading the 'myth' of representativeness can be; it should also be indicated how diversionary it can be. It can suggest to citizens that since they all have the vote and since they use their votes with relatively equal weights, then there must be in their society an equality in the distribution of power. This illusion is strengthened by beliefs in the centrality of government – as if 'power' is uniquely resident within the government administration, which has an independent (some-times arbitrating) existence and represents an agreed common good. And it can also suggest that there can be something 'undemocratic' in protest by citizens against the government, because the government is the repository of the people's will.

In fact 'the people' are significantly missing from the symbolic display in practically all of the buildings that house the legislatures of the liberal-democratic societies. Some of them are palaces converted to new purposes. The National Assembly in Paris (formerly the Palais Bourbon) has one significant reference to the 1789 revolution – Mirabeau's defence of the Third Estate – and there are two statues of the Republic, two of Liberty and one of Montesquieu (now relegated to the garden), but the dominant political references are to great men of France (Charlemagne, St Louis, etc.) and great men of Greece and Rome (Solon, Brutus, etc.); however, the greatest emphasis, in reds and ivories and golds, in chandeliers and painted ceilings, is on the sumptuous elegance of the aristocratic past. The Chamber of Deputies in Rome (constructed around a palace), with its marble floors, third-rate Old Masters, tapestries, glass cases of old pots and painted allegorical ceilings, provides a parody of a patrician *palazzo*; the chamber itself, with its sumptuous oaken columns and red velvet curtains, celebrates the concept of the nineteenth-century Opera House. In the Hague the principal house of the States General is located in a former palace, in a celebration of the eighteenth-century ballroom experience. Some of the parlia-ments are in new palaces. In London the Houses of Parliament are principally a celebration of royalty and aristocracy; the parliament in Vienna, in its façade and on its roof, is a museum of all of the forms of nineteenth-century classical revivals. A few of the parliaments (notably in Berne, and in Oslo) exist with a kind of democratic plainness; in Stockholm, parliament moved itself away from a plain, modern building back to a more aristocratic past. Even in the United States, whose Constitution begins with the words 'We the People', scarcely any of the legislative buildings acknowledge the symbolic presence of 'the people'. Even the Capitol building in Washington does not effectively include in its symbolism a reference to the 'myth' of 'the people'. Outside, along with many of the surrounding buildings, from the Federal Triangle to Union Station, it is a reminder of the virtues of Imperial Rome; inside it is a baroque monument to aristocratic style. In its principal art works, it celebrates the European conquest of America.

There is another element in some of the buildings of the United States legislature: there can be architecturally eloquent expressions of Republican Roman virtue and even Latin tags stressing the duties to the state of the Roman Senate. With this sense of Romanness can come the idea of law-making: the walls of the House of Representatives in Washington are ringed with 23 marble plaques of great law-makers, beginning with Hammurabi, Solon and Moses, and including Suleiman the Magnificent. Only one of them, Thomas Jefferson, professed democratic principles. With its monumental marble steps, colonnades and sweeps of marble floor, the Supreme Court, built in the 1930s, went even further than Adolph Hitler in his plans for using neo-classical architecture to inspire in the people an acquiescent sense of awe. In liberal-democratic societies the 'myth' of 'the rule of law' can be diversionary. But it can also be simply autocratic. The Constitution of the United States may have begun with the phrase 'We the people' but for 76 years it was interpreted as permitting slavery. For conservatives in a liberal-democratic society 'the rule of law' may be the most acceptable liberal-democratic 'myth'. They

can appear most at home when carrying out a 'law-and-order'
campaign to defend 'freedom'.

'Myths' of collectivism

As things stand, the liberal-democratic 'myths' provide the
characteristic 'legitimations' of economic and political power
in modern industrial societies that are capitalist. The executives
of the large corporations and the owners of small businesses
conduct their affairs in a 'reality' that, as projected in the public
culture, purports to explain and justify their power over
material and human resources. The 'realities' of what is seen as
an economic marketplace are also to be found in what is seen as
a political marketplace, projected in the public culture and
purporting to explain and justify the actions of the various
sections of the apparatus of the state – legislative assemblies,
governments, bureaucratic administrations, government corporations, the courts and the coercive and surveillance forces
(the military, the police, the intelligence services). They are also
projected as explaining and justifying the existence of the
political parties as the mediating units of the political system,
although often with considerable strain among those who see
party politics as 'dirty', or who see their own party as legitimate
and the others as a threat to society.

It is obviously not the case that liberal-democratic 'myths'
are the only 'legitimations' of economic power in capitalist
societies. For example, there are also Greece under the
colonels, Spain and Portugal under Franco and Salazar,
Germany under Hitler, Japan under Togo, and the whole
patronalist and *étatiste* traditions of Latin America. What is
'legitimated' in fascist or *étatiste* societies are the leader and the
state itself. It is they who lend their 'legitimacy' to the
capitalists. It may, however, be true that when the liberal-
democratic 'myths' operate effectively (when they are not
merely asserted, but permeate the society, becoming its
'common sense') capitalist societies run more smoothly; it
might be easier to run a labour force imbued with the work

ethic and the consumer ethic and housed in suburbs than a labour force of slaves housed in concentration camps. For that matter, versions of the liberal-democratic 'myths' could operate in the public culture of a Communist society. However, that is not how things stand at present. Equally it does not seem self-evident that collectivist 'myths' could not operate in the public cultures of capitalist societies. In fact they do. But in its most simple form it is in the Communist societies that the collectivist 'myth' at present dominates the public culture. It is in that form that it will be considered here.

The Soviet Constitution explains and justifies the power of the Communist Party in the Soviet Union in precise Leninist terms. The aims of the dictatorship of the proletariat having been fulfilled in destroying the capitalist system and establishing the Bolshevik Party as the vanguard party of the working class, the Soviet state has become a 'state of the whole people'. 'All power belongs to the people', who, in the system of 'democratic centralism', exercise power through Soviets of peoples' deputies and in general through electing 'all bodies of state authority from the lowest to the highest'. And since state property ('the common property of the Soviet people') is the principal form of socialist property the people thereby exercise their power over property by this means, or through control in collective farms or co-operative property. So far, what has been put forward is similar to part of the 'myth' of representative government, except that on paper it is more thorough, with more positions up for election. More rituals of voting go on. More hands are raised. But even if the voting were not as pre-arranged as it is known to be, this *is* merely the representative principle, with all of its weaknesses. The Yugoslav Constitution is more ambitious in its 'myth' of collectivity. It additionally offers the participatory rather than the representative principle, on the basis of 'social relations based on self-management by the working people' in which 'socially owned means of production' are 'managed directly by associated workers working within these means in their own interests and in the interests of the working class and the socialist society'. This would seem to be an essential element in a thoroughgoing 'myth' of collectivity.

The Soviet Constitution also refers, however, to the leading role of the party, 'the vanguard of all the people'. The leading and guiding force of Soviet society and the nucleus of its political system and all state organizations and public organizations is the Communist Party of the Soviet Union, which 'exists for the people and serves the people'. So, although the 'myth' of the representative principle is firmly entrenched, and, in the case of the Yugoslavs, the 'myth' of the participatory principle as well, there is no liberal 'myth' of choice in political parties. The Communist Party is the vanguard party of all the people. Why would the people need any other parties? Wouldn't these parties necessarily be enemies of the people? For those socialists who simply do not believe that the Communist Party *is* the vanguard party of all the people, a most troubling question remains: how is it possible to imagine a socialist modern industrial state with more than one political party? (Some Communist states do have more than one party, but the relations between the minor parties and the Communist parties are pre-arranged.) Is it possible to imagine a socialist modern industrial state with *anti*-socialist parties? Is it possible to imagine a socialist state in which socialism could be legislated out of existence? I would think the answer lies in asking the same question of the capitalist societies: is it possible to imagine a capitalist society in which capitalism could be legislated out of existence?

So far, at least apart from Yugoslavia, the 'myths' of collectivism in Communist modern industrial states have left vagueness as to what collectivism might mean as a primary organizing basis for society. There is no doubt that in their public cultures direct 'myths' of individualism are absent. (The excesses of the personality cult were not individualistic but fascist: the people lent their will to a leader, through whom they then lived.) There are various expressions of social control based on social utility, but beyond that there is the difficulty that there are not many usable Marxist–Leninist references:

Marx did not have much to say about the classless society, and some of what he did say could seem rather like the general humanist 'myths' of progress: human nature was essentially good and, once social constraints were removed, that goodness would be liberated.

What fills some of the gap in the public culture is the 'myth' of revolution. There actually were, at least in a conventional although not necessarily Marxist sense, revolutions in Russia, Yugoslavia, Albania and Bulgaria, and in various ways the struggles involved can make credible appeals to a national patriotism of revolution – especially in the Soviet Union, where, following the breakdown of the state and the rise of Bolshevik leadership, there was the civil war, with intervention from four imperialist powers; and in Yugoslavia, where Tito and the Partisans are a convincingly heroic legend. There were no working-class revolutions, in any ordinary sense, in the other European Communist nations, but 'revolutions' have nevertheless been invented for them in the public culture. In the Klement Gottwald Museum in Prague this is done by presenting wartime Czech resistance to the Nazis not as resistance (which makes it the same as resistance in capitalist Europe) but as a 'national and democratic revolution': this is then followed, in February 1948, by 'the culminating phase of the class struggle in modern Czechoslovak history'. In Bucharest, in the Museum of the History of the Communist Party and the Revolutionary and Democratic Movement of Romania, the transition is also made by simple audio-visual proclamations: one set of photographs and other relics shows the establishment, through 'revolution', of a 'popular democratic regime'; dated two and a half years later, another set of photographs and relics asserts 'the transition from bourgeois democratic to socialist revolution'. Whether or not these sacred (and legitimizing) 'revolutions' *were*, in any conventional sense, revolutions varies from one country to another, but in all these countries there is a curiously frozen and detached quality about them. There it is – that was the revolution (which, like the crucifixion, made possible human salvation). That is now the end of revolution. It is only in non-Communist countries that the revolution can still flourish. With its millennialist belief that by one great turning of things upside down human nature will be liberated and human society will be saved, it has been one of the most impelling 'myths' of modernism. In *Pyramids of Sacrifice* Peter Berger suggests that the 'myth' of revolution is equalled only by the 'myth' of economic growth. Like the 'myth' of economic growth, the 'myth' of revolution can offer guarantees of material and social improvement and, in its most ambitious modes, the prospect of paradise on earth and human perfectibility. The national creation 'myths' of a number of capitalist modern industrial nation-states feature legends of bold uprisings, still commemorated in paintings, sculptures, patriotic songs, national days and school history texts; the French, on the whole a conservative people, nevertheless have as part of their permanent political repertoire the occasional painless enactment of brief, quasi-revolutionary episodes – a theatrical technique that can ensure the changing of some things while the important things can remain the same. In the world outside the modern industrial regimes, whether capitalist or Communist, the 'myth' of revolution can have more credibility than the 'myth' of economic growth: it is the basic creation 'myth' of most of the nation-states of Africa, the Middle East, Asia and Latin America. In Mexico the party that has won all elections since 1929 is called 'the Institutional Revolutionary Party'. Even in the capitalist modern industrial societies, revolution – now mainly in Marxist versions or what purport to be Marxist versions – can seem the only possible redemptive process.

It was only in China that there was an attempt within a Communist society – in the 'cultural revolution' – to re-invent revolution as a salvationary force. Except in China, Cuba and Vietnam the received Communist view of revolution became exceptionally narrow, an heroicization of Lenin's 'Great October Revolution' – even if this was not in itself a revolution at all but as Barrington Moore put it in his book *Injustice*, a 'changing of the guard' in front of a series of government buildings in Leningrad. Yet the simplest legend can see the revolution completed with the 'storming' of the Winter Palace (an event that in fact took place after the occupation of other government buildings was over). Having portrayed this heroic episode, the official paintings then show the triumphal Lenin a few hours later handing down to the Second Congress of Soviets the Decree on Peace and the Decree on Land. This particular legend of the Great October Revolution has frozen the 'myth' of revolution in the Communist modern industrial states to a narrow, mechanistic determinism in which, as if in a series of chemical equations, certain changes in the ownership of productive property will necessarily produce certain types of social change and change in human consciousness. (In fact the Great October Revolution was not even an economic change. It was a sharp *political* change – or *coup*.) The usual Soviet explanation of almost any social change or lack of social change is to make an analysis of material circumstances. Paradoxically, this crass determinism is combined with an equally crass voluntarism in which all kinds of exhortations are made for an increased exercise of the human will. A 'Marxist–Leninist' purity of revolutionary doctrine is preserved: the great questions of revolution remain undiscussed.

In the 'legitimations' of the Communist nation-states it remains essential that there should be maintained an ever-present sense of the presence of the working people. They are present in the public art and other symbolism of the state, in the official rhetoric, in the newspapers and in the television programmes. From movies to museums of revolution, their role is commemorated in historical reconstructions of their sufferings under capitalism, of the formation of labour parties and trade unions, the correctness of party lines, heroic legends of strikes, protests or wartime resistance. But it is as *workers* rather than as *people* that the working people are likely to become manifest in the contemporary public culture. They are part of a great drama, not of human liberation, but of plans for economic production. The museums of revolution are likely to end with exhibits of power houses, blast furnaces and, in the more prosperous

Communist states, of consumer goods – motor cars and refrigerators.

In the Soviet Union the greatest 'legitimation' of power is the leadership of Lenin. Tens of thousands of statues, from granite colossi to small plaster casts, flood the Soviet Union. There are tens of thousands of reproductions of the most famous paintings of Lenin: his face appears on vases, in tapestry, in glass, in ceramics. On tens of thousands of walls are lettered quotations from Lenin's works. His name honours hundreds of towns and city districts, hundreds of industrial enterprises and recreation centres, and thousands of squares and streets. There is a Lenin Strait, a Lenin Mountain, a Lenin Atomic Icebreaker. There are hundreds of Lenin museums and memorials. (It is in these that the schoolchildren 'Pioneers' stand in their red caps and scarves, flowers in their hands and dedicate themselves to the ideals of Lenin.) The party leaders explain each change in course as one in which they are being faithful to 'the correct Leninist path'. The great slogans proclaim Lenin's supreme virtue: 'Lenin is with us.' 'Lenin Lived. Lenin Lives. Lenin Will Live.' 'Lenin's name and Lenin's case will live forever.'

7. The Variant Repertoires of the Public Culture

Repertoires

In the last chapter I began with the general outline of the 'myths' of modernity and of industrialism that are the tickets of entry into this discussion. Then there was a listing of two pre-industrial 'myths', the chauvinism of sex and race, that existed before the industrial era but that have survived it and that may have both affected it and been affected by it. Then came a consideration of the 'myths' of national identity, some national-chauvinist, some not: all of them provide definitions of a nation-state which can be a basis for thought and action but they also provide vehicles for chauvinisms of sex and race and ethnicity, and for general 'legitimations' of other kinds of claims to privilege in a society. After that came a concern with what are, for the moment, the two main streams of 'myths' that purport to explain and legitimate the control of those social resources that we think of as 'economic' and as 'political'. In the liberal-democratic societies this fuzzy distinction is itself a 'myth', diverting attention from 'economic' power to power that is seen as 'political' – an illusion maintained by much of the 'political science' teaching in the universities in many capitalist societies. I have so far not used the word 'class', but what we are talking about here are divisions based not only on sex, race and ethnicity but also on how people work and/or how they gain their incomes (which I take to be the areas of concern that people have when they use the word 'class').

However, as well as those discussed there are at least five other repertoires available in modern industrial societies –

what I will call 'the labour culture', 'the neo-traditional culture', 'the religious culture', 'the ethnic compromise' and 'the critics' culture', each of which has a potential to colour a public culture.

The religious culture

In speaking of 'the religious culture' of modern industrial societies we are speaking, very largely, of what is left over in secular societies from the previous hegemony of the 'myths' of the Christian religion. In saying 'Christian', I have not suddenly slipped into ethnocentrism. The point is that with the exception of Japan, and a few small nations (Israel, for example, or Singapore), all the other modern industrial states developed out of what was once Christendom.

Until the Protestant revolts, or, more exactly, until 'toleration' and then secularization, religious culture was the dominant 'language' of what we now think of as art, entertainment and ceremony, and political and economic life. Christendom could be cleft by secular conflicts and by heresies and schisms, but these were all differences within a Christian 'reality'. It was the churchmen who decided what the facts were and stored the bodies of knowledge: if there was to be a dispute it would be a dispute between churchmen who, in the great scriptoriums, copied knowledge from one manuscript to the next. The Church controlled all teaching, most scholarship and, at periods, virtually all writing. The Church was the main patron of what we now think of as the arts, although these were not seen as 'art' but as devotional and institutional techniques, and it was the principal master of the ceremonies of state and, to some extent, of folk ceremonies as well. Churchmen held a monopoly in reaching out to the people by preaching, and they commanded the unique technique of the confessional. They could warn, authoritatively, of the details of damnation; their monasteries could offer an exclusive model of what goodness might be like; and in their exclusive control of the sacraments the Church held a monopoly on salvation.

To what extent this dominance influenced people's thoughts and provided their only effective 'common sense' is something that we can only guess about from what has haphazardly survived in written records. The main point is that the Church held a virtual monopoly of public statements of 'myth' about what life was like. It was God who was invoked as the great legitimator, both of the powers of princes and of sex and ethnic discriminations. If there was a challenge to some earthly power, this would also be explained as part of God's work. The first great revolt against the Church, the fifteenth-century Hussite rebellion in Bohemia that held Christendom at bay for 15 years, was seen by its 'fraternities' as a return to the early Church, with aspirations of simplicity and equality.

The basic 'reality' that explained the world was the *supernatural*. This was supported by an enormous weight of legends and icons and rituals – of which, in earthly affairs, the most important was prayer. Whether by prayer, or by making an offering, or both, seeking supernatural intercession in earthly affairs was the practical way to get things done in Christendom as in almost all other societies. Even those who did not accept the Church's monopoly were likely also to appeal to the supernatural, although through sorcery.

With the Reformation, Europeans divided into several camps in their view of the supernatural, but this was merely a struggle between rival certainties. It was not until the seventeenth century that the Netherlander, Spinoza, put forward his extraordinary view that the liberty of the individual should be the basis of the state. It was in the Netherlands of the late seventeenth century – perhaps partly because sectarianism could impede trade and Amsterdam was the trading centre of the world – that toleration first became manifest, but it was not really until the eighteenth century that an accompanying secularism began to transform society. People began to speak of the future as if it could be in their own hands, not in the hands of God. This is the time when what we now think of as 'political' and 'economic' conflict began to be expressed in thoroughly secular 'myths'. As the Australian historian Alan

Gilbert puts it in his book *The Making of Post-Christian Britain*, one can see the difference by comparing the rhetoric of the Netherlands and English revolts in the early seventeenth century (which were drenched in religious justification), with that of the North American and French revolts of the late eighteenth century (which were not). In the North American revolt, orators were still polite about God but they presented 'the people' (by whom they meant people like themselves) as prime movers in their own affairs; in the French revolt God became an eighteenth-century logical abstraction, a mere Supreme Deity or epitome of Reason. Bonaparte later put God back into the churches that had been secularized in the revolution, but this was a tame, nineteenth-century God, whose function it was to keep the people acquiescent.

As Gilbert presents it, a modern 'secular society' is not an atheist society, but a society where the supernatural, if believed to exist, is seen primarily as a matter for the hereafter. A modern secular society is one in which the world is interpreted mainly in its own material, earthly terms and in which humans see humans, not God, as masters of human destiny. Whether or not they also pray for supernatural assistance is a matter of taste, but, at best, supernatural intervention as evoked by prayer is usually an ancillary resource. If Christianity remains part of the public culture (which it can do, if tenuously, even in some of the Communist societies), it no longer provides the *language* of the public culture and it may be significant mainly in secular terms, in its relationship to the structure of the state. In the secularizing processes of the nineteenth century, religion met its match in the newly developing 'myths' of liberalism, conservatism, radicalism, socialism, nationalism, imperialism, each of which provided an alternative explanation of the world to that of religion and all of which offered alternative ways of getting things done to those of prayer, and all of which provided alternative forms of social mobilization. Even the religious political parties tended to be redefined in political terms. They were not only Calvinist or Lutheran or Catholic: they were also seen as 'conservative' or 'centrist'.

In the great social changes of the nineteenth century churches tended to take the side of the powerful, but not without conflicts. Those churches that were conservative and supported the old order could become what Alan Gilbert describes as 'prophetic critics of modernity' (as the Catholic Church did), and could sometimes attack the materialism, secularism, hedonism, liberalism and individualism of the new capitalist order. Others, most notably some of the Protestant Churches, with their emphasis on the work ethic, individualism and self-help, became capitalism at prayer, and movements such as Anglican 'evangelicalism' or Lutheran 'pietism' could also provide sustenance in the new drives for respectability. As the church of compassion, the Catholic Church could hold out hope, at least in the afterlife, for the poor and the powerless in a world where all humans were united in being sinners, and it could still offer powerful folk appeals of communal ceremony. Revivalist Protestants (the Wesleyans, for example, or the Salvation Army) could also offer communal solace, by re-workings of Protestantism into an optimistic creed of salvation through prayer, good works, decorum and temperance and, by folk creation, also provide communal ceremonies.

In the United States, revivalism moved furthest, both for whites and for blacks. In the other new European societies transplanted to the Americas and Oceania, the European religious denominations adjusted to new circumstances but remained recognizably European. In the United States revivalism created a new product. With torchlit camp meetings, shoutings, sittings, stampings, week-long festivals, 'old time religion' projected a frontier of faith of ostensibly literal interpretations of the Bible, equality among believers, salvation through individual worth and the continuing folk excitements of constant ceremonies of affirmation and conversion carried out in contemporary entertainment styles, with a tribal combination of life, art, religion and entertainment in a way that could seem distinctively 'American'. Among the black people, revivalism created an even greater definition of 'reality': the black churches became the main institutional definers of what being a black in the United States might mean, with entirely new art forms – communal preaching, gospel song, the blues. In both cases, new religious movements had been created with new styles that could tie people into communal life and also provide an opening for contemporary forms of social intervention.

As faith drains out of theologians (apart from fundamentalists and traditionally minded Catholics), it may be partly this communal, folk appeal that can hold churches together. There is a joke in Italy that there are more Catholics in Poland than in Italy and more Communists in Italy than in Poland. When I put this to a Communist senator he said, 'That's no joke. Both the Church in Poland and the Party in Italy provide people with a sense of belonging.'

The Christian churches – almost all of them – had taken on imperialist colorations as they articulated a 'myth' of the great mission given by God to various European races to civilize the world. In the Great War of 1914–18 they led the litanies in the national cults of blood. In each nation the war was expected to provide, by its great sacrifices, a redemptive cleansing for the nation as it was washed in the blood of young men. It is doubtful if, in their interventions in the life of the state, the churches ever recovered from these excesses. Now, even in the non-Communist societies, with the exception of the United States, God seems, very largely, to have abandoned affairs of state. It is usually no longer as master of ceremonies, but as one of the officiants, that God is now most visible in the public culture, and as a recorder of births, marriages and deaths.

In none of the modern industrial societies does religion dominate the public culture and it is in only a few of them (Ireland, for example) that it provides, even residually, elements of the language of the public culture. With a few exceptions, most notably Italy, where the Pope is a celebrated figure, constantly on television, church dignitaries do not even appear with any frequency in the public culture. In Amsterdam the two most prestigious churches have now been secularized to become cultural centres. They can be hired for religious services.

In Japan, after the Second World War, there were a number of expressions of religious revivalism in the so-called 'new religions'. Superficially these might seem similar to what happened in the United States – but there is little or no concern in the 'new religions' with the supernatural. If they are a revival of anything it is of ideas of what it might mean to be 'Japanese'. There are the group rituals and group expressiveness of religion-belonging, but these exist with only touches of religious belief. It is in the United States – shown by surveys to be perhaps the most religious-believing of the modern industrial societies – that 'new religions' still have a wider meaning. The black churches were the principal institutional base for the civil rights movement and, on the whole, they continue to spearhead the drive by black people to gain some space of their own in United States politics and public culture. From Martin Luther King to Jesse Jackson, most of the black leaders have been preachers; in the speech that at the 1984 Democratic National Convention stained with tears many a televized Democratic cheek, Jackson actually performed, as a politician among politicians, an act of Christian contrition. The styles of black revivalism are so strong that they have become part of the repertoire of liberation. In one climactic sequence at that Democratic Convention, after the tear-stained cheeks there came the soft rock, and the disco dancing, then a sound-and-light show when the '1812 Overture' played to a background of strobe-lighting and fireworks, then the 'Battle Hymn of the Republic', then a gospel song, with the delegates holding hands and swaying, and more television close-ups of damp cheeks. It was significant, however, that although the Democratic voter-registration drive was conducted with gospel-song fervour, the counter-registration drive from the Republicans was conducted with equal fervour by white religious fundamentalists protecting 'the American way of life', creationist beliefs that the world was made by God in six days several thousand years ago, and millennialist beliefs in the imminence of Christ's second coming. But there is a difficulty in invoking God in a country where people of all denominations are seen as influential voters. It is: what is God's religion? With Jewish voters, for instance, seen as marginally significant, God cannot be presented as Christian. At the Republican Convention a plan to include a copy of the New Testament in the delegates' kits was abandoned after protests from the American Jewish Committee.

There are still religious practices in the Soviet Union, although in its public culture it proclaims itself atheist. As in the French Revolution, the churches in Russia were seized and put to secular purposes, and many of them have not been given back; a Museum of Atheism was established in one of Leningrad's greatest cathedrals; only 45 churches are still open in all Moscow; new towns are built without any churches. Yet churches are still attended and although the large audiences at the Easter services may be there more for the theatrical than the religious qualities of these occasions, there are still signs of minority belief. But in the public culture, the Orthodox Church is a resource controlled by the state and given whatever exposure reasons of state demand: the Patriarch is deployed in and out of the public culture according to political needs. And it is mainly the Russian Orthodox Church (with its symbolic Russianness) that gains even this exposure. Islam (perhaps with more active adherents now than the Orthodox faith) is almost completely invisible in much of the public culture. In Bulgaria, the Orthodox Church is given a place in the public culture in its context as initiator of Slavonic civilization, as a nation-definer in the nineteenth-century struggle against the Ottomans and as a bearer of national art forms – icons, church music, architectural styles. In Yugoslavia the toleration (although not the encouragement) of religious faith – Orthodox, Catholic, Islamic – is part of that public acceptance of ethnic difference that is seen as essential to the survival of the Yugoslav state. In the German Democratic Republic, where Marxist views of Luther are undergoing change, the Evangelical Church has been given some ill-defined place in the public culture. In Poland, where the Catholic Church has been a state within a state, part of the church's essential strategy has been to extend its visibility in the public culture.

Apart from whatever vestigial role the churches may play in the ceremonies of civil religion and whatever vestigial 'newsworthiness' remains in their own activities, provoked usually by internal disagreements, novelties or 'personalities' (the Mother Theresa syndrome), a church in a liberal-democratic society becomes, as it were, merely one 'lobby group' amongst others in that society's public space. (It may not even be 'the Church' itself that speaks, but elements of it.) It enters a secular public culture on secular terms.

And in this the churches (or elements of them) are no longer necessarily on the right. Recently the Catholic bishops in the United States made a (qualified) assault on capitalism; clergymen of all denominations are on all the peace platforms; some Church of England dignitaries declined to bay with the pack in the Falkland Islands celebrations in London; clergymen speak up for gays, women's rights, the environment, the poor. In Latin American countries the church of compassion and of the martyred Christ has become a principal articulator of social discontent and, in doing so, provides new theology and new martyrs.

There is, however, still also a strong religious 'lobby' of the right, and not only in the United States, which can appear in the public cultures of the liberal-democratic societies because of its resistance to 'permissiveness' and the disintegration of religious rules for conduct. There has been a dismantling of the Protestant 'myths' of restraint that occupied such a strong position in public culture in northern Europe, in the Protestant-dominated societies of North America and Oceania, and in some Catholic societes (Ireland, for example). These were the 'myths' of the holiness of the Sabbath, the need for decorum in manners and attire, and abstinence from evils such as dancing, smoking and drinking. These Protestant 'myths' were, all of them, threats to the commercial base of a consumer society and their relegation within the public culture occurred without much friction – although there are exceptions, such as the still strong temperance movement in Sweden or the minority fundamentalist movement in the Netherlands. There was also in the public culture, to varying degrees in various countries, a casting aside of some of the 'myths' of sexuality – the belief in sex as provided by God for procreation in marriage, not for random recreation, the belief in chastity, the (coded) belief in the sexual passivity of women – and these assaults on the public culture, accompanied, to some extent, by actual changes in sexual practice, aroused the Catholics as well. The related but different question of abortion brought out the greatest passions, in some countries producing a fusion in which Protestant clergymen led secular anti-abortion movements, with many or most of their supporters Catholic. In the United States, the conservative faith contains both disbelief in abortion choice and a belief in laissez-faire capitalism. Beyond all of these anxieties there were also concerns, not always stated as such, about threats, in the public culture, to the 'myths' of woman being intended, by God and/or by Nature, to be 'feminine'.

To those affronted by change, all of these changes could seem to be portents of a general decline and fall. Religious belief and puritan practice were seen as the cement of the social order: when they began to disintegrate in the public culture, it was assumed that society was rotting. Sometimes, by contrast, the puritanism of the Communists was praised. Yet the modern industrial state that could seem most homogeneous and that could also seem to be working and thinking hardest about production for profit had for three centuries lacked any strongly proclaimed religious faith. Japan had 'Confucianized' the supernatural out of its ruling-class culture in the seventeenth century. Following China, the 'myths' by which Japan's rulers ordered their actions were not those of the supernatural but of a belief in a rational order of things here on earth (not in this respect unlike that of eighteenth-century Enlightenment, but lacking the accompanying belief in progress) and also with a belief in government, in filial loyalties and hard work. It is true that the Japanese rulers added a revised Shinto, with its shrines and festivals, but this was not much concerned with the supernatural: it was the Japanese version of imperialism, elegantly understated. After the war, Shinto almost disappeared from the public culture; a few of the shrines are now national monuments, others are principally reminders of nature, order and beauty. The 'myths' by which the Japanese work and that hold things together in Japan are secular – a belief in group loyalty and in hard work, in achievement, and in the purchase of consumer goods. What holds the modern industrial societies together is not religious faith, but the beliefs and practices of modernity and industralism. The 'religious culture' is one of the ingredients of a public culture; its significance is most likely to lie in the secular effects of a religious presence.

The neo-traditional culture

As the European countries and Japan in varying degrees exploded into modernity and industrialism, their old ruling-class culture was necessarily changed.

The first of these metamorphoses of the 'myths' of traditional ruling-class culture came with the construction of the creeds of 'conservatism' and 'imperialism' in nineteenth-century and early twentieth-century Europe. These new 'myths' came from the need to mobilize the masses in what was becoming a 'democratic' age (one in which it was seen as necessary to colour the opinions of the masses as well as to coerce them, since working-class males were gaining the franchise and being conscripted into armies). Their construction was a means of gaining new 'legitimations' for the old privileges of dynasties and nobilities. The method was to develop the 'myths' of national chauvinism (as distinguished from nationality) and, in the case of nations with colonies, an enlargement of this into the 'myths' of imperialism, which is to say the 'myths' of European national chauvinism operating in the world beyond Europe – the world of 'the natives'. The nation was not to be found, rhetorically, in 'the people', except in the United States and in the French Third Republic (and in the latter with the opposition of the royalist parties and the Catholic Church). In all these other industrializing nations – with their railway systems and their power-driven factories, their telegraph and telephone systems, their gas and electricity, their new economic classes, their programmes for universal literacy – the 'nation' was to be found in the monarchs in their medieval garments and in the leaders of the military forces in their eighteenth-century uniforms. Monarch and state were seen as one, and in the conscript armies it was to the monarch, as to a medieval prince, that allegiance was sworn. The gallant soldier laid down his life for monarch as much as for country. In the public culture, for all the peoples of the Russian, British, Austro-Hungarian, Japanese and German Empires, life was offered its greatest secular meaning in the absorption of selfhood into loyalty to Crown and Empire. The greatest honour available to mankind was to lay down one's life for God and Emperor. It was only in the France of the Third Republic and in the United States that honour could be achieved by laying down one's life for 'the people'.

As principal embodiments of the honour of the nation, both monarchy and military were seen as inspired by a spirit of 'chivalry' that had been resuscitated and revamped and made manifest in a flow of works of third-rate stereotyped art portraying St George and other legendary characters (and in Japan the samurai) and given continuing life in the invention of many new chivalric Orders, from the Norwegian Order of St Olaf to the Japanese Order of the Chrysanthemum. There was a general taste for the medieval and a considerable flaunting of colourful costumes and uniforms. The church (and, in Japan, Shinto) was also seen as imbued with the spirit of the past and often with the spirit of 'the nation'; the spirit of the nation might also be found in the certainties of rural life and in the peasantry, both of them much glorified in paintings. Old ethnocentrisms became magnified in great chauvinist boasts and great xenophobic fears. This was the age of terrors of what might come, if there was a weakening of the national will, from catastrophes such as 'the yellow peril', 'the Cossack invasion', 'the American challenge', 'the Zionist conspiracy' or a general 'decline of the West'. There was an accompanying intellectual conservatism which, in contradiction to the optimism of modernity, maintained a pessimistic view of a world seen through the Christian doctrine of Original Sin as necessarily a vale of tears. In this predicament, it was not the 'myth' of optimism but the 'myth' of fatalism that was needed for acceptance of the inevitably unsatisfactory nature of 'man's lot'. Along with this, as already discussed, went a nostalgic regret for the passing of what was seen as an organic society, in which everyone, high or low, had 'his' 'proper place'.

It was the new 'myth' of the democratic conservatism of a state honoured by monarch and nobility and of military forces honoured by chivalry that formed the 'myth' of the Right in the nineteenth century. (The whole idea of 'the Right' was, of course, a nineteenth-century invention.) I have said 'democratic' because this conservatism developed as a response to various needs of social mobilization, most openly expressed by Napoleon III ('Other French governments have ruled with the support of perhaps one million of the educated masses: I have called in the other twenty-nine million'), but consciously understood by many others. Conservative 'myths' appeared to be in opposition to the perceived greed and disruptiveness of capitalism. To some extent Disraeli, for instance, purported to be summoning the strength of the people against the havoc brought to Britain by unbridled capitalism; Bismarck's inauguration of a welfare state was an intervention against perceived excesses of capitalism.

In societies where the bourgeois programme of the Declaration of Rights was not in operation, the new capitalists might find themselves on the 'left'. In Britain, where even the nobility were divided between conservatism and liberalism, liberalism was nevertheless seen as the specific doctrine of business. But although the conservative–liberal juxtaposition could still have meaning in some nations (most strongly perhaps in the Scandinavian nations and most savagely repressed in Britain, by the bias of the voting system) there was a transformation in all the liberal-democratic societies when the socialist parties began to form as to what 'the Right' was supposed to be.

Conservatism came to mean, essentially, capitalism, opposed to a perceived socialism. Even in the countries where religious parties became the principal conservatives, they also became the principal parties of capital. In Italy, where the Christian Democrats still remained a party of the Catholic Church, they nevertheless also became the representatives of capitalism, Italian-style, although with tensions. In the Federal Republic of Germany, where the Christian Democrats were really no longer a religious party but represented a symbolic fusion between the old Catholic and Lutheran differences, that is to say, an end to religious parties, the Christian Democratic Party became, for a season with Ludwig Erhardt as Economics Minister, the principal capitalist 'myth'-maker of post-1945 Europe.

By mid-twentieth century, the new 'traditions' of Europe that had been fabricated in the nineteenth century to serve the interests of the old nobility had gone through further transformations. In the Communist nation-states they had simply been cleared away, except that, varying from one state to the next, there was some residual presence left for the churches. In liberal-democratic states the old ruling-class culture was shattered in its old forms, but, as with other explosions, fragments of its 'myths' might remain drifting in the social culture where they could take new forms and acquire new functions and serve new interests. In some of the capitalist states some of these fragments re-shaped and coalesced in new ways and, without either liberal-democratic or capitalist-individualist 'myths', became the principal 'legitimations' of power. This was in the fascist states. In the New World of the Americas and Oceania, it would be only a slight exaggeration to say that some of these 'new societies' (the United States, Canada, Australia, New Zealand) were born modern – they were settled at the time when Britain's modernization was beginning – but even in these, especially in 'the old dominions', there could remain substantial fragments of the old 'myths'. The Latin American societies were, however, settled in the pre-modern period and, unlike even their founding societies, they seemed isolated from the way things were going, remaining un-'modern', yet not 'traditional' either – partly museum cultures, repeating old themes.

In all of these societies, where fragments of once-traditional culture survived, those fragments were *transformed*, just as an exhibit in a museum is transformed by becoming an 'exhibit', or a 'monument' is transformed by existing in a society different from the one that produced it. Even if one element of a society does not appear to change and other elements of that society do change, the unchanging element does, in fact, also change, because it is interacting not with the traditional but with the modern. The 'traditional' is irretrievable. A feudal survival in a modern industrial society is no longer feudal. That is why, to explain a range of authoritative figures in a spectrum ranging from Adolph Hitler to a New Zealand Governor-General, I will use the expression 'neo-traditional'. In any non-Communist modern industrial state one can inspect its public culture for evidence of the 'neo-traditional'.

In liberal-democratic countries that became republics most of the 'myths' of neo-traditionalism had to die, although the state might still clothe itself with other memories of the past – as in the nineteenth-century uniforms of the Guardes Républicaines in Paris or the eighteenth-century uniforms of re-enactments in episodes in the United States War of Independence. A decisive battle of the 'myths' was first fought in the French Third Republic where supporters of 'myths' of neo-traditionalism were seen as enemies of the state. The army had ceased to be largely an army of the people, with careers open to talent, as it was seen to be during the Revolution and under Napoleon; it had become, again, in the opening decades of the Third Republic, an army of the nobility. As such it was a threat to the republican regime, as was royalist neo-traditionalism. The battle of the 'myths' in France is demonstrated in the Pantheon where there is something like a 50–50 division between the paintings and sculptures representing a royalist and Catholic France and those representing a France that is secular and republican. When it controlled the state, each side produced changes in the representational art of the Pantheon. A republic cannot be royalist. Nor (as was discovered in the Weimar Republic) can a republic remain liberal-democratic unless it tames its military 'myths'. It may be significant that it is only in the societies where the liberal-democratic 'myths' and the Communist 'myths' are strongest in the public culture that the military have been tamed and the force of civilian power acknowledged, so that even if a general does emerge into a central position in the state – Eisenhower, for example, or Jaruzelski in Poland – it is known that his authority comes from a political party.

What is likely to remain of neo-traditionalism in the public culture of a liberal-democratic society? In some of them, a continued presence of the church as a reminder of the past – as, for example, in the form in which the Catholic Church still remains a repository of 'myth' in the public culture of Italy. In all of them, fragments of the aristocratic myth – perhaps simply, in its picture magazine form, in curiosity about those surviving members of the nobility who can combine an imagined glamour from the past with some form of modern 'celebrity'; or in the intellectual form of equating 'art' with the aristocracy, so that democracy can seem to make 'art' impossible; or in the form of tourism, which is, in part, organized around nostalgia for an aristocratic life that never existed: tourists visit a restored palace that becomes itself a work of 'art', made pure form now that it has no social contact. Even the restorations (in fact 'innovations') in the White House, to which Jacqueline Kennedy first gave great prominence, have, by re-carpeting, re-panelling and the careful disposition of expertly selected specimens of antique (mainly nineteenth-century neo-classical) furniture, 're-created' in the White House an elegant past of aristocratic good taste that never existed. When Abraham Lincoln arrived there in 1861 he said the basement had 'the air of an old and unsuccessful hotel': now it is made up of five exquisitely decorated reception rooms in which treasures are artfully displayed in a way quite new to the building.

With the 'constitutional monarchies', however, the neo-traditional is a central part of the 'legitimations' of state. In Britain, the monarchic presence suffuses the public culture with its glow, in the palaces, the bright uniforms of the guards regiments, the royal coaches, the ceremonies of state, the continuing display of diamonds on royal females and the continued presence of the crown jewels themselves, safe in the Tower, guarded by Beefeaters. These relics of the old ruling-class culture help sustain many other games of feudal dressing-up in towns and cities throughout the land, in the robes and processions of mayors and lord mayors, lord-lieutenants of counties, judges at assizes, Knights of the Thistle, Knight Grand Commanders of the Order of the Bath, Lord Wardens of the Cinque Ports; they also give continued meaning to the hereditary aristocracy, whose power is displayed in tours of palaces set in large estates. The overall effect of this dazzle can help sustain illusions of English 'greatness' (it is the English, not the French, who can seem obsessed with '*la gloire*') and in other ways support 'realities' far removed from those meta-phorical embodiments of 'the people' that, according to some liberal-democratic theory, might be expected from the displays of state. In fact it is remarkable that in England there are left scarcely any of the ceremonies of the old folk culture that elsewhere in Europe can be one of the principal forms of providing neo-traditionalist 'colour'. In England, even nostalgia is something that people do not do for themselves; instead they have it done to them.

In the other monarchic countries – Spain seems an exception – monarchic neo-traditionalism glows much more modestly and can sometimes take a popularist flavour, as in Norway or the Netherlands where some of the remaining symbolic strength of the monarchy can come because the monarch is seen as a metaphor for 'the people' (or even as quaint: in a Netherlands events calendar the opening of parliament by the monarch is listed under 'Folk Traditions'). The Swedish and the Japanese constitutions expressly declare their monarchs to be powerless. (Although the maintenance of the monarchy itself helps give credibility to the Swedish nobility and general sense of social hierarchy, in Japan the old nobility has virtually disappeared, and the monarchy floats almost alone through the public culture, with a touch or two here and there of Shinto, as a neo-traditionalist relic.) In Denmark, although the Folketing meets in a royal palace, the monarch's only role in the opening of parliament is to sit in a royal box, as if parliament were an opera. In the 'old dominions' of Canada, Australia and New Zealand the monarchy lives on in a kind of export-only neo-traditionalism – physically remote, except for regular local appearances of the 'radiant presence' by a succession of members of the dynasty, but ever-present as a symbolic statement by these nations of their own self-imposed incompleteness: the monarchy becomes, in effect, a symbol of national second-ratedness.

Most of the symbolic forms of fascism were neo-traditional. The trappings and insignia, the great processions, the elaborate hierarchies, the glittering orders and decorations, the gradations of uniforms, the national hymns, the bombastic public art, the emphasis on 'blood' were all replays of old imperial dreams even if much of it was larger in concept than the earlier imperialism, with the displays magnified to fit the age of film and radio. Equally imperial was the emphasis on the army as the heart of the nation. And so, above all, was the racism. It was a turning in, on to Europe itself, of the long-held European contempt for 'the natives'. New devices were added: the liking of the Nazis for meetings at night, with flaming torches, could appeal to neo-traditionalist fantasies, with touches also of a Teuton pride in barbarism. Above all, there were the trial oaths to the leader, and the leader cult itself – a form of neo-traditionalism offering relief from all the predicaments of secular humanism and of the individualism of the person by allowing absorption into the larger-than-life individualism of the leader. It was the leader who absolved the people of the need for decision and put on a great show of personal power, to the background of the majesty of the state. Nazism's opening appeal lay partly in its apparent opposition to modern industrialism. It was this that provided a simple set of tableaux in the public culture that distracted attention from what was still the high bureaucratization of a modern industrial state.

Fascism is only part of the repertoire of neo-traditional 'legitimations' of a capitalist state. As a replay of nineteenth-century imperialism, it may have gone out of fashion. But some other forms of the leader cult, or forms of state worship, military glamour or idealized corporatism can also operate as 'legitimations' of a society in which most of the productive resources are privately owned. In Latin America, the specifically capitalist 'legitimations' of capitalism have not taken root. Capitalists thrive, but they are not celebrated as benefactors in the public culture. The pre-modern traditions of the Latin American states – their mercantilism, their patronalism, their sense of an organic corporatism – have led to other 'legitimations'. In all these societies, and perhaps, on the whole, also in the European authoritarian nation-states, while there have been few, if any, 'myths' of free enterprise and the importance of the profit motive, a kind of 'concessionaire capitalism' has flourished. It is not the same as the 'crony capitalism' of the Third World, in which the regimes simply rig up profitable rackets for themselves and their cronies, but it is one in which most of the rich continue to gain concessions from the state to make themselves more rich. Their price, and it is an easy one, is to allow the state, or the military, or the leader, to take all the honour.

The ethnic compromise

For most of Hawaii's history as a tourist island a prime symbol of the tourist business has been of a woman in a grass skirt doing a hula; leis are placed around the necks of members of group tourists as they arrive in their tens of thousands; in the stores women buy muu-muus and men buy aloha shirts (in a recent marketing device these now come in his-and-hers matching patterns); as the coach tours set off, the driver will begin his spiel with a ceremonial 'aloha'; at the hotel desks reservations are made for luaus. Other than these travesties, nothing much else is projected to the tourist of the life of native Hawaiians. The actual circumstances of their life are concealed by these appropriations, which characterize the native Hawaiians as a tourist gimmick along with the Glass Bottom Boat Cruise, the Hawaiian Love Boat Cruise and the Aloha Air Adventure. Until the 1970s, even to the people who lived there (in origin, mainly Europeans, Chinese, Japanese as well as native Hawaiians), this was part of the 'ethnic compromise' in Hawaii.

In using the phrase 'ethnic compromise' I have this in mind: that in many nations (or smaller communities such as the state of Hawaii) there is still much unfinished business in the conflicts between ethnic groups. In the showings of the public culture some ethnic groups will be dominant; some may not be there at all; others may be present, but not on their own terms.

Sometimes there is no 'ethnic compromise'. In various forms of 'master race' philosophies it has been asserted that only one form of ethnicity should be the natural condition of the whole nation. Such a view of ethnicity then dominates the public culture as portraying all national life. This was the language of imperialism, in which one 'race' was given by God or by biological necessity the manifest destiny (to use the United States term) of being the principal expander and upholder of civilization in a vast territorial expansion or even a world mission. There was nothing unusual in most of the Nazi rhetoric about the Aryans as master race. Its social Darwinism was the common sense of many people in the later nineteenth and early twentieth centuries. ('Mankind has grown great in eternal struggle', 'The stronger must dominate', 'The right to victory goes to the best and strongest in the world' and other such phrases of Hitler's were the kind of thing millions of people grew up with.) And if the culture claims for the Aryans as master race were somewhat ahead of other imperial rhetoric that was only because the concept of 'Aryanism' was so broad and imprecise that it could be presented as a central theme in history. ('The Aryan is the Prometheus of mankind from whose shining brow the divine spark of genius has sprung at all times, forever kindling anew that fire of knowledge which illumined the night of silent mysteries and thus caused man to climb the path to mastery over the other beings of this earth', etc. etc.) It is not unusual that certain 'races' (in this case Slavs, Jews and gypsies) should be chosen as sub-human (*Untermenschen*). What was unusual (although not unique) was the total extermination programme for Jews and gypsies. The approach to the Slavs as the other principal *Untermenschen* in Europe was one of limited extermination prompted partly by policy (eliminating the upper classes and intelligentsia) and partly by brutality and muddle, for in Hitler's New Order, the Slavs as sub-humans were to have been given an ordered role as slave labour. The public culture would have glorified Aryanism as the unifying feature of European and for that matter world civilization; Slavs would have existed in their segregated communities, but in the presentation of national life they would not have existed, except as those chosen by nature to be inferior, as 'Negroes' were for most of the history of the United States.

In South Africa the Afrikaners do, in fact, regard themselves as the master race in southern Africa and in the world at large as a morally superior race and as a people who, alone of the European colonists, created their own language and went the furthest in creating their own culture – a culture of struggle, informed by religion, against the land and poverty and against the blacks and the British, with the central thread of *Kradadidheid* (resolve to survive). And this sense of superiority extends beyond 'Bantus', 'Asians' and 'Coloureds' to a sense of superiority over the South African English, who are not seen as a new 'race' like the Afrikaners, but mere homeward-looking expatriates. However, it is not expedient in the public culture of South Africa to project directly a master-race Afrikaner view of national life, although of course there can be many coded references. What occurs in the public culture is a presentation of a multi-lingual, multi-racial society, but a society of white supremacy, proclaimed, above all, by superior visibility. In this there is the curiosity that the (now declining) English-language press has been the freest in Africa, giving the relics of a liberal look to the white part of the public culture, even if what the English-language press said was of no concern to the government or to most Afrikaners. And in 1984 there was an attempt to add to this 'liberality' by giving the Asians and Coloureds a kind of play space in the political culture. However, off-setting this public culture is what might be thought of as the clandestine 'public culture' of Afrikaner supremacy, carried out in the Dutch Reformed Church, in the *Bruderbund* and other secret societies, in the folk festivals, and in many private but influential places in Afrikaner life.

At the other end of the scale from the declaration of a master race is the declaration of multiculturalism in a public culture. There are many reasons why the Austro-Hungarian empire collapsed: one of them was that when it became a modern nation-state it was unable to reach an ethnic compromise in its public culture for the ten or so nationalities in the empire.

In contrast, the very foundation of Singapore was built on multiculturalism (Chinese, Malay, Indian, English): seen as the only alternative to communal bloodshed, it was the reason for Singapore's existence. In Switzerland there has been an intricate interlacing of languages, so that multi-lingualism becomes part of what it means to be 'Swiss'.

In Finland and Canada, bilingualism reflects earlier conditions of settlement. In Finland, the Swedish language is a reminder of the days of the Swedish empire, although the development of Finnish as a language in the nineteenth century came partly from a Swedish upper class who, when Finland as part of the post-Napoleon settlement was passed from Sweden to Russia, preferred Finland to be culturally and then independently Finnish, rather than politically Russian. In Canada the policy of bilingualism was so long coming because the French Canadians were seen by the English Canadians as an 'inferior race' which should have been assimilated, and the French Canadians – although aware of having a separate culture as well as a separate language – were slow in ambition. It was only in the 1960s as part of a change in new French-speaking elites to a more modern and industrial vision of French Canada that things began to move in Quebec. This came in traditional nationalist style, with a renaissance of intellectual and artistic life, a new political party (*le parti Quebecois*), bombs and foreign support (de Gaulle). Official bilingualism arrived in 1969 but it is doubtful whether a bilingual 'Canada' has yet been created: Canadians can speak of themselves as having 'two official languages but no official culture'. Another idea approaches – that of 'multiculturalism within a bilingual framework', as an acknowledgement that the post-war immigration brought people from many ethnic backgrounds. For the same reason (multi-ethnic immigration), in Australia – for so long celebrated as 'White Australia' and as more British than the British – multiculturalism became a bipartisan policy in the two main political parties in the 1970s, although with strong resistance from those who still saw Australia as 'British'.

In Yugoslavia, Belgium, Czechoslovakia and Spain mixed ethnicity is embedded in regional divisions, so that although only Yugoslavia and Czechoslovakia are constitutionally federations, Belgium and now Spain are also, in effect, federal. Catalan was a co-language with Castilian in Spain until the early eighteenth century and, despite almost continuing repression thereafter (including, under Franco, the banning of books in Catalan), after Franco's death the acceptance of the separateness of Catalonia, along with the acceptance of the separateness of the Basque country, seemed essential to maintain a liberal-democratic regime. In Belgium, the nine-teenth-century attempt of the French-speaking Belgians to turn all Belgium into a country of French culture was, almost from the start, resisted by the Dutch-speaking Belgians. They participated in a Flemish cultural awakening, then obtained at the end of the nineteenth century the acceptance of Dutch as the second language of Belgium. Later came unilingualism in the dominantly French and Dutch regions: now almost every-thing is divided in Belgium on language lines. After the suppression of 'the Prague Spring' in 1968, Czechoslovakia became a federal republic, with at last an acceptance that the Czechs and the Slovaks saw themselves as separate nations, with their own languages and culture, and historical memories. In Yugoslavia, multiculturalism is built into the foundations of a federal state as firmly and for much the same reasons as it is built into a unitary Singapore – in a nation with ten ethnic groups, five official languages and three principal religions, multiculturalism seems essential for survival. In each of the six republics that make up the federation there is one dominant ethnic group.

In Yugoslavia, Belgium and Czechoslovakia the lucky ethnic groups are also allowed their own *histories*. In some countries, there can be an official biculturalism in the public cultures, but this falls short of allowing an ethnic group to preserve its own history (its own 'reality'). Romania is an example. There has been a public policy of 'co-habiting nationalities' in which the minority Magyar, German and Serbian ethnic groups maintained language and other cultural rights: but these groups lost their history. This was most significant in Transylvania which, with its large Magyar minority, has two histories (two 'realities') – a Romanian history and a Hungarian history. Only the Romanian version of Transylvania's history is permitted to survive in the public culture.

With its hundred nationalities, the Soviet Union provides the most complex of all the ethnic compromises. At one extreme are the Crimean Tartars and the Volga Germans, who were simply deported from their own territories. At the other extreme is the Armenian Republic, which has many of the characteristics of national cultural autonomy. Multiculturalism – in the sense of a recognition of diverse art forms – is endemic in the Soviet entertainment industry, and in the Soviet public culture generally. In no other nation-state is there such detailed and specialist concern with the preservation of such a diversity of national art forms. In Leningrad what was once a trophy museum of the tsarist imperial conquest became the Ethnological Museum of the Peoples of the USSR, by far the most ambitiously diverse ethnographic museum in the world. The 1980 Olympic Games in Moscow provided the world's most expensive folk art festival. Yet in the Ukrainian Republic, Catholicism has been very largely suppressed, the Ukrainian language downgraded; and the culture and history that are taught are Russian, not Ukrainian. Yet in the Georgian Republic Georgian is the language of instruction in most schools, and there is a Georgian perspective in the teaching of history and culture. In the Latvian Republic there has been a fairly brutal Russification; in the schools of the Estonian Republic Russian is only the second language. In the Armenian Republic patriotic memories are stirred not by the monuments to the 'Great Patriotic War' of 1941–45 but to a monument, on a hill above the Armenian capital, to the 1,500,000 Armenians killed and 500,000 deported in the Turkish holocaust against the Armenians in 1915. The Armenian Church plays a greater part in public culture than any other church in the Soviet Union, and it is Armenian history that is taught in schools. Marxist–Leninism does not come into the syllabus until grade 10.

The 'realities' of an ethnic group can be maintained partly by the wisdoms of family traditions and surviving folk art forms, but if a group has no lively communal ceremonies there can come about a 'cultural atrophy', in which, as Herbert Gans put it in *Commentary*, the ethnic culture can lose its meaning and become an 'objects culture', objectifying ethnicity into, as it were, a few souvenirs, or it might become a festival culture of certain entertainment art forms. Even where meaning remains, it may be as a 'residue culture', preserving as an antiquarian curiosity what has already been changed. It is in these museum forms, as harmless curiosities, that minority ethnic cultures are most easily admitted into a public culture.

This is why to take away its history from an ethnic group can be so dangerous. Most ethnic groups in the United States have nothing much left to them other than festival cultures or object cultures. They get slotted into the public culture in certain harmless stereotypings ('Pennsylvania Dutch') or festivals

('Columbus Day'). The two main troublesome groups that are left (apart from the native Americans) are the blacks and the Latinos. The blacks have communal forms (churches, for example) and cultural forms (gospel song, for example) to keep alive their culture. The Latinos have close to nothing. For the 1960s rebels there was the self-definition of the murals movement. Then other protestors took up murals. Even Mexican American eating and musical habits become titillating additions to the general restaurant and entertainment businesses. What some Mexican Americans want is to regain a history of 'America' in which the United States has *not* been 'America', but merely one part of the story. In Australia, through the long period of Protestant ascendancy, the Irish kept some of their Irishness through the Catholic Church and through their separate Catholic schools which taught a history somewhat different from that of the prevailing Protestant and imperialist vision. In London, about one-sixth of the population is Irish but, unrecognized as an ethnic minority, they are constantly caricatured in the media as clowns and/or murderers, and their children are given in schools an entirely English view of history. 'Great Britain', or at least its public culture, is held together by the Anglicization of Ireland – in the language itself, and in images of history. This may be even more the case in France. In Britain, part of the ethnic compromise is a recognition of Scotland and Wales, at least as separate cultural regions (although objectified in the public culture into harmlessness with tourist industry stereotypes – the Eistedfodd, the Highland fling, etc.) – a compromise, however, that failed in Northern Ireland. France has been even more absolutist, so that, at the best, the self-perceived occupied territories (perhaps with the exception of Corsica) are seen not as 'nations' but as fringe eccentrics. It may be Italy, divided by so many language and regional differences, that may nevertheless be more coherent. A special resilience may come from the fact that the Italian history taught in schools *begins* with the recognition of religious diversity – as the 'pillarization' principle in the Netherlands began by defining Dutch society as divided between Catholicism, Calvinism and humanist secularism (to such an extent that even the broadcasting service was divided on these lines). Yet it is now from the Netherlands that there comes some of the strongest support for the idea of a common 'European' television service, as if all 'Europe' were the one thing, with the one public culture.

The struggle has now begun for aboriginal inhabitants to claim a place in the ethnic compromises of the public culture. Eskimos, Amerindians, Hawaiians, Australian Aborigines and Lapps attempt to make their incursions, with somewhat similar strategies. In New Zealand, the Maoris, already more advanced in their claims than the others, still lead the way. But in Western Europe, some of the most suppressed elements are not the oldest inhabitants, but the newest – the 'guest workers', or the 'migrant workers', making up to a quarter of the Swiss workforce and up to 10 per cent of the workforce of some of the other most industrialized Western European nations. For centuries a territory of emigration, Western Europe became an area of immigration. Yet in the public cultures of these societies most of the immigrants are simply not there – except as a threat. In Switzerland, one of the harshest countries in its treatment of guest workers, they speak of the problem as *Uberfremdung* (overforeignization). In the Federal Republic of Germany, where there is a migrant population of four and a half million, the West German Cabinet issued a statement in October 1984 that began: 'The Federal German Republic is not a country of immigration.'

The labour culture

Even slave societies (if masters wish to get a good return on slaves as property) can develop a resilience in their slave culture: slaves are accommodated to their masters, but there can also be effects on how masters behave with their slaves. In the convict colonies that marked the British occupation of Australia in the eighteenth century there soon developed amongst the convicts certain habits of work and self-definition that affected how the authorities treated them. Similarly, peasant societies can be exploited, but only in some ways, not all. It is only where there is concern with absolute control but little or no concern with getting a good return on forced labour (as in the concentration camps) that a labour force can be drained of all potential to affect its conditions of work.

But although the oppressed can often get some terms from the oppressor, there has never been anything to equal that great social transformation of the nineteenth century that produced 'the labour movement'. What was extraordinary about the creation of a wage proletariat was that it developed so quickly such feelings of independence and consciousness of the wage earner *as* wage earner, and out of this developed some of the most potent organizations of the twentieth century – and also some of the most potent 'myths' of twentieth-century public culture. The very indifference of the laissez-faire attitudes to labour of the industrializers of the nineteenth century allowed sufficient organization amongst the new wage earners for them at least to begin their great battles against the police and soldiers set against them by the state. Perhaps the only way to have stopped this might have been if the nineteenth-century industrializers had used as their way of controlling labour the techniques of the twentieth-century concentration camps, but this could involve a very low return on labour and, of course, a reduction in demand for consumer goods.

This consciousness of being a wage earner did not usually produce the liberating consciousness anticipated by Marx: at its most basic it was simply an awareness of class conflict in the economic sense – which still exists even in the United States – that there are 'owners' and 'wage-earners', or 'masters' and 'hands', or 'bosses' and 'workers', or, as the division also came to be known, 'management' and 'employees', and that there are necessarily conflicts of interest between them. It was out of this recognition that aspirations to form trade unions were born and, after heroic struggles, made real. These aspirations were never purely economic, but what other hopes of a better world became attached to them would vary. Perhaps the most frequent was the desire for greater respectability (both self-respect and social respect) and for a slightly more generous share of material comforts – both of these within the existing social order. Such hopes could be clothed in institutions such as temperance societies, or in worker education organizations such as the 'mechanics institutes' of Britain or the *folket hus* movement of Sweden, or they might take the form of building societies and friendly societies. They might also be found in co-operative movements. These were aspirations that could be accommodated by liberal or radical parties, and for that matter by conservative or religious parties. Where the labour movement became attached to a distinctive 'political' creation was in the support many sections of it gave to a new 'myth' – that of socialism, a body of belief that was not concerned simply with fitting wage earners more comfortably into the existing social order, but with changing the social order itself.

Like liberalism or conservatism, socialism spoke for all society. It was presented as a better way of ordering the world to secure human happiness and fulfilment. As the parties of socialism formed in all of the industrializing nation-states and, with only a few exceptions (most notably the United States), began to take their places in parliamentary assemblies – in Social Democratic Parties, Socialist Parties, Labour Parties – the future could seem reasonably clear: history demanded a transition to socialism. In extreme cases, as with most of the German Social Democrats, it was as if there were nothing much more they had to do about this: the passage to socialism would be determined by history, and so would the answers to the puzzle of what a socialist society would be. It was, of course, Lenin's most significant contribution to this discussion (celebrated in all the V.I. Lenin Museums and the Museums of the Revolution) to argue that, if left to themselves, the workers would merely engage in narrow trade union activities: a vanguard party was essential to awaken the workers' consciousness so that they might then participate in that millennial release of the revolutionary potential which, Marx had prophesied, was the role of the proletariat in history.

Both the followers of Lenin (who were, of course, nothing much more than a minor sect until their extraordinary success in 1917) and the socialist parliamentarians, in their own ways, developed a considerable 'myth' of the working class for whom they spoke (and to which many of them belonged), and of the 'realities' that seemed to make the workers decisive in history. Within the unions and their ancillary organizations a whole culture developed – 'myths', rituals, icons, ceremonies, legends, organizational techniques. The working class had, by now, its many martyrs. The red flag, the clenched fist, the singing of the 'Internationale' could seem profoundly moving symbols of the future, and something for which people were ready to die. In some of the industrializing societies, notably Imperial Germany, this labour movement with its culture could seem not only an 'alternative culture', but almost a 'state within the state', and it is still, more or less, the Gramscian ideal of the Italian Communist Party that it should be seen as community leader, as it is the ideal of the Swedish Democratic Party (if in different ways). Just as a church could be an alternative society within a society, with its own schools, its own 'myths' and 'realities', its own rituals, its own basis for a separate sense of community, and its own relations to the state, to political parties and to other organizations, so could the labour movement.

So another of the variants in the public cultures of modern industrial societies is what we might call 'the labour culture'. The labour force is there. Its existence cannot be denied. In some way, even in a fascist society, it must be accounted for. The forms of accounting differ greatly, however, between Communist societies, liberal-democratic capitalist societies and capitalist societies that are not liberal-democratic.

In the Communist societies we have already discussed the fundamental importance of working-class 'myth' to the 'legitimation' of the Party and the state. Thus, the opening paragraph of the Soviet Constitution:

The Great October Socialist Revolution made by the

workers and peasants of Russia, under the leadership of
the Communist Party headed by Lenin, overthrew
capitalist and landowner rule, broke the fetters of
oppression, established the dictatorship of the proletariat,
and created the Soviet state, a new type of state, the basic
instrument for defending the gains of the revolution and
for building socialism and communism. Humanity thereby
began the epoch-making turn from capitalism to socialism.

In the rhetoric of fascism, labour is honoured, but mainly for
its sense of duty in serving the state. The aim of the Nazis'
'Labour Front' ('the organization of creative Germans of brain
and fist') was 'to create a true social and productive community
of all Germans', whose task was 'to see that every single
individual should be able to perform the maximum of work'.
The 'Charter of Labour' proclaimed that it was the responsibility
of 'the leader of the enterprise' to make decisions and to be
responsible for the well-being of the workers; it was the
responsibility of the workers 'to owe him their faithfulness'. In
reward, they were able to gain strength through joy in the
organized leisure facilities of the Labour Front's recreational
organization.

In all the liberal-democratic capitalist societies other than
the United States, parties of the labour movement now engage
in parliamentary politics and in most of them a significant
proportion of the workforce is in trade unions. Even in the
United States, where only about a fifth of the workforce is
unionized, where there *are* unions they can be successful
bargainers, although perhaps decreasingly so. But in most of
these societies the labour movement is not united. There can be
splits between right and left, divisions within the union
movement, weak connections between the unions and the
political parties. In most of them the labour movement is
overwhelmingly specialist in organization and lacks a strong
community base. It does not usually play a part in neighbourhood life, for example. And it lacks a wide sense of or even
concern for rank-and-file participation. In most of them the

political parties of the labour movement do not dominate the public theatre of politics. And in most of them (therefore?) the labour movement plays a weak, or at best a tolerated and restricted part in the public culture.

A useful test in these societies is to discover on what terms the trade unions, political parties and other organizations speaking in the name of labour are, as it were, 'allowed' to appear in the public culture. In some of them a considerable part of the 'labour movement' may normally remain submerged, and if these concealed aspects do appear in the public culture it is likely they will be perceived as deviant, or threatening. In some countries (Britain and Australia, for example) trade union activity is scarcely ever reported in 'the news' as a normal part of what 'the news' projects as the 'reality' of 'national life'. Union activities are likely to appear in 'the news' only if there are strikes, and these are usually projected as threats to consumers, probably to 'the economy' and not infrequently to the whole social order. In such a country, the opinion surveys may show perceptions of national 'reality' in which a majority of those interviewed are likely to see the unions as having too much power and a significant minority are likely to see unions as *the* most powerful force in national life. One of the tensions in liberal-democratic societies can be in this ambivalence about trade unions, in which the unions can be presented as a principal threat to liberal democracy, whilst, at the same time, it is recognized that a wholesale suppression of the trade union movement would necessarily transform the nature of state and society. The result of this, ironically, is that one of the most effective tests of liberal democracy (which can stand any number of 'nationalizations' of business) is non-suppression of the whole trade union movement (although there is room for the suppression of individual unions).

Another test of the terms in which the labour movement is 'allowed' into a public culture can come from observing the degree of acceptance (if any) of discussion in the public culture of socialism by socialists. In some of these societies socialism can be rejected in the public culture as a fit subject only for denunciation. The very word can exist in the public culture only as a scare word: in such a public culture it may also be the case that the word 'capitalism' becomes taboo. To use the word is to be radical. Capitalism is not thought of as 'capitalism', but as 'free enterprise' or some other soft, outward-going benefit-offering phrase. In some countries the better part of the meaning of the magically glowing word 'freedom' is that it is a nice way of saying 'capitalism', without actually saying it. Capitalism can even seem such a natural way of running things that it does not need a word. In such a society, leaders in a party of the labour movement may even be concerned with demons-trating that they are not really 'socialist', or they may define 'socialism' in such a watered-down way that it is something that every reasonable, concerned person might wish to be.

These societies in which the 'myths' of the labour movement are weakly and selectively present in the public culture are those in which there prevails what Francis Castles calls in *The Social Democratic Image of Society* a 'capitalist image of society'. He suggests that this is amplified where there is a large and united party of the right and where the labour movement (political party, trade unions and ancillary movements) is not united and lacks a strong community base. In such a case, he says (and it is the majority one), the large and united party of the right can act as the political amplifier of the 'myths' of the rich, maintaining a 'reality' in which their special interests are magnified as though they were the interests of all, dominating the political processes, dominating the apparatus of the state and setting the overall pattern of what politics should seem to be about so successfully that these definitions may prevail even when the right is not in office.

The Australian culture critic Hugh Stretton evoked this dominance of the capitalist 'myth' in his essay 'Has the Welfare State All Been a Terrible Mistake?' when he said:

The commonest trick is this: of people's individual spending mention *only the goods they get*, but of their collective spending, mention *only the prices they pay*. When they buy a private car and a public road to drive it on, present the car as a benefit and the road as a tax or cost. Tell how the private sector is the productive sector which gives us food, clothing, houses, cars, holidays and all good things, while the public sector gives us nothing but red tape and tax demands.

Where a labour movement is partly submerged, with some aspects of it appearing in the public culture only as a threat, one can inspect the public culture to find out which kinds of performers in the labour movement are seen as normal players; which of them never or scarcely ever appear in the public culture; and which appear only as fools or villains. It is likely to be found that certain types of leftist 'critics' may appear as regular players – but because they *are* critics (in the sense in which that word will be used in the next section of this chapter) and therefore to some extent tolerated – but examination of the parts performed by the other, and perhaps main, players (principally political and union leaders) can show to what extent their appearances reinforce the central, directive elements in the public culture.

These labour leaders are unlikely to question the basic 'myths' of modernity and industrialism, for example. In fact, if they show a rational, technocratic, modernizing faith in the state (as they are likely to do), they may express these 'myths' in a purer form than their opponents, who are likely to use a more oblique language. In use of the widest-based liberal-democratic 'myths' of representative democracy and the rule of law and in response to other political 'myths' they may be more, or less, liberal than their opponents, according to time and place. They are likely to speak the same language of national identity as their political opponents and usually they will see the world through much the same strategic imagination. In the past they have been as chauvinistic as their opponents in perspectives of sex, race and ethnicity: at a time of shifting perspectives such as the present, they are, on the whole, likely to have shifted somewhat further than their opponents. They are likely to be more explicitly concerned with welfare than their opponents and more open in plans for certain types of government intervention in 'the economy'. They will accept capitalism, in the form of 'the mixed economy', but they will present themselves as being better able to make it work (in 'economic management').

There can also be, however, what Francis Castles calls a 'social-democratic image of society', to be found most clearly in the Scandinavian countries:

Social Democrats and their sympathisers are integrated into every major political instrumentality in Scandinavia. Exactly the same is true at the local and intermediate levels. Within the schools, the decisive voice in administration is as likely to be Social Democratic as bourgeois. In the factories, recent legislation has given the decisive responsibility in regard to safety to the workers rather than the employer . . . In Scandinavia the dominant political class is not capitalist in orientation. Some of the agencies of political socialisation – for instance, a substantial portion of the press – remain in private hands. However many others do not. Radio and television are administered by a 'politically neutral' agency, which like virtually every 'politically neutral' body in Scandinavia, attains that status in virtue of its reflection of the prevailing political balance: in other words, Social Democratic dominance.

One of the most telling comparisons is this: in Britain, there is still a tendency to see welfare as abnormal, as not really deserved, or even as charity. In Sweden, part of the school curriculum involves social studies courses which teach students about the range of benefits to which the citizen is *entitled*.

The critics' culture

Somewhere in the fifteenth century in Europe something new begins to move. There is the entry of a new element – that of criticism – that was different from the former styles of theological disputation, which argued from a dogmatic base that could not in itself be disputed, except in interpretation. Of course much arguing from dogma still goes on: both Marxist talmudism and modern scholarship would not be possible without it. But several things are new.

One is the 'myth' of criticism itself as an essential force in society, both liberating and rational. This becomes a question not only of what one says, but of a characteristically questioning approach to existence which received its most famous epitomization in Voltaire's *mot* that he might disagree with what one said but would fight to the death for one's right to say it. Voltaire himself became one of the most legendary figures of the Enlightenment. Thomas Jefferson, author of the Declaration of Independence and sceptical towards the proposed United States Constitution until a Bill of Rights was appended to it, bought a bust of Voltaire when he was in Paris which still stands in the hall of Monticello, Jefferson's Virginian mansion. It is almost the only reminder, apart from the intelligent design of the building itself, that Jefferson was also one of the great figures of the Enlightenment. As fundamentalists, creationists, millennialists, born-again Christians and other United States tourists admire Monticello as a reminder of what they see as the graciousness of more stable days, it can seem as if Voltaire (a notorious 'liberal', of whom they have not heard) is standing in a corner, mocking them. Yet Jefferson himself moved beyond Voltaire's sense of enlightened rationality and beyond the concepts of freedom as civil liberty based on property rights. When he wrote the Declaration of Independence it was not life, liberty and property on which he imagined building his new society, but life, liberty and the pursuit of happiness.

Another of the novelties of criticism as a characteristic technique in approaching existence is the development of legends of martyrdom for unorthodox opinion. There is a famous painting by Jacques Louis David of Socrates as he lectures his sorrowful disciples before taking the hemlock: it provides an exemplary scene of the martyrdom of one who believed that the unexamined life was not worth living. The silencing of Galileo, another of the strongest images of the persecution of a critic, brings up another theme – that of the critic-martyrs, or the critics who are mocked as critics 'before their time'. With this can be associated the 'modern' and optimistic side of the critics' culture – that in the end reason must prevail. The legend of the Salon de Refusés is a popular example. A new style of painting is mocked and can find no place in the Academy; its proponents set up their own paintings exhibition; the new style prevails. Even the secularization of aspects of the Passion of Christ can show him as the critic questioning his judges, a man before his time.

The idea of criticism inevitably elides into the idea of protest – of the retaliation the critic must take when reason does not prevail. Uprisings are as old as human history, but it has been a special talent of the critics to give them clear secular meanings, with the result that much of modern history can seem to be in the hands of the critics. Both in 1776 and 1789 documents of explanation and justification ('legitimations') were produced, of a kind that continues to have an enormous simplifying power. Theories of protest as an intellectual form have developed: for the protest movements of the 1960s publishers reprinted Thoreau's essay 'On the Duty of Civil Disobedience'.

Intellectual and art forms could, in themselves, be regarded as protest. 'Modern art' was seen as an attack on the social order – at least until the rich began buying it. It continues to be seen in this way in the Soviet Union. On 15 September 1974, when a group of unofficial artists tried to put on an outdoor show in Moscow, it was broken up by police disguised as workers, using bulldozers and garbage trucks. But this happened at the time of *détente* and the reports of this incident in the Western media induced the authorities a couple of weeks later to permit a one-day exhibition. This was how the critics imagined it should be. Later attempts to repeat such exhibitions were broken up.

Another of the novelties of the operations of criticism in public cultures is the 'myth' of novelty itself. It can become an expectation of the age that there should be a continuing wave of new 'realities'. To take one example, in *The American Left in the Twentieth Century*, John P. Diggins delineates the three waves of leftism in the United States, each of them articulating new historical visions, new 'myths', new senses of 'reality', of the possible. Each of them identified a generation as if it were unified by common historical ideals (although there were variations among these in their degree of amplification in the public culture).

What is also characteristic of the operations of criticism in the public culture is that with a new perspective there can be an arguing for an entirely new critical base, a new style, a new way of approaching existence. One example would be the creation of 'realism' in the French novel, as one can see it develop with Balzac and reach its limits with Zola. Sometimes parts of a Balzac novel can seem like great heaps of rubbish backlit by one of those melodramatically romantic studio skies used by the 1930s Hollywood movie-makers, but what also comes through is Balzac's conception of modern 'society'. This is why Oscar Wilde said that Balzac 'created the nineteenth century'. He introduced the technique of imagining a whole 'society'; he introduced the idea of *milieu* (literally, in his *Avant-Propos*); he gave obsessive attention to that technique of 'description' that partly transforms a novelist into a stage carpenter, constantly making new sets; he was a determined propagandist for the realist 'myth' that the 'reality' he was constructing had an exact match in outside existence. ('French society was going to be the historian,' he said of *Comédie Humaine*; 'I had only to become its secretary.') And he introduced to the new idea of realist novel-writing a concern with the material base of existence ('Tell me what you have, and I will tell you what you are') as fundamental as the similar concern Marx introduced to sociology. Cleaning up the mess, and concentrating on these techniques of 'realism' without Balzac's other distractions, two decades later Zola was able to invent 'realities' of a most precise kind of class conflict (*Germinal*), of conscript armies (*La Débâcle*), of lumpen urbanization (*L'Assommoir*) that both defined the modern in terms in which we can still see it and asserted 'naturalism' as a technique for constructing (or, as he would put it, discovering) 'reality' in ways in which we can still see it.

Only 10 years after Zola died, in the *Neue Sezession* some of the painters who were loosely to be thought of as 'the expressionists' were suggesting an entirely different critical base for constructing 'reality', rejecting the imitation of nature ('Photography relieved painting of the necessity of being objective,' said the photographer Edward Steichen) and replacing it with the idea that paintings were 'expressions', not of nature, but of feeling. Throughout the century, this struggle continued, in 'popular culture', as in 'high art'. The hand-held camera, the incoherence effect (as in Robert Altman's *Nashville*), and the introduction to some movies and even television drama of open endings, were all examples of new forms of 'realism'.

The concept of there being 'critics' in a public culture goes further than the concept of being an 'intellectual' that I discussed in the first chapter. Whatever their potential as intellectuals, most people are, as it were, 'passive' intellectuals. They may be part of general social maintenance systems upholding certain 'realities' but, except in their own immediate environments (where they *can* be 'active') or in their interactions with the products of the culture industries, this may be all they can do about it. It is certainly all that they are expected to do about it. But there are also active performers who, in practising criticism, may see unorthodoxy as an essential force in society and who may even be critics of criticism, in that they are arguing for a new critical base. Many (most?) of these are, one way or the other, suppressed. A few are imprisoned, tortured, killed. In some societies, however, some of them do enter the public culture, some of them, it is true, as paid performers (with varying degrees of freedom), or as gatecrashers who may later become paid performers.

So one of the ways of examining the public culture of a modern industrial society is to examine it for traces of a 'critics' culture' (whilst recognizing that more 'criticizing' might be going on within the society than is 'permitted' to appear in the public culture). What we are looking for is the extent to which the notion of criticism itself is seen in the public culture as an essential and liberating force; then the extent to which dissident opinions regularly penetrate the public culture, and the kind of opposition they meet.

In fascist societies, of course, there is no public critics' culture, just as there is no public neo-traditional culture in Communist societies. One of the benefits offered by a fascist society is to relieve people of the perplexities of critical thinking. The critics become, instead, enemies of the state, whose books must be burned, whose paintings, if they are to be shown at all, must be shown in derision; the private role of the critic is to shut up or be shut up; the public role is to recant, or to be the object of an exemplary court trial followed by an exemplary punishment. It is part of the central principle of a fascist state that there should be no critics' culture. Criticism is part of the filth that is being cleaned away. However in *étatiste* societies of the right that are less than fascist there can be, in varying degrees, at different times, considerable manifestations of a critics' culture, given special zest by physical danger.

In Communist societies, according to Lenin, there would be free debate within the party, but once decisions were reached members would follow the party line. In practice, the party 'debate' has usually been manipulated. Nevertheless (in contradiction to fascist societies) there is usually maintained, in varying degrees, the *public* notion that (responsible) criticism is a creative force. Even in the Soviet Union there is not absolute uniformity in the newspapers and magazines; some of them, however prudently, run exposés that seem to have developed within their own resources and there is a positive cult for readers' letters as part of the practice of *samokritika* (self-criticism). *Pravda* gets something like 40,000 readers' letters a month and has 45 people in its letters department. In the other European Communist societies the public presentation of criticism varies from regime to regime. In none of them are there such imposed orthodoxies in the arts as in the Soviet

Union. Many of the exhibitions of paintings, for example, put on in other Communist countries, are the kind of art that in the Soviet Union would bring out the bulldozers.

In the liberal-democratic societies, since 'myths' of freedom are one of the central 'legitimations' of the distribution of power, there *must* be some evidence of a public critics' culture. Even in periods when these societies have been marked by censorship and other forms of coercion, there must be, even within a narrow area, debate. As I suggested earlier, even within the white community in South Africa, there is, within a certain range, public debate. The legitimacy of that regime depends on it. In circumstances where there is considerable coercion in a society with a purportedly liberal-democratic political system the accepted players in the political system have essential roles to perform: it can be made to seem that what the acceptable political parties choose to disagree on is all that need be discussed controversially. Criticism is something the citizens watch other people perform, on their behalf.

But at other times there can be a much wider range of critical opinion. For one thing, in the entertainment industry (including most of the 'news' services) even commercial considerations can mean meeting new types of 'reality': there can be a feeling for new moods in audiences. In *Inside Prime Time* Todd Gitlin shows how out of the protest turbulence of the late 1960s the television industry in the early 1970s moved towards a certain liberalism and sense of social relevance, meeting a mood of anti-authoritarianism and a desire for the authentic. He quotes one producer as saying: 'Coming out of the sixties, the climate was right, the kids were letting it all hang out, the kids didn't want to see Doris Day: "Quit jerking us off and give us something real." ' When he was researching his book Gitlin found that some of the television controllers 'half-recognized that, in television, success often comes from finding the main fault lines of value conflict in the society, and bridging them'.

'Protest' movements can at times meet 'news' standards and get a hearing, although not necessarily on their own terms. And not only is there usually within the culture industries a predisposition amongst many of the practitioners towards the standards of the critics' culture, there are also roads to expression, perhaps especially in book publishing and the theatre where there is not such an overwhelming emphasis on numbers as in broadcasting and print mass media. And there are small presses, little theatres, little magazines, community radio. This kind of approach can also exist within a liberal Communist regime.

One might imagine the public critics' culture in a liberal-democratic society (or in a liberalizing Communist society) as consisting of a proclaimed belief in the notion of criticism itself and then list the kinds of dissident opinions that regularly penetrate the public culture. The dissidence of these opinions is usually selective rather than total and it is much more likely to be reformist than revolutionary, although it might sometimes be highly radical in style. Such dissident opinions may become so widespread in certain fields (in parts of the education and entertainment industries, for example) that they can be seen by their opponents as clandestine 'establishments'.

There is another function of a critics' culture. It can be a kind of acclimatization society for newly introduced ideas, so that at times new 'realities', after their domestication in a 'critics' culture', became part of the central directive 'myths' in the public culture, if sometimes in a weaker form. For example, at present in all the liberal-democratic capitalist societies overt antagonism to declared race chauvinism is likely to appear in a critics' culture and then transfer, in varying forms and strengths, to most varieties of the central, directive 'myths' in the public culture, producing a new 'ethnic compromise'. It is the 'critics' culture' which is an important part of the process by which public cultures can go through such remarkable changes. One of the roles of the 'critics' is to act as translators of change.

The usual radical reply to such an argument is, of course, that other things do not change. In particular, capitalist societies remain capitalist. Or males still remain dominant. That is an argument to which there is no end since its answer lies in the future: if you are looking for how present events can lead to future transformation it becomes an act of faith whether you see a reform as hastening further change or arresting the possibility of fundamental change. What we can note here is that it is of the very essence of liberal-democratic societies that there should be this tension between stability and change. As with trade unions, if a 'critics' culture' were altogether suppressed, the society ceases to be liberal-democratic. So a liberal-democratic society continues to live in contradiction and tension.

The kind of part a 'critics' culture' can play in a liberal-democratic society is nicely demonstrated by the anecdote of the 1946 United States State Department 'Advancing American Art' exhibition. The exhibition was put together at a time when a number of painters in the United States were going through the classic 'critics'' process of reconsidering their critical base. A few of the paintings were social-realist; the dominant perspectives were expressionist or abstract. These styles were chosen, instead of the styles that were still seen in the United States as 'truly American', to indicate to sophisticated foreigners that the United States was not a cultural wasteland, that the country 'which produced brilliant scientists and engineers also produced artists'. The exhibition was praised when it began its foreign tour, but at home it was soon attacked as 'radical', 'leftish', 'alien', 'vulgar', a 'travesty of art' and even, because of the emphasis on the expressionist and the abstract, 'Communist' (although it was years since the Soviets had locked up all their abstract and expressionist paintings because of their 'bourgeois decadence'). In 1947, the House Appropriations Committee defended the purity of the 'truly American' by cutting off the money to finance the exhibition and by abolishing the division in the State Department that had mounted it. A year later the paintings were sold off as surplus goods.

Yet in 1984 the National Museum of American Art in Washington re-assembled most of the exhibition and put it on again, in the traditional resting place of United States painting, as yet another example of the legend of critics who were 'before their time'.

The modern phenomenon of 'high culture'

Associated with the critics' culture is the concept of 'high culture' – in which the world of the intellect, of scholarship and of the arts is regarded as being a minority, specialist concern. 'High culture' is, I believe, a peculiarly modern phenomenon, but it is often presented as necessarily relating to a ruling class, and therefore as a permanent condition of history. (This, in turn, can then be seen as a good thing – art is elitist – or as a bad thing – art is elitist.) Against this, I would argue that with the arrival of modern industrial societies there occurred a critical shift and that, whatever may have happened in the past, the 'high culture' of modern industrial societies is not necessarily (at least not all of it) the culture of the rulers; nor is it necessarily part of the public culture.

Obviously, the concept of a ruling-class culture is of no use in thinking about tribal societies of the participatory kind, such as that of the Australian Aborigines. In these societies, although there were secret and restricted elements of initiation into knowledge and ritual, much of what we now think of as the intellectual and the artistic were matters of common knowledge and common practice, shared by everyone. However, the idea of a ruling-class culture (that also dominated public display) is extremely useful in understanding pre-industrial societies more complex than tribal societies. In such societies, as Herbert Gans put it, there was a division between the culture of the rulers, who had the time and the resources for its sponsorship, and the culture of the folk. The rulers used many elements of their culture to display their own importance, and it was their display arts that dominated the public scene. But this ruling-class culture was not the same as the 'high culture' of a modern industrial society, although some of the relics surviving from that culture have now been appropriated by the 'high culture' of modern societies.

Consider how unlike a modern industrial society is Gans's description of a pre-industrial society. In a modern society there is no longer the dichotomy of ruling-class culture and folk culture. In modern industrial societies (if in varying degrees) traditional folk culture has been attenuated into a few last souvenirs. The culture that dominates the public scene is not a ruling-class culture of triumphal display, but a fabricated 'public culture' that purports to be the culture not just of the rulers but of all the people.

In such a society 'high culture' (which might be thought of as the specialist world of the arts and the intellect) has both a unique and an ambiguous role. Most aspects have never been known before.

One of these is the enormous bulk of the 'classics' – the vast libraries, the huge museums, the tens of thousands of reprints of 'great books', the tens of thousands of art reproductions, the tens of thousands of discs, tapes and cassettes of 'great music', the immense archives, the continuing quest for the discovery of new 'classics', whether in old manuscripts, old music scores or old reputations revised. The bulk of the 'classics' becomes so great that for many people lifetime careers of creativity are found simply in new interpretations of the 'classics'.

In the continuing processes of metamorphosis suggested by Malraux in *Antimemoirs*, the 'classics' are constantly turned to new, modern purposes, because, although there is reverence for the 'classics', there is also continuing reverence for novelty ('originality'). Now that there are far more 'classics' than can be held in any single human imagination, they are treated as new material for 'research'.

A second aspect unique to high culture is the enormous bulk of 'research' and, of this, research into the 'classics' is only a minority section. Most of the 'research' done by social scientists and, above all, by physical scientists, is new. Whole sections of libraries are devoted to journals of 'research': hundreds of thousands of careers depend on the careful weighing up of 'research' papers. To aid this process, there is 'research' into 'research'. In each field each year careful estimates are made of all the citations made in new 'research' papers from old 'research' papers and scholars are graded according to these citations. In the United States there is another level of this 'research' into 'research': the worth of whole universities is quantified by measuring their 'research' contributions. Other scholars can make reputations by researching even the world's 'research', nation by nation; figures are given to each nation and then nations are graded, to show their ranking as contributors to 'world knowledge', just as they are graded in terms of economic 'growth'.

This concern with novelty in research is related to a third (and most extraordinary) aspect of modern 'high culture' – the idea of the avant-garde. In itself the metaphor is misleading. The idea is not of an advance guard moving into new territory, seeking out a way for the main army. If anything, the idea is that an avant-garde advances into new territory, alone. There is no main army behind it. If the territory is seized the avant-garde itself becomes the main army – at least until another avant-garde materializes, seizes new territory, and in turn becomes a main army. (Even the idea of seizing territory is misleading. An avant-garde creates new territory.) The continuing concern of 'modernism' with the new is also unprecedented. As Clement Greenberg said in his book *Art and Culture*, there is an understanding that no society is eternal. Nothing is 'natural'. What there is, is the latest. Even the success of an avant-garde movement – its transformation into a main army – can be seen as failure.

There is another exceptional characteristic of the avant-garde: a 'true artist', or a true thinker, does not accept the prevailing values of the rulers. It is no longer seen as the role of true artist or true thinker to serve the rulers and the prevailing social order.

'High culture', overall, is not the culture of rulers. Some rulers may appropriate parts of it: in both capitalist and Communist societies the lavishness of the opera, for example, can attract them. In capitalist societies the costliness of paintings by celebrated artists can appeal to the rich. But rulers can now see many aspects of 'high culture' as, simply, beyond their intellectual power, perhaps as challenging their social prestige, perhaps as challenging the social order. And there is certainly no society where the public culture is dominated by 'high culture', as the public scene of pre-industrial societies was dominated by ruling-class culture. Parts of a high culture may be tolerated in a public culture; other fragments of it – certain economic and political orthodoxies, for instance – may be central; and the mystifying specialist priestliness often associated with high culture can help keep ordinary people in their place. But there are always elements of a 'high culture' that are subversive to the social order. And if a 'high culture' dominated a public culture, because of its diversity it would destroy it.

Part Three:

A Declaration of Cultural Rights for the Citizen

8. Who Wins? Who Loses?

A show for the victors?

The public culture of a modern industrial society is not a representation of that society. A public culture is simply a limited set of representations of a society in the more general setting of what existence might be. Or, as we have already put it, a public culture is a dominating or perhaps monopolizing assertion, in representations and enactments, of a limited number of 'realities' over all others. How could it be otherwise? *There is not room in a public culture for all of a society's 'realities'.* If they were all 'there', then there would not be a public culture. A public culture is a form of limiting and organizing 'realities'.

Even in the more restricted sense of 'facts and figures', a public culture will not be a representation of the society – partly because those who control the public construction of 'facts' and 'figures' may, simply, lie, but mainly because there are prevailing assumptions about which 'facts' and 'figures' matter. Governments set up great manufactories of 'facts' and 'figures': in some societies they may hold the manufacturing monopoly; in others they share this monopoly with controllers of 'the news' (whose treatment of the governments' facts and figures may determine how they appear in the public culture) and/or controllers of research facilities. (But the final appearance in the public culture of research 'facts' and 'figures' may also be determined by the media and/or the government.) A prime example of this has already been given in the enormous concentration on figures of 'economic growth': the concentration on these figures seems to give a concrete underpinning to the whole 'myth' of investment and the accumulation of capital and to the myth of society as something which can be 'accounted for'.

It also gives a concrete underpinning to the all-containing 'myth' of 'reality' as fundamentally 'economic'. Within the range of 'the economic' there can, it is true, be a battle between one kind of figures and another. In the United States in the 1960s there was an essential relationship (too close for chronological ordering) between new types of research figures and 'the war on poverty', and for a season there was an enormous research concentration on poverty figures, popularized in the metaphor of 'the poverty line'. In the long crises following the end of the post-war boom there was a contest as to which mattered – figures about growth and inflation or figures about unemployment and deficits. Unfortunately, most of the audience in some such contest of the 'figures' do not know much about what the 'figures' mean. The main result of this kind of contest can be to reinforce the kind of 'reality' in which the 'economic' is what politics, and, for that matter, existence, is 'really' about. Consider the enormous symbolic significance given to a government's 'budget': by its apparent openness it can appear to proclaim the democratic nature of government. Look! The government is opening its books! In some countries, most notably the United States, the books are even made up in public. The 'budget' also projects the impression (despite alternative evidence) that the government is really 'managing the economy'. And it also proclaims that this kind of figuring is what government is 'really' about, or what existence is 'really' about.

There is an even simpler sense in which a public culture is not a representation of a society – that of the head count. Certain kinds of people are likely to be missing. They will simply not appear in the public culture. For example, until recently, the very existence of homosexuals was not recognized in the puritan public cultures of the liberal-democratic societies and the possibility of lesbianism was so unmentionable that in some countries the repressive legislation against homosexuality was confined to men. Or take the example already given of Mexican Americans in southern California. And until recently, under the weight of the myth of the family, single parents have not been visible in the public culture. There was a whole period before poverty statistics came back into fashion when in a number of liberal-democratic societies, from inspecting the public culture of those societies one might have assumed that the poor had ceased to exist. In some societies there is an attempt to keep the existence of *all* dissenters out of the public culture. Until Zola wrote *Germinal*, the modern industrial proletariat did not exist, as such, in the 'realist novel'. In the golden years of Hollywood, sexual activity did not exist: a husband and wife did not even share a bed.

Often certain kinds of people may not be altogether missing, but they won't appear in the public cultures to anything like the degree of their proportion in the population. In liberal-democratic societies, for instance, the industrial proletariat, *as such*, is scarcely evident (whereas in the Communist societies, along with the long boring lecture recitals by party leaders, there are continuing displays of the presence of workers in their workplaces). There are whole areas of the public culture (the areas of what is presented as 'power') where women are very largely obscured. Regional and ethnic representation is always skewed. Certain groups (for example, Europe's 15 million 'guest workers') would seem scarely to be there at all. And, of course, the way in which people appear in the public culture is not necessarily as *they* see themselves. If they belong to some unfavoured group, when they do appear it may be only as entertainers, or as sporting stars, or as victims, or as criminals, or as lovable clowns or calculating villains. Something like 10 per cent of Londoners are Irish, yet in the public culture if the Irish appear at all it is likely to be as terrorists, or as clowns.

Not only is a public culture not a representation of a society: it is not even a representation of all the principal actors in the power relationships of that society. This can be particularly the case in 'the news' in the capitalist societies. In 'the news' in the

Communist societies one may not see much of the kinds of bureaucrats who handle detail, but at least one can see their political leaders, attending parades, greeting dignitaries, being applauded on foreign missions, addressing delegates, reading speeches, going to funerals; but there is a particular form of invisibility in the capitalist societies – by and large, the capitalists themselves are not there, as capitalists. When 'the news' presents what are perceived as areas of power, executives of the large corporations are rarely among the main players. What is presented is a power arena occupied very largely by political leaders and public affairs interviewers and commentators. In the liberal-democratic societies, however, more complex pictures of power, including business power, can be given in books and in art and entertainment forms (there can be plenty of businessmen in these), whereas in the existing Communist societies such treatment of top party leaders is unimaginable.

It should be repeated that one reason a public culture is not representational of the 'realities' of a society is the mechanical one: that there is not enough space in a public culture to fit everything in. For this reason alone, it is, of necessity, a form of limiting and organizing 'realities'. It must by its very nature be representationally repressive. In a more equal world there would not be a public culture: as the United States culture critic Alan Lomax suggested in his essay, 'An Appeal for Cultural Equity', there would be a 'multi-culture' – a world in which 'many civilizations each with its own support systems of education and communication could live'. Within any modern society there are more 'cultures' than the public culture admits – more ways of giving meaning to existence by the construction of 'realities' that provide a basis for thought and action – than are visible in what is presented as 'the national life'.

For example, in all the Communist nation-states there are 'contra-systems' existing within the society, of which there may be no mention in the public culture – except, now and again, as criminal activity. In *Dissent in Eastern Europe*, Jane Leftwich Curry lists some of them: in all of them there flourishes, partly legally, partly illegally, a 'second economy' of private enterprise that does not get a fair representation in the public culture (no more than the significance of state economic activity does in some of the capitalist countries); in each of them, in varying strengths, there is a religious system that will usually be largely subterranean; there is within all of them, although in varying degrees, a widespread and unsocialist tendency to privatization unreflected in the public culture; in those where art activities are most firmly controlled by the state there is a 'parallel culture' of opposition to censorship and artistic unorthodoxy, just as there can be, in intellectual life, a small underground 'open university' – the *samizdats* in the Soviet Union, for example, or the 'Padlock Press' in Czechoslovakia; and there can be small, politically dissident movements – the 'second society' in the Soviet Union, for example, or the 'Parallel Polis' in Czechoslovakia. In Poland, the position goes furthest: the Church, the intelligentsia, the peasantry and, after the coming of Solidarity, parts of the labour movement, were so resilient that they provided almost a parallel existence to that of the party and the state – but they did not have an equal share of the public culture, although they fought for it.

The degree of repression of activities themselves may be greater in the present kind of Communist state than in the present kind of liberal-democratic capitalist state. But although there are not the same physical repressions, the selectivity of a public culture is just as present in a liberal-democratic capitalist state. There can be, for instance, the almost complete absence of an industrial proletariat, as such, in the public culture. There can be the restrictive representation of women mainly as wives, shoppers, whores, mothers, girlfriends. There can be the absence of whole ethnic groups from the public culture, or selective representation of them, usually as fools or rogues. In the public culture of Communist societies the importance of private economic activity is very largely suppressed; in some of the capitalist societies the importance of state economic activity can equally be very largely suppressed. ('Thatcherism' and 'Reaganomics' took to its rhetorical conclusion a habit that already characterized the common-sense 'realities' of their societies.) Whole art forms and intellectual styles may be almost completely missing – or altogether missing – from the public culture. The very idea of the 'typical household' is not representational: the nuclear family of working father, home-making mother and two or three children is no longer 'normal', yet single-parent households, working-parent households, elderly-person households, gay-couple households, single-person households, divorced-person households, extra-marital households and communal or singles-sharing households receive little space in the public culture.

In almost all social conflicts there are losers and winners. One can always ask of a public culture (since it must be limited in what it represents): to what extent is this a show for the victors? But this does not necessarily mean that there is a triumphal show. Except in a fascist state, where the surrender of the will to the leader can turn the public culture into a continuing triumph for the leader, finding the answer is a more subtle matter. A public culture can act as a kind of shadow play, distracting attention from the differences and conflicts of a society. It need not be be a triumphal presentation of the victors. It can distract attention from the victors.

One example is Switzerland. In the public culture, at one of the most simple levels of presentations of 'national life', Switzerland is the simple-hearted land of the Alps, of cowbell music and yodelling clubs, chalets and cosiness, and 'true Swiss freedom'. In international affairs, with the tradition of 'Swiss neutrality' it can be presented as a light of the world; internally it can be seen as a land of consensus, equality and 'Swiss democracy'. These are some of the principal shadow plays of the Swiss public culture. There is nothing triumphal about them: they are carried out with an assured modesty. But they conceal the triumphs of Swiss capitalism. The 'myth' of consensus is a distraction from the weakness of the trade unions and the taming of the Socialist Party. The 'myth' of equality is a distraction from the fact that women did not get the vote until 1971, that something like a quarter of the workforce consists of foreign workers, many of whom live in ghettoes, with no mobility about where they may live or what they may do, without the right to bring in their families, and without the right eventually to 'claim' citizenship. This is a form of colonialism practised at home. It is, in fact, also backed up by colonialism practised abroad: Switzerland is the second-largest foreign investor (after the United States), in South Africa. The 'myth' of neutrality distracts attention from the actions of Switzerland's huge transnational companies and the world power of its banks. It also distracts attention from the way in which, as Jean Ziegler put it in *Switzerland Exposed*, these banks act as fences for some of the world's greatest crooks and as launderers for some of the shadiest dealings of many of the world's greatest companies.

The alternative and the oppositional

When speaking of submerged cultures it has now become conventional to make a distinction between the 'alternative' cultures that diverge from but are capable of co-existing with the norms of the public culture, and the 'oppositional' cultures that appear to challenge the fundamental 'myths' of the public culture. At first sight this distinction may appear to be useful. The argument can go something like this.

One can assume that guardians of the public culture exist. Whether they are operating from an ingrained, institutional 'common sense' or from conscious deceit does not matter. Even whether they see themselves as guardians does not matter. People *do* act in ways that guard public cultures. In the liberal-democratic capitalist societies they may even excuse what they are doing by speaking in the calculating language of the 'myth' of market self-interest. 'Well, of course,' some media controller might say, 'if we were putting this on for people like *us* – of course. But *the public* wouldn't stand for it.' Given the assumption that there are guardians at the gates of the city of the public culture, the assumption then is that if they let new elements into the public culture that may have seemed inimical to it, they do this because they are accommodating to changes in the society; either on grounds of credibility or of market opportunity or both, these changes seem impossible to ignore. In the most tightly controlled societies even such accommodating changes may be ignored; it can appear better to keep all wickedness out, and to some extent lose credibility, than to let the face of change or opposition appear in any form, but, as Todd Gitlin suggests, in a liberal-democratic society certain elements of a submerged 'alternative' culture may, if the time is ripe, emerge in a 'domesticated' form that has made them safe for the mass entertainment industries. The assumption can then become that *any* element of a submerged culture that gains entry into the public culture must necessarily *not* be 'oppositional'.

This argument, as well as running the risk of leading back on to itself, can also lead to those theories mentioned before that suggest that all changes that occur within a system must therefore not be real changes and must merely 'strengthen the system'. The difficulty with this position is that it leads either to a pessimistic view that no 'real' change is possible, or to an adventurist and jacobinical view that 'real' change is possible only after the system, in its entirety, is overthrown, presumably in one apocalyptic event because any change less than the apocalypse is not real change. But if it is the apocalypse or nothing, there comes the puzzle: if there have been no 'real' changes before, including changes in 'reality', how can the apocalyptic overthrowing of the system be anything more than a changing of the guards?

In millennial movements the usual answer is supernatural. God will provide. Before Lenin's theory of a vanguard party the general answer among socialists was that material destiny would provide. As in chemical change, there was a formula: if certain material changes occurred they would therefore produce certain social changes. Lenin's theory did not leave so much to destiny, but since the October Revolution it has been interpreted as a simple act of faith that the vanguard party, once in command, will work for the people's liberation.

To put it mildly, this is not self-evident. Ultimately those who have policies of change may be left with the necessity to make some acts of secular faith ('myths'), but how can one still retain faith in the liberating role of a vanguard party when this now means, in effect, that human liberation will occur by changing the guards on *the system of industrialism* – by changing ownership in a way that moves from bureaucratic oligopolies to one bureaucratic monopoly?

If one abandons a single 'big bang' theory of change one may have to see change occurring not in events but in processes, ebbing and flowing, and one may also have to accept that in some ways this will be mysterious, so that there is need for 'myths'; but if changes are occurring in processes, ebbing and flowing, and if this is the only way change occurs, how can we say that any change that does occur is therefore, from its very occurring, not a 'real' change? A romantic answer would be that a new, counter-hegemonic 'reality' was growing so strong among the potential liberators in a society that when these liberators arose, and changed the guards, they had already also been changing their consciousness. That seems to me the best answer. But even in this case there would be struggle: it would be unlikely that the counter-hegemonists could develop their new 'reality' as conspirators in isolated basements and then arise and seize the streets unless they had previously engaged in some public performance. Their counter-hegemonic views would develop in social conflict, and in these conflicts (which might include a struggle for the public culture) they might sometimes win.

Another difficulty about the distinction between 'oppositional' and 'alternative' is that in practice this can depend on what lies in the minds of the guardians. The 'oppositional' books of Lenin are (these days) likely to be on the shelves of public libraries in a liberal-democratic capitalist society. They don't (any longer) get burnt and the people who read them are not (any longer) imprisoned. But what might be burnt, or at least confiscated, is an 'alternative' protest form – an 'obscene' or 'blasphemous' poster, for instance, paraded in front of the library – and it may be the 'alternative lifestyle' people who have their heads batoned by cops on the steps of the public library. To the guardians, the 'alternative' can seem 'oppositional'. It depends on what they think they are guarding. In the Soviet Union, abstract art is 'oppositional' enough for the authorities to bring out the bulldozers. In the Bible Belt in the United States Darwinism is still seen as threatening to the social order.

Another criticism is that the distinction between 'oppositional' and 'alternative' does not take into account that the public culture is merely an assembled 'reality' that provides a publicly dominant shadow play of what existence is supposed to be and how humans should behave. Unlike the old ruling-class culture it is mainly something put on for the public amorphously. *It is not inextricably part of the daily life of the rulers*, as ceremonial display and sign display were in a ruling-class culture. It is not actually performed by rulers, courts, their immediate retainers and priests, or performed in front of them. Nor must it be associated *only* with rulers. In fact, it is essential that this should not be so. It is projected as a culture *for all*: it is 'the national life'; it is the way everyone should behave. Some parts of it *are* enacted by almost everyone – the work ethic, the home ethic, voting, for example – but other parts have a vicarious quality in which enactments are made *for* us and (in a distinction I have referred to before and shall return to shortly) although some parts of it may be *dominant* they may not be *pervasive* throughout society, and may not become its common sense.

In other words, it is the public culture of a nation-state, but it is not necessarily the culture of the whole nation. But when one comes to the submerged cultures (or as it is usually, although I think misleadingly put, the 'sub-cultures') within a nation there can also be a dissociation between the repertoires of meanings and 'realities' thought of as 'sub-cultures' and the groups that actually form a 'society within a society'. There are very few cases where 'society within a society' and 'sub-culture' are terms related exactly to the same minority group. A particular minority group may have its own, as it were, 'selections' from the cultural repertoires, but many or most of the cultural repertoires from which the 'selections' are made will run more widely through the society. For example, in the heroic days of Jewish immigration, the Lower East Side in New York was a Jewish enclave – but it was an enclave where some Jews taught other Jews how to be 'American'. Where this is not the case the group, unless it can live in regional isolation, will be culturally destroyed. One of the moral battles of the nineteenth century was fought in Australia in the seizing by the British of the lands of the Aborigines. It was a moral battle because Aboriginal society was communal, reciprocal and traditional and British society was individualistic, competitive and industrial. Given the confident imperialism of the time there was no possibility of compromise. As with the native Americans in the United States and Canada, this alien culture had to be destroyed. In fact, this destruction could be spoken of openly: in social Darwinist terms of the survival of the fittest it was seen as the passing of an inferior species too unintelligent to adapt to the methodical life of industrial 'work'.

The distinction that will be made here is not between the 'oppositional' and the 'alternative', but – when it is relevant – between what is dominant or monopolistic in the public culture (itself an important matter), and what is also very largely pervasive throughout the society, constructing for many or most people in the society their 'common sense'. For the rest of this chapter the principal concern, however, will be to consider how to apply the *Who benefits?* question to public cultures.

The momentum of industrialism

To state the distinction between the dominant and the pervasive is easier than finding it. Some of it is surveyable, but, if the surveys were to be 'scientific', it would be only in enormous programmes, both qualitative and quantitative, regularly repeated, and in a whole range of nations some of which would not allow the survey anyway. Does that leave us hopeless? Only if you believe that we can discuss only questions that are surveyable.

Or is it as difficult as that?

At least in the case of the 'myths' of industrialism (with which I will therefore begin) is there any difficulty? Anyone who doubts that in the societies we have been discussing the acceptance of 'the accumulation of capital' and 'the accumulation of men' is so widely and deeply pervasive that it is ingrained in bodily habits would have to explain how, otherwise, these societies could operate as they do. They are distinguished from Third World societies precisely because of the strength of these habits. (And in this the conjunction of the 'myths' of industrialism with the 'myths' of modernity with their belief in the inevitability of progress is usually assumed to be relevant.) Not only is there the 'normalization' of the human body in work: there is also the 'normalization' of the human mind which makes 'work' (paid labour) appear as the only way. It is as if the prisoners can accept only their chains. As André Gorz points out in *Farewell to the Working Class*, 'Instead of demanding the abolition of wage labour, the proletariat has come to demand the abolition of all non-wage labour. The height of alienation is reached when it becomes impossible to conceive that an activity should have a goal other than its wage.'

I have suggested that, although much else in these nation-states may be different, industrialism is common to both capitalist and Communist societies. The difference is one of *who* should control the accumulation of capital and the accumulation of labour. To those who believe as an act of faith (a 'myth') that state control of industrialism in the workers' name makes industrialism in itself different in the Communist states from the capitalist states, it seems to me (since this *is* the expression of an act of faith) that there is no useful answer other than the mild one that after almost 70 years the truth of this 'myth' is not yet self-evident.

If one takes a more complex view, there is this problem: if both societies are concerned with capital accumulation, the normalization of a labour force and a belief in salvation through work, who are the winners? An easy answer for one side is to say 'the capitalists' and for the other side to say 'the party bosses'. But then one can extend it, and reply 'the generals', or 'the colonels', or 'the fascists', or 'the nationalists', or perhaps even 'the mullahs', or whatever else it might be. In other words, as a system of 'myths' and power relations industrialism may not be related necessarily to a particular class of victors. It is related to *any* class of victors.

And it is a system maintained by the willing collaboration of its victims, who, on the whole, can imagine no other way. Even 'myths' of worker self-management have the difficulty that, as with concern with wages as the main system of honour in a society, it can turn those who practise it into accomplices of the system. I don't see that as a reason for not supporting self-management, but those who engage in it might contemplate some of its intractabilities, as André Gorz does when he says:

> The obstacle standing in the way of workers' control, power and autonomy is not merely legal or institutional. It is also a material obstacle . . . For the great secret of large scale industry, as of any vast bureaucratic or military machine, is that *nobody holds power* . . . All that can be found – from the bottom right up to the top of an industrial or administrative hierarchy – are agents obeying the categorical imperatives and inertias of the material system they serve . . . In the modern state, the bearers of power enforce obedience in the name of objective necessities for which no one can be held responsible.

And this is a process that can seem as natural to those who take the orders as to those who give them. They are both part of the same thing. Aboriginal Americans and Australians are often given as examples of 'alternative' cultures in modern industrial societies. Yet they, almost alone, are truly 'oppositional'. Even members of the wage proletariat in a capitalist society who see themselves as revolutionary socialists will nevertheless be imbued with part of the cultural repertoires of a modern industrial state. Unlike aboriginal Americans or Australians, they can, with their very bodies, accept the work ethic that is essential to modern industrialism. Where they they see redemption is not in the destruction of the 'myths' of industrialism but in a change of legal ownership and control of modern industrial activity. Then, if they seek change, this change in ownership and control will do it for them. It may be that the *only* 'oppositional' cultures that are really oppositional in an industrial state are the anti-'industrial' cultures. All of the others may be concerned with changing some of the characteristics of an industrial state, but they are not concerned with changing it *as* an industrial state.

In the meantime, if we believe in continuing possibilities for human liberation, we need strong, simple perspectives on equality. We largely have them already, in concepts of gender, race and ethnic equality and in recognition of economic inequality. We do not yet have equally strong and simple perspectives on the implications of the 'myths' of 'work' in the industrial societies and on the concepts of 'home' as nothing but a private, recuperative place and on 'leisure' as a private time of recuperation in either indolence or spectatorship or mere 'hobbies'.

'Legitimations' of power: sex, race, ethnicity

The 'legitimations' of the privileges of males over females were carried over from the pre-industrial societies. (In sexual activity itself we create 'realities' with our bodies.) Male privileges were dominant in both ruling-class and folk cultures and they passed into the industrial societies, with some biology added to theology and with some deployments necessary to legitimize new types of male privileges. In this case, there is no doubt about who the victors are. They are males. The enactments of the naturalness of male superiority – even *triumphal* enactments – are still commonplace in all the public cultures. In some of them there are now challenges. But, as things stand, it is usually *only* as challenges that they will appear in the public culture. 'First times' for women began to appear almost a hundred years ago, towards the end of the nineteenth century, as part of what was known as 'the woman question'. There is still a 'woman question'. An interesting test would be to rate what kinds of appearances of women in the public culture now, compared with 1900, have really become 'natural'.

Whether in politics or in television serials there is not likely to be much enactment of the *naturalness* of sex equality. And when there is, it is worth looking at critically, to speculate about what else it is that these appearances of women 'say'. Women have probably become more accepted as television news readers and interviewers, for instance. In different nations different kinds of attempts are made by the people who run the television news and public affairs programmes to produce a somewhat more diverse presentation of national identity (their motives in doing this vary) and in these programmes women may even have begun to appear more 'natural', as performers, than do, say, men with black faces or accents that suggest a submerged ethnic or class origin. But one should ask: on what conditions do these women appear? If the women are staged in subordinate roles, the answer is obvious. But there is something even more important: there will almost certainly be some special attention to the extent to which the faces and bodies of these women convey current conventions of youth and beauty. How many newscasters are old women, or bear faces that show stereotypes of 'character' (which is what is required in males) instead of stereotypes of beauty? In other words, the mere appearance of women playing parts in the public culture not previously played by females does not put an end to the 'feminine' stereotype: it can give it new strength.

When 'permissiveness' became commercially exploitable in most of the liberal-democratic capitalist societies, a lot of what was worked out both in entertainment ('explicit' films and so forth) and in the kind of material provided in some of the new and more 'liberated' women's magazines could be seen as an inducement to young women to make themselves more sexually available to males. The 'explicitness' itself in any case continued the division between young women and old. It was only young women who were shown enjoying what were seen as new freedoms. Again, there was also the emphasis on conventional feminine beauty: it was only beautiful young women who were presented as enjoying sex. The new 'explicitness', in style, was just as romantic as the old reticence. It simply revealed more: literally. At a time when the display of female flesh to the male beholder had gone out of fashion in painting, it came into fashion in the movies.

The question as to the degree that these 'myths' also still pervade the society as 'common sense' requires slightly more guessing, but, surely, not much, at least so far as males are concerned. Almost all the impressions that have surfaced suggest that there are only certain enlightened and almost always 'educated' segments of society where male *attitudes* are changing, and perhaps even fewer were male *conduct* is changing. It may not be insignificant that in the 1980s a commercial reaction began against the kind of commercial exploitation made in the 1970s of the non-triumphal male – the 'sensitive' male, sometimes even the inadequate male, of whom the paradigm, at least in the cinemas of some of the capitalist societies, became Woody Allen. By the mid-1980s the fictional presentation of males seemed to be returning to the strong and masterful. The sensitive male, at least in the United States, was becoming 'the wimp'.

What of the way in which women also accept the 'myths' of male superiority and of a 'feminine' role so deeply that they are collaborators, as it were, in their own domination and not merely coerced by economic or physical force? Well, yes there has been plenty of evidence for that, too, but there can always be a residue of doubt: were some women dissimulating? We know that some women do now see the world from what could be called a feminist perspective and that evidence of this comes into the public cultures in both Communist and capitalist societies, but we don't really know much about the extent of this. The spread throughout most of the capitalist societies of more information about female sexuality presumably makes some difference to what happens between some women and men. And one can wonder how much longer in two-income homes women can be expected to play both income-earning (male) roles and household-maintaining (female) roles. Neither of these questions receives much concern in the public culture. In *The Russians* Hedrick Smith recalls a gender role-reversal skit shown by a satirical troupe in Leningrad in which women are shown acting around the house like men while the men act like women. He said Russian audiences found it 'deliciously funny'. Audiences in liberal-democratic societies would probably also find it 'deliciously funny'.

There is less overt race chauvinism now in the public cultures of all the modern industrial states, except, of course, South Africa, in the sense that there is no longer likely to be sheer racist abuse ('cunning oriental', 'nigger', 'lesser breeds', etc.). At least, this abuse is no longer articulated *as* abuse. At least not in public. But none of the public cultures of the old imperial societies is yet colour-blind. To take one example: it is the Jews who are commemorated in memories of the Holocaust – never the gipsies. In any case, the killings and torturings of Hitler come to be seen as an aberration; but the killings and torturings of Pol Pot can be seen as typically 'Asian'. Likewise, the attempted assassination of Mrs Thatcher was seen as symptomatic of new tensions in British society, but the assassination of Mrs Gandhi that followed a few weeks later was seen as normal for a place like India. When revolution (a European concept) spread to the Third World countries it was sometimes accompanied by blood-letting; but so it was, also, in Europe. The making of 'new nations' in Africa and Asia has been difficult: but in Europe there were equal disasters, and part of the 'making' of the United States was one of history's most savage civil wars. The old imperial centres of Western Europe, North America and Oceania can still retain (as Disneyland does) monuments to white triumphalism: in the civic museum of

Liverpool respect is still paid to the commercial success of the slave trade. History is still likely to be taught as an extension of white civilization; the economic aid programmes to poor countries are often expressed in the patronizing terms of charity when in fact the 'aid' is often 'bought' at huge economic and social cost. The United States' response at a conference in Mexico City on Third World over-population was to recommend the free market as a form of birth control: by increasing material prosperity it would increase the tendency to limit the size of families. In Japan contempt for 'lesser' peoples may be even stronger than in the European nations. In the Soviet Union (where, as in the United States, Canada, Australia and New Zealand the whites retained their empire) there is no overt racism in the public culture – but it is Europeans who are the masters: Soviet citizens who are Asian are even less evident in the public culture than black Americans are in the public culture of the United States. The Moslem Church stands second to the Orthodox Church in adherents but receives no space at all in the public culture – not even in 'art' relics or the tourist trade.

In some societies there are continued struggles to gain space in the public culture by ethnic minority groups. Sometimes they may even use the same methods. Just as in Australia at the beginning of the 1970s the Aborigines pitched a protest tent outside the parliament in Canberra as part of their struggle for land rights, at the end of the 1970s Lapps pitched a tent outside the parliament in Helsinki as part of the struggle for preservation of their lands. It is in the United States that the struggle can reach its most heroic to gain that place in the public culture that Jesse Jackson calls 'respect'. But while this struggle is a beginning, it is not an end: the question remains to what extent an entry into the public culture by blacks is made merely on the prevailing terms of the whites.

There is no doubt that celebrations of white triumphalism were as dominant in the white societies as celebrations of male triumphalism were dominant in all societies. It might also appear that just as the victors of sexism were males, the victors of racism were whites, but the position was somewhat more complex. Males were victors down to the lowest levels of society: from the top of a society to its bottom men did well out of male chauvinism. But in race chauvinism, while economic exploitation of non-whites may have benefited many or most whites, for many whites racism was merely a consolation in their failure: it told them they were better than 'niggers', 'chows', 'wogs', etc., but that didn't put any butter on their bread. It merely gave them the consolations of poor people who are supporting a winning sporting team. If they happened to live in a society where there were coloured people, there was the extra consolation that they could despise them in person and they could sometimes kick them or beat them; but, as in the United States South (as Jesse Jackson and others still point out), all this pride was, for the poor whites, a way of preventing them from recognizing their economic identity with poor blacks against their common masters.

It should also be recognized, of course, that even if there are ameliorations of racism in the public culture, they do not necessarily become pervasive. Just because some of the language of anti-racism is used in a public culture it does not mean that anti-racism has become the common sense of people throughout that society. At times even some of those who speak the language of anti-racism in the public culture may still use the language of racist 'reality' when they are off-stage. In a modern industrial society changes in the public culture are only the beginnings of change. The same is true of struggles to gain greater space in the ethnic compromise of a public culture. But here we face head on a central question. In a complex modern industrial society there simply isn't space for everything. A true multi-ethnicity would mean the end of a public culture.

'Legitimations' of power: class

The University of California at Santa Barbara is an adjunct to a 'laid-back' rich persons' city. Its pale buildings are set on the coast amongst wide lawns, where students lie around sunning themselves as if they are on an expensive holiday. Near the elevator I saw an advertisement for a discussion on 'Gender – Race – Ethnicity'. 'At an Australian university,' I said to my host, as we entered the elevator, 'we would probably add another word to those three – Class.' I was probably wrong in imagining that everyone in the elevator went silent. But one student did say, in a loud voice, to no one in particular: 'In America we have a classless society.'

At the period when the industrial societies and their public cultures were forming, the existence of class could be seen as a natural and indeed orderly aspect of society: it was a recognition that all the classes of a society had their proper place. It then became usual in the public cultures of most of the liberal-democratic capitalist societies for them to be projected as 'classless', or for what remained of class-consciousness to be seen as a 'problem' that must be solved. (In the Communist societies, of course, the state is seen as classless on the grounds that there cannot be classes when private ownership of productive property has been abolished.) The reason for the change from an acceptance of class to an avoidance of it is that class division could once be seen as orderly, but now it is seen as threatening conflict. In a state where 'the capitalist image of society' strongly prevails (and there is no society of which that is more true than the United States, with no labour party and, in most areas of paid labour, a weak or non-existent union movement) the idea of 'class' seems to upset the natural order.

There is a voluminous literature on the word 'class'. Here I am using the word loosely to discuss matters associated with how people gain their incomes and/or how they work. (Some people – *rentiers* of the classic sort, for example – can gain income without working. Others – 'housewives', for example, or 'hobbyists' – can work without gaining an income.)

With this kind of meaning, one cannot describe a modern industrial society as 'classless' but one can go beyond the obsession with *owning*. There are several reasons why I haven't wished to confine the question of 'class' to the question of owning or not owning productive property. One is that this concern leaves out all people who are not either owners or wage earners. Another is that it leaves many of the conflicts of Communist societies undiscussable. Another is that it does not allow sufficiently for the difference between ownership and control and does not allow for access to power on grounds other than ownership. Another is that it does not allow for direct qualitative observations (as distinguished from *a priori* deductions) on the nature of different kinds of work.

This is not to say that ownership is not in itself important. What we own, how much we own and how we own it are matters that can divide human beings. People can spend their lives struggling, accumulating, planning, saving and borrowing, buying and owning. Acquisition can come to seem the better part of life. And belief in individual owning can be one of the organizing principles of a society, as in the 'myth', already discussed, of 'a home-owning democracy'. In a country such as Australia where the votes of home owners in what are called 'the mortgage belts' of the cities are seen as crucial, 'common sense' can give such enormous importance to home ownership that political campaigns and public policies are directed much more to house-owning than to housing programmes. Non-owners get a worse deal than they do in countries such as the Netherlands with a strong tradition of government concern about housing; in a society such as Australia, home owners are among the beneficiaries of the public culture.

But if one wants to talk about 'legitimations' of power in modern industrial states the traditional concept of class as related primarily to ownership may be useful in one case only – the case of the liberal-democratic capitalist societies, and that in an unexpected way, connected with the possibility that when looking at the great bureaucratic agglomerates of modern industrial states, what becomes remarkable is how unimportant ownership may be.

Some of the densest bureaucratic agglomerations, after all, occur in 'classless' societies in which there is no private ownership of large-scale productive resources. And if we are concerned with representations of 'the national life' in the modern industrial states, what becomes remarkable in almost all of them is the comparative invisibility of the principal administrators. These bureaucratized societies are 'run', at least up to their second-highest level, by specialists and administrators with high bureaucratic/technocratic skills to whom what is common, whatever kind of society they are in, is that their negotiable assets are expertise and the prudent skills of bureaucrat-courtiers. Yet on the whole they suffer a kind of cultural captivity. They have made the vertical ascent in their 'careers', through education-based expertness and/or a talent in bureaucratic styles, but honour does not come to expertness and prudence. They are likely to live in societies in which the public culture is still dominated by other values. In Communist societies it is the 'myth' of the liberating working class and the vanguard party that are honoured; in fascist societies, the 'myth' of the leader; in other non-liberal capitalist societies, varying forms of the 'myth' of the state; and in the liberal-democratic capitalist societies, the 'myths' of the capitalists. There are exceptions – in Japan in particular there is high esteem for the idea of dedicated teams of expert functionaries in the bureaucracies of government and business who serve 'Japan', and in some of the European nations there was a season in the 1960s in which it was fashionable to speak of 'technocrats' and 'meritocracies', and there is certainly respect for them in Singapore – but, generally speaking, the idea of 'bureaucracy' is negative when it appears in the public culture. The 'bureaucrats' are seen as impeding the will of the party, or of the leader, or as impeding the rationality of 'free enterprise'. So, very largely, most of the directive class are not honoured, as such, in the directive culture. Their honour comes from a transfer of 'myth' – and in the liberal-democratic societies these 'myths' tend to be those of capitalist ownership.

In fascist societies and in capitalist societies that are *étatiste* in some form, the rich can lead the lives of concessionaires without, on the whole, having to be justified in the public culture. Hitler did not make speeches praising the free market. A military president does not attribute the glories of the state to the profit motive. But in the liberal-democratic societies, where, in varying degrees, the 'myths' of capitalist enterprise become 'legitimations' of the social order, they can, by osmosis, also help 'legitimate' the executives – most of them administrators with expertise and bureaucratic skills – who on the whole actually run businesses, and most of whom are not themselves owners. The companies they preside over are so large that they do not run the risks of failure of a corner grocery. Their main personal risk is from intrigue in bureaucratic court life. But they speak the language of profit. (Its practice is somewhat more difficult: what they can really be concerned with is survival, and even attributing blame or praise for losses or profits can be a question of bureaucratic manoeuvre.) And they are honoured in the public culture as if they really were (owning, risk-taking) capitalists. They can still be suffused with the honour of the risk-taking and potentially bankruptable small firm. We might call them 'pseudo-capitalists'.

The 'myths' of free enterprise can also, of course, 'legitimate' private ownership in general, and, to their great advantage, the rich. This 'legitimation' is slightly complex. If productive activity were largely provided by small, family-owned firms controlled by their owners operating as risk-taking entrepreneurs in a relatively free market with a strong sense of personal creative involvement, there could be a direct relationship between the 'myths' of free enterprise and these firms. They would be given honour by the principle of utility. However, how the rich gain their incomes is not necessarily related to this kind of utility. Many of them have inherited wealth. Most of them are not risk-taking entrepreneurs and controllers of small businesses, but investors, or speculators in shares, in real estate, or in any of the various forms of money-lending. How they gain an income is not honourable by many of the standards of 'the traditional virtues', nor by the standards of utility of the free enterprise 'myth'. Now, unless they gain through their wealth some position in the corporation-bureaucracies, the rich themselves are often 'alienated' from their own property. It can be sheer, speculative gambling that can feed their sense of individualism. In their takeover battles, the most powerful of them can become punters who sit in the members' stand and manipulate races in which even the losers win. They continue to gain honour, however, because private ownership seems to work, because the large corporations run mainly by the pseudo-capitalists seem to work, and because small owners in their family firms or corner groceries can still honour the system with their thousands of sacrificial bankruptcies. It is this relatively small group of people – the rich – whom the public culture of a liberal-democratic capitalist society can, by the magic of its free enterprise 'myths', most ingeniously protect.

'Myths' of the labour movement, of varying sorts, usually play their part in 'legitimating' political and economic power. In the Communist societies, of course, the party acts in the name of labour. But even in neo-traditionalist states labour can play its part in lending magic to power, usually in the 'myth' of the nobility of labour, the purification of work and the loyalty of the labour force in serving the will of leader, junta, state, monarch or nation. In some of the Latin American societies the trade union movement has been part of a corporatist compromise in which, along with a peasant movement, it might have been seen as fitting into a general equilibrium that 'legitimated' the state or, as in the case of the Peronist movement in Argentina, claimed the right to determine the leadership of the state or withdraw its support for a regime's legitimacy. It is only in the liberal-democratic capitalist societies, or some of them, that a labour movement can live without honour, in the public culture, or at least without the honour of sharing in the 'legitimation' of the state. According to Francis Castles, in his book *The Social Democratic Image of Society*, in Sweden the Social Democrats have a distinct image as a party of the working class. (Certainly, on May Day, with the red flags and the old songs and signs, one might imagine Stockholm in the grip of revolution.) The party projects itself *as* a class party countering capitalism, and its high visibility is seen as essential to the legitimacy of the state, as is the presence of the trade union movement. This could seem to be so in a few other countries, where the 'consent' of the unions can be seen as an essential part of an imagined social contract and the visibility of the labour parties is accepted as essential to images of 'national life', but it is just as usual, or more usual, for the unions to appear as divisive and for the labour party to be concerned with denying that it is only party of 'the workers'.

'Legitimations' of power: the neo-traditional

Not surprisingly, the rich are winners in the range of manifestations in the public culture that might be thought of as right wing: the conservative, the neo-traditional and some forms of religious backlash.

'Conservatism' is now little more than an enlargement of the capitalist image of society, with a more than usually open expression of the laissez-faire 'myth'. It is not necessarily accompanied by any extension of laissez-faire in practice. It is not likely to mean, for instance, a dismantling of 'the welfare state', because, as Bismarck knew, welfare can be a useful form for controlling the 'useless' – it stops them rioting, or dying in the streets. It might, however, mean a lessening of welfare, but there is the complication that welfare extends to those thought of as the middle class: it is not only a form of income redistribution; it is also a way in which, as a group, the financial affairs of the 'middle class' can be re-arranged to see them through their non-earning periods. Conservatism may not even mean less government intervention. It can mean *more* government intervention. What changes is the direction in which the government intervenes. The state intervenes more effectively to help the rich.

In its milder form ('constitutional monarchies' and so forth) neo-traditionalism might also be seen as aiding the rich. If some of the perceptions of national life presented on television are suffused with the warm glow of neo-feudal ceremony, for instance, this can be a distraction from contemplations of inequalities, or present them as natural to humankind – after all, this is what the symbolical use of a hierarchical system apparently based on heredity is 'saying'. More generally it can be one of the inducements for the overall acceptance of the familiarity of things as they are. In this it can, of course, also serve (or at least appear to *them* to be serving) social-democratic governments, whose reform programmes may partly operate on the assumption that if certain sections of the public culture remain reassuringly the same it may be easier to achieve 'real' change. This has been a belief in the Scandinavian societies, where it has been associated with a 'democratization' of the monarchy, in which royal performers are photographed riding bicycles or going shopping, and thus celebrating ordinariness and family virtue, so that it might be understood that when they do dress up it is simply because they are performing certain ceremonies of state, a situation quite different from that in Britain where part of the magic of the monarchic family is that they are great aristocrats leading a life not available even to others as rich as they are. In Spain, the return of the monarchy to the public culture was seen (probably correctly) as a stabilizer in the period after Franco's death.

Neo-traditionalism, however, as the fascist regimes have shown, can also be thought of as a reservoir of those passions which can find many devout believers amongst the ordinary people and are mobilizable at some time of apparent threat. This does not harm the rich, as a class. It is true that in a fascist or highly militarized regime or a regime 'legitimized' by some other form of neo-traditionalism some of the rich might be imprisoned or hung or shot. But the rest of them, along with various party or military leaders, can fatten on the pickings of concessionaire capitalism. The repertoires of hyper-neo-traditionalism are not 'essential' to capitalism, but they can remain one of the repertoires of a capitalist society, providing a potential for rousing passions that under special circumstances can be used by right-wing political entrepreneurs.

Religious backlash (attempts to desecularize at least some parts of the public culture) might also, tangentially, appear to operate in the interests of the rich. In the United States God can become a laissez-faire capitalist fighting all the evils of liberal secular humanism – from abortion choice to food stamps. The revivalists on United States radio or television with their vehement curses against the satanic evil of liberalism are curiously reminiscent, in their mixture of religion and politics, of Khomeini's Iran. And in so far as religious leaders preach quiescence they provide a general 'legitimation' of the status quo. Or, more generally – this would also apply to some of Japan's 'new religions' – by providing forms of group enthusiasm, religious sects can help accommodate people to an industrial society. But then so do mass sporting events. (And the Soka Gakkai, the most popular of the Japanese 'new religions', and its associated political party, the Komeito, can really be seen more in secular than religious terms – as an enthusiast manifestation of neo-traditionalism.) However the potential of Christianity, with the ambiguous figure of Christ as both triumphant judge and sacrificed victim, would still seem wide enough to leave other possibilities open. In criticizing 'liberation theology' for its Marxism, a Vatican pronouncement nevertheless spoke of 'the seizure in certain parts of Latin America of the vast majority of the wealth by an oligarchy of owners bereft of social consciousness', of 'military dictators who make a mockery of elementary human rights' and of 'the savage predatoriness of some foreign capital interests'. This is a type of language that would be seen as satanic liberal-humanism on a United States revivalist radio station.

'Legitimations' of power: political 'myth'

In the distinction between what is merely dominant in the public culture and what permeates the society – becoming its common sense – we have already speculated about how pervasive in industrial societies are gender, race and ethnic chauvinism. This is guesswork about which we can be fairly confident because the stereotypes are so simple. It is much more difficult to speculate about how pervasive are the 'myths' that in the public culture appear to justify those elements of power relations that we think of as 'political' and 'economic'. These relations are also, of course, sexist, ethnocentric or racist, but we also think of them in terms such as free enterprise, or socialism, or the *Führerprinzip* (leader-worship). To what extent do most people in a society 'believe' in capitalism, Communism, fascism?

We know that people can 'believe' in industrialism; they show this belief with the 'common sense' of their bodies as well as their minds. The rest of the answer, it seems to me, must probably remain beyond the scope of serious research. Within one society there could be many different meanings, and the diversity of meanings would become even greater when we began to compare societies.

Gramsci was right when he said of the United States that it was the best example of a society in which the ruling classes had historically established almost complete ideological hegemony (not only dominant in the public culture, but pervading the society, providing its common sense). Even so, the idea of individualism, for example, might have different meanings among different social groups. In other capitalist societies, as in Italy and Sweden, there is a clearly articulated anti-capitalism with a mass following. Even where the socialist base is weaker, there may be within a capitalist society whole ranges of scepticism and hostility; and the particular parts of free enterprise 'myth' that can be persuasive in, say, party politics, may be much less than the whole doctrine – perhaps just a few simple images and phrases. In the Solidarity movement, and in the Prague Spring, we saw how, beneath the observed public culture of a Communist society, there can be strongly reasoned opposition trends. In Germany under Hitler fascism seemed to pervade much of the society, while fascism in Italy seemed much less pervasive, as the Italian resistance showed. Then, when Hitler was defeated, Germany was transformed and began to operate in the West as a liberal democracy and in the East as a people's democracy.

There are personality appeals that can be stronger than

national belief. Hitler and Mussolini, for example, had personal as well as ideological appeal. In the liberal democracies life can seem to change with a strong political personality. Elections can be decided on the whimsical ignorance of quite small numbers of people. Where there are monarchs, they can distract attention from a naked concentration of power. So can sporting victories, entertainment stars, 'celebrities', popes. And all of the time, in almost all of these societies, attention is deflected from their bureaucratic-industrial nature. In this sense, capitalism, socialism and fascism can all divert the gaze from industrialism.

It might be useful to go back to the idea of national identity. People within a nation-state that is not disintegrating can 'see' the nation in ways that can confirm sexist, racist or ethnocentric chauvinism – or that proclaim some compromise between these tensions. In their imaginations there also dance around many other images – from a 'typical' tree to a 'typical' home. There are legends that almost all of them know. Personalities come into their view who excite their dreams or their nightmares. From time to time there can be a 'national achievement'. (Every industrial state can produce, now and again, some 'national achievement'.) Amongst these images of 'the nation', some constant, some passing, float simple bits and pieces of political and economic belief that can also seem part of 'the nation'.

9. Constructing New 'Myths'

Changing 'reality'

To see paid labour as the main form of usefulness and the only proper avenue to welfare and dignity is itself to urge a form of 'unemployment': it means that a large part of human potential lies unused, locked up in what Alvin Gouldner called 'the unemployed self'. Both education and work patterns develop only a part, and in many cases a very small part, of the 'self'. A concern for human liberation could be viewed as a 'full employment policy' for the self. This means that as well as concern for the discriminations of sex, ethnic and economic inequality, those who seek human liberation must pass beyond the 'reality' of industrialism, whether of the Communist or the capitalist kind, into the magic of new 'myths', new ways of looking at things, so that the 'measurements' by which our activities are regulated in industrial societies could be replaced as *the* 'reality' by a different basis for thought and action.

To say this is not to suggest that material comfort is of no consequence. In fact one could begin by recognizing the failures of industrialism in spreading material comfort. The potentials of science, of technology and of intellectual enlightenment and inventiveness are lavish, but these are not industrialism. In fact industrialism can restrict them with its narrow emphases. For instance, in an industrial society the findings of medical science are directed, on the whole, not towards health, but towards hospitals. Industrialism, as a system, has been possible only as a result of human inventiveness, but it also becomes a principal curb on inventiveness.

Over a restricted part of the earth it has produced great engineering triumphs, and for a restricted part of the world's human population it has produced many material goods (which can then become for some of those people the central meaning of their lives.) But who now can believe, as seemed the case until the end of the 1960s, that 'economic growth' would continue forever, and that out of this growth the materially deprived would, in due course, if they remained patient, get their modest share?

It was towards the end of that same decade that pundits began to detect a 'post-industrial society' in which the problem of production (in the sense of manufactured goods) had been solved – as indeed, in technical terms, in the advanced capitalist societies, it had – and there would now begin a more enlightened society in which the principal 'economic' dynamic would become a concern with services and amenities, 'quality of life', the arts, leisure, etc. If predictions are ways of attempting to organize the future, perhaps those who have some concern with human liberation should go back to the more humane of the predictions that were then made about the post-industrial society. Those predictions were 'realistic', in that they were within the range of material possibilities. Automation, for instance, does not, in its own material terms, necessarily mean unemployment. There is nothing in the material conditions of automation that could not mean that work was shared out in shorter working weeks, or that there could be a 'productivity tax' so that those who were doing well out of automation shared with the deprived some of what they had gained, or that since working in automated factories could be so boring, we could all do our turn, one day a week perhaps, for a common minimum payment. Nor was there anything in the nature of the 'economies' of the capitalist post-industrial societies that meant that taxation should not be increased to help establish the kinds of service industries that would 'enhance the quality of life'. It was only the 'realities' of industrialism that made such ideas seem impractical. The result is that the post-industrial society becomes one in which factories close down and the promised growth in service industries can mean that at a time of greater unemployment more people get part-time jobs in supermarkets.

In the capitalist societies, over the long period of the post-war boom in which there was full employment with only low inflation, the 'myth' of the work ethnic could at least seem to be functioning in ways that would satisfy the 'myth' of the consumer ethic engendered by those societies and on which full employment came to be based. But now this charmed circle has broken. It no longer seems likely that these societies can go back to the days of full employment and low inflation. Nor is there any creative potential in most of the new jobs which replace lost jobs. Increasingly, the new employment is insecure, much of it part-time, so that we now have junk jobs as well as junk food. For those who seek forms of human liberation it becomes even more imperative to find ways of passing beyond the 'reality' of the work ethic to find a new kind of 'reality', in which it is imaginable that human productivity and human creativity are 'cultural rights'. These 'cultural rights' need to be 'declared' with the verve with which civil rights were 'declared' by Thomas Jefferson in the Declaration of Independence he drafted in 17 days in Philadelphia in 1776 or in the Declaration of the Rights of Man and of the Citizen drafted in a week for the National Assembly in Paris in 1789 and with the verve with which the rights of the toiling masses were proclaimed in the 'Manifesto' that Marx and Engels wrote in the winter of 1847–8.

To propose such things is to move into an unknown where some of the 'myths' and 'realities' of parts of eighteenth-century enlightenment and nineteenth-century socialism would be extended into a late twentieth-century redef-inition of the world. But they would only have imagi-native power if what was being articulated was already in the minds of the people. I suspect that an imaginative force of that kind would come only at some time of perceived catastrophe.

It may be that the bureaucratic entanglements of industrial

societies have become so intractable that for the rest of human existence there will be no more 'Declarations' and no more 'Manifestos', but I don't think we need take that as self-evident. What we may have to lose is a belief that there will be a repeat of 1776 or 1789 or 1848 – or, for that matter, 1917. We can keep in mind the enormous outflowings of secular humanism, the great triumphs in extending the human potential of science and the enlightenment. We can also keep in mind that the problems of production (in the sense of manufactured goods) have, in fact, been solved. Then we can wonder why these vast potentials have been so restricted in application, and have become so distorted; and why it is that the potentials of science, of enlightenment, of humanism and of humane uses of technology have not been liberated in forms that go beyond our present view of 'reality' seen as 'economic' to a 'reality' seen as 'social'.

In recent years, there has been a backlash against enlightened, humanist views of potential progress. These can be rejected as the dreams of the late period of 'affluence' at the end of the late 1960s and the early 1970s, the time of the various new 'movements' – of feminism and environmentalism, of movements for civil rights and 'permissiveness', of 'wars' against poverty and against race and ethnic prejudice, and of reactions to the failures of industrialism that ranged from hippie communes to scholarly inventions of concepts such as that of the post-industrial society or the poverty line. Part of this backlash has been 'legitimated' by suggesting that these movements were somehow a luxury that can no longer be afforded with the unexpected coming together of inflation and unemployment. It can even be suggested that these various movements somehow 'caused' present economic predicaments. To this, one can reply that perhaps what we can no longer afford are the traditional 'realities' of industrialism. In so far as the 'movements' of the late 1960s/early 1970s were experiments in casting up new 'realities', new shapes of what the world is and what is possible, some of them might be seen as eminently practical. They were responding to change, rather than maintaining a 'reality' that did not account for change. And it should be remembered that all of these movements still exist (even if the idea of a 'war' against poverty became weak – because its techniques were those of the 'affluent' era); however, they are no longer so frequently seen as being all part of one big, inevitable movement into the future.

I am aware that, although we need new 'myths', ideas do not themselves produce change; there are also changes in social institutions and material circumstances. But without changes in 'myth', the changes in social institutions can become little more than changes in mechanical balance: new kinds of people may go on doing old types of things. I am also aware of the conflicting bodies of knowledge that are stored in the intellectual arsenals of those on the left – each proclaiming that there is only one way to gain change – and that these ways range from apocalyptic revolutionary millennialism to reform movements so cautious that their main effect can be to inhibit change. What I am suggesting is that whether aspirations are revolutionary or reformist, what is needed are new 'myths' – not just 'myths' about techniques of change, but new 'myths' about human predicaments and human potential. The 'myths' of 'the economic' have not, for the vast majority, worked.

If change is seen as occurring not in discrete events, but in processes, ebbing and flowing, and in various ways necessarily mysterious, what can be seen as most practical are not specific programmes, but changes in people's 'realities', in the 'myths' into which they shape existence and which give them their general posture towards events. The future is unpredictable, but it may hold circumstances that will favour certain changes: what may matter most when such a time comes is not a specific programme (which may be unworkable in the actual circumstances that are offered), but a general attitude towards existence that will seize its good where it finds it.

Under all these circumstances what is sought is not merely new hands at the helm, but new definitions of 'reality' in the public culture. We don't know much about change in bureaucratically controlled modern industrial nation-states, but we are gaining experience of it. There are some models. The

Prague Spring and Solidarity may, in their own terms, have failed, but they are two examples of how change *could* occur in a Communist society, if attempted with greater prudence. With both of them part of the change that was sought was a change in public 'reality'; in Poland that change continued to be sought even after the repression of Solidarity. (One small measure of its success was that after a Solidarity priest had been murdered by security police, the details of this came through on television and that, later, there was a public trial.) How change other than change from the top could occur in the Soviet Union itself is not obvious – but it is also difficult to imagine a modern society that will never change, and in the 'movements' of the late 1960s/early 1970s there may be paradigms of change in liberal-democratic states because all of these 'movements' were concerned with re-creating the world.

New 'worlds'

Some of the new approaches to museums among ethnic minorities in the United States offer a small example of how a new 'movement' attempts to create a new 'world'. One instructive contrast is between three Indian museums I visited in the south-west.

The Southwest Indian Museum in Los Angeles has a trophy-hall approach to the life of the native Americans. It is mainly an artefacts collection: the two largest galleries show selections from 'one of the largest basket collections in the world' and selections from the museum's collection of prehistoric pottery. This old-style museum emphasis on categories and authenticity can be boringly repetitive to some visitors, but it gives a satisfying emotional basis to the concern that many people have in the south-west with the authenticity of the Indian artefacts that they buy and with which they decorate themselves or their houses. In the museum shop there is a book, *Are You Sure?*, to give shoppers advice on authenticity. When I asked for material on the history of the white treatment of the Indians, there was nothing, and when I asked for material on the treatment of Indians today I was given a seminar programme advertising attractions such as a concert of Indian flute music or a demonstration of Indian basket-making. There is no concern with the fate of Indians as human beings. The main interest is in their 'art' (a concept that, for Indians, did not exist).

The State Indian Museum at Sacramento, concerned exclusively with the Californian Indians, is also mainly a collection of artefacts – feather headdresses, bows and arrows, redwood dugouts, nets and other trophies. Here some feeling is given that it was human beings who made and used these objects, but, like the Southwest Indian Museum, it also is partly an adjunct to the museum shop – especially with its emphasis on beadwork and baskets ('The State of California owns one of the largest basket collections in the world'). The sign on the display case containing Ohlone basketry is headed: THESE ARE VERY RARE BASKETS. There are two main attempts to humanize the Indians: one is 'quaint' – the emphasis among Californian Indians on the humble acorn as a basic food. The second is on a Californian Indian called Ishi, who was that most romantic of Indians, 'the last of his tribe' (and when he was 'found' he 'lived' for five years in the University of California Museum of Anthropology). In the three books about him in the museum shop he is described as 'the one survivor of the lost Yahi tribe' – as if what happened to the Yahi tribe was not that they were destroyed by the whites, but that they took the wrong path one day and disappeared. The museum, as such, makes no statement about the present position of Indians in California, and scarcely any statement about white treatment of them in the past.

The Indian Pueblo Center at Albuquerque is a museum not of the whites, but of 19 Indian communities ('pueblos') in that part of New Mexico. The building (intended to evoke the form of Pueblo Monito in Chaco Canyon, 'one of the great pueblo architectural achievements') was constructed on the basis of community donations and a government grant; the museum is run by the Indians as a non-profit tax-exempt enterprise funded by entrance donations, arts and crafts sales, direct donations and support from a 'Friends' organization. Apart from its ownership there are two remarkable aspects of the Center: it presents objects 'in such a manner as to provide the viewer with insight into the people and forces that produced the objects'; even more important, it presents a pueblo, rather than a white, 'reality'. The presentation in the basement of the museum, 'Our Land, Our Culture, Our Story', gives a pueblo construction of pueblo history. It begins with pueblo creation myths, then a reconstruction of pueblo life before the white invasion, with descriptive panels, drawings and paintings as well as authentic objects. In the course of presenting the white invasion, it celebrates the Pueblo Uprising of 1680 (against the Spanish) in heroic style as 'the first recorded revolt for freedom in the United States, a fact little known to Americans of today'; the Pueblo Bonito is described as 'until the late 1800s the largest single structure in the New World'. In other words, it provides the same kind of boasting as is found in the white museums, but this is pueblo boasting. It also produces 'the documents' showing how the pueblos were swindled out of their land rights.

As a pueblo presentation of pueblo 'reality' the museum has the remarkable weakness of having nothing to say about the continued existence of life in the pueblos apart from the presentations (splendid, in themselves) of arts and crafts from each pueblo: what might come through from seeing the galleries and shops is of a people happy in their culture, devoted to their arts – a 'reality' that seems far from the actualities of modern pueblo life. And while the bright, contemporary style of presentation reflects modern museum styles, one wonders if it reflects modern styles in the pueblos. Nevertheless, as with Mexican American murals, the museum is an example of the powerful effect created when submerged minorities seize space in the public culture to proclaim their own 'reality'.

United States black communities have now produced more than 100 African American museums, of varying sizes. I visited two of them.

In San Francisco, the San Francisco African American

Historical and Cultural Society began in 1955, prompted by the realization that nowhere in the public culture of the United States was there any serious presence of the life and history of the blacks. (Blacks did not appear at all in most museums.) The society has been concerned mainly with black consciousness-raising. It has a small museum space used for special exhibitions, which are then sent on tour; there are regular workshops for writers and painters which emphasize African art as well as American; there is a continuing concern, culminating each year in 'Black History Week', with sponsoring the presentation of the history of the blacks; there are walking tours of San Francisco that concentrate on the black presence there in the nineteenth century.

Chicago's Dusable Museum of African American History, established in 1961, is more ambitious as a museum. It too is intended to be a consciousness-raising experience for blacks, reminding them of slavery, but telling of black resistance against slavery; it also shows blacks as 'regular guys' by presenting black achievements in the American War of Independence, in other wars, in business and the professions and in the opening of the West (including memories of black cowboys); there are displays of art objects produced by Chicago blacks and demonstrations of African culture. One room is devoted to stereotypes from the popular culture of blacks as seen by whites – sheets of songs ('The Toughest Coon in Town', etc.), dolls of blacks ('Aunt Jemima', etc.), joke postcards of blacks (blacks as comic cuties or as watermelon eaters), the use of blacks in advertisements or on packages, the portrayal of blacks in toys ('Sambo', 'Topsy Turvy'), books about blacks (*The Ten Little Niggers*).

From the African American museums, a movement amongst blacks themselves, there then developed plans for two large state-supported African American museums that will take their place in the more 'official' part of the public culture: one opened in Los Angeles in 1984; the other, part of the Smithsonian museum complex in Washington, opens this year.

The protest movements

The new movements of the 1960s and early 1970s provide an encyclopedia of forms of 'myth'-making. In books such as Shulamith Firestone's *The Dialectic of Sex* or John Kenneth Galbraith's *The Affluent Society*, or Dennis Altman's *Homosexual: Oppressions and Liberation*, or Paul Ehrlich's *The Population Bomb*, or Michael Harrington's *The Other Americans*, or Masters and Johnson's *Human Sexual Inadequacy*, or Rachel Carson's *Silent Spring*, new bodies of knowledge were created. Humans were given a new history. There was an enormous proliferation of key words. Consider just a few of them, and the new world they pointed to: 'activist', 'alternative lifestyle', 'biosphere', 'black power', 'body language', 'chairperson', 'cityscape', 'civil rights', 'commune', 'consciousness-raising', 'conservationist', 'consumerism', 'counter-culture', 'demonstration', 'demystification', 'de-schooling', 'de-segregation', 'do-your-own-thing', 'dropout', 'ecological disaster', 'environmentalist', 'freedom ride', 'fulfilment', 'gay liberation', 'hidden curriculum', 'human scale', 'involvement', 'male chauvinism', 'moratorium', 'nuclear family', 'patriarchal society', 'permissive society', 'pollution', 'post-industrial society', 'poverty line', 'protest', 'quality of life', 'racist', 'relevance', 'sex object', 'togetherness', 'unstructured', 'urban guerrilla', 'urban renewal', 'wilderness area', 'women's liberation', 'ZPG'. The colour 'green' became a symbol of hope: there was to be a 'greening' of America; in Australia for a season a Communist-led builders' union enforced an environmentalist policy by imposing 'green bans'; later, a political party in the Federal German Republic was to become 'the Greens'. There were new icons, new legends, new heroes, new rituals and festivals.

In asserting new 'myths' against old, what must be enacted is good drama. An established 'reality' is strong, not necessarily because it is practical – often it isn't – but because of its imaginative appeal: what the imagination gives, the imagination can take away. New 'realities' can replace old. What made the old 'realities' strong can make the new 'realities' stronger. This theatrical quality of 'reality' was well brought out by Peter Berger in *Invitation to Sociology*:

> Stage, theatre, circus and even carnival – here we have the imagery of our dramatic model, with a conception of society as precarious, uncertain, often unpredictable. The institutions of society, while they do in fact constrain and coerce us, appear at the same time as dramatic conventions, even fictions. They have been invented by past impresarios, and future ones may cast them back into nothingness. Acting out the social drama, we keep pretending that these precarious conventions are eternal verities. We act *as if* there is no other way of being a man, a political subject, a religious devotee or one who exercises a certain profession – yet at times the thought passes through the mind of even the dimmest among us that we could do very, very different things.

In *Symbolic Leaders* O.E. Klapp recognized how the very existence of that modern 'public drama' that is a feature of modern public cultures can assist change: the very dramatic structure can sometimes take over. He suggested that the public drama could be unsettling, with unpredictable alignments, so that very different kinds of people, or at least people who saw themselves as very different in one kind of structuring of society, might see themselves, under some new perspective, as the same kind of people. (The women's movement provides an example.) Following a now much misquoted usage of Max Weber's, Klapp saw in this a 'charismatic' quality that could break down existing arrangements in a society. When Weber spoke of 'charisma' he had in mind an obsessive devotion to a person that could go beyond normal human qualities and break through normal social routines (Gandhi, for example), but Klapp suggested that public drama itself could have the force of charisma. One might imagine not that leaders are in themselves charismatic, but that situations are charismatic – dramatically magical in their imaginative power, so that people follow a new wave. Under such a situation, if there is a leader, and this is not always so, it is the charismatic force of new drama *that gives charisma to the leader*. So public drama can provide the scenes within which important changes occur, changing the location of things in the world, providing new 'realities' and new ranges of the possible.

It is in this context of the 'public drama' that the 'protest movements' of the late 1960s and early 1970s can seem a cultural form particularly appropriate to liberal-democratic societies (because in these societies it can sometimes be possible to gain space in the public culture). To say this is not to suggest that there could or should be maintained all the rages and styles of the earlier protest movements. In fact, in the book-keeping of importance, the widest importance of a 'movement' might lie not in whether there is this or that success, but whether over a period, in these ebbing and flowing dramas, dominant 'myths' and 'realities' are changed. In this, the culmination of some individual cause, whether success or failure, is important above all in its symbolic force – and in this particular type of drama symbolic failures can be particularly appealing, martyrdoms most of all.

Not much that is worth reading has been written about protest movements, and much of it has been written from a point of view that has tried to estimate their success in a direct relationship of Protest/Change. You protest: then you get what you want. But social affairs being so intractable and mysterious, not every protest can be followed by what is wanted. Even from this point of view, not enough has been written, yet, as Jo Freeman recognized in *The Politics of Women's Liberation*, the policy successes of the protest movements demanded an important re-writing of liberal-democratic theory, going beyond interactions of pressure groups and political parties. As she put it:

(1) the American political system encompasses the potential for new elements as well as the reality of established ones; (2) these new elements, while they form

in varying ways, usually involve what is commonly labeled
as 'disorderly' behaviour; (3) such behaviour, rather than
taking place outside the normal limits of political action, is
part and parcel of the American political process.

From the perspective of changes in 'reality', however, these
policy changes are not only important in themselves but
important beyond themselves, as part of the wider drama.
Legislation against sex or ethnic discrimination, for example, is
not only a positive policy achievement; it is also part of the
symbolic drama of changing the 'realities' with which people
regard sex and ethnicity. In taking this view, we can look at
'movements' in a way much wider than the views of many or
most of those who participate in them. We can see individuals
coming together or seeing themselves as having come together
for this or that special cause. Some of them may take up only
one cause in their lifetime. But we can know that they are also
playing their part in this wider drama.

For an example of this, take the changing of the developmentalist 'myth' by environmentalists in Australia. Almost
from the beginning of British 'settlement', 'national development' had become one of the principal 'realities' of Australians:
it could seem the very reason for Australia being there. When
one of the first school histories of Australia was published, in
1909, it concluded that where the course of Australian history
had led was to 'the developing of the country's natural
resources by cultivating its richer soils, irrigating its drier,
exploiting the fisheries along its coasts, opening up and
thoroughly working the mines hidden below its surface . . . To
do these things methodically, scientifically, is Australia's task
for the future.' In an election in 1919 it was said, 'You are all the
shareholders in the great company of Australia Unlimited, the
greatest firm in the world.' In 1944 a radical bureaucrat said,
'In a very real sense public works contribute to a fullness in the
national life by adding a sense of achievement and a consciousness of growth to the life of an individual.' In the early 1960s a
Labor Party leader could say, 'To no other nation in the world

has the opportunity been granted for the sole possession and development of a sea-girt land-mass by a single people . . . This feeling owes much to the hard, factual ideas of the economists or the strategists; it is a sentiment, and the best and most honest name for it is nationalism . . . There is a continent awaiting our conquest, and its name is Australia.' In the early 1970s a Labor Party Minerals and Energy Minister became so obsessed with a crusade against nature with gas pipelines, uranium enrichment, petrochemical plants, coal hydrogenation and rail electrification that he went around the political bend and helped to destroy a government. (But when the political ineptitudes brought on by his holy vision forced him to resign, he went down reciting a developmental ballad, 'Give me men to match my mountains, give me men to match my plans, men with freedom in their vision, and creation in their brains.')

But by then new 'myths' were being made. An Australian Conservation Foundation had formed, with 320 separate conservation groups. There was a new secular faith – the preservation of irreplaceable forests, vast wildernesses, precious beaches, rivers, swamps, lakes and caves, whole stretches of mountain ranges, islands, reefs. And along with it sometimes went a scepticism about the economic value of some of the 'development': in its own terms, some of it was costing more than it was worth. Petitions circulated; books appeared; advertisements were endorsed by eminent citizens; leaflets were handed around; posters went up; law court actions were instituted; at mass meetings guitarists sang songs about excess profits and the simple life; the arrest of protesting 'conservationists' became a routine scene on television news. By the 1983 national election something happened that for most of Australia's history as a European nation would have seemed beyond belief. In a nation where elections were won by political parties promising to build new dams, an election was won by a political party that promised to stop the construction of a new dam. Australians were acquiring a new history and a new 'reality'.

A declaration of 'cultural rights'

C. Wright Mills used to speak of 'the labour metaphysic': the belief that there was something in the nature of existence that meant the working class would lead humankind from capitalism into socialism. This was the transcendent 'myth' that could lift the hearts and minds of the people who, in one nation after another, constructed the social formations that came together as a 'labour movement'. In the Communist societies, with certain Leninist changes as interpreted by the party leaders, this 'myth' is still the basic 'legitimation' of the state, and in the capitalist societies, in varying degrees, it can still seem the way ahead to some of those who seek a better world.

Yet there is a paradox for those who accept 'the labour metaphysic' if they are doing so because they believe in the liberation of human potential. On the one hand, there can be the recognition that in industrial societies the cult of 'work' means that a large part of the self is 'unemployed', but the 'myth' most concerned with human liberation from 'work' (as paid labour in an industrial society) places the source of liberation in the workers, *as such, as* workers, as if, after all, 'work' really were the centre of life. It was not the great mass of the people to whom Marx and Engels appealed in *The Communist Manifesto* but *the workers* of the world. Not their families, not the unemployed or the unemployable, not the dispossessed, but *the workers*. The area that in an industrial society most limits human potential – the workplace – can still be seen by some as the area where the movement would come for liberation. Yet, as André Gorz sums it up, 'the collective worker, structured by the capitalist division of labour and adapted to the inert requirements of the machinery it serves, has come to function like a machine'.

In the liberal-democratic capitalist societies, the trade union movements, which make up the potentially most powerful organization of the masses ever known, are with a few exceptions (mainly Scandinavian), concerned only for employed persons – not for the families of the employed, not for the neighbourhoods in which the employed live, not for the sick or the old or the young, not for the unemployed, not, very largely, even for women, not even for their own unemployed members, certainly not for the great mass of humanity, but for the *employed*. And not even the employed as a class with special concerns ('employment' being a state from which they might be cured), but those who are employed in certain trades or industries – and only in so far as their work in those industries goes. There is no concern with them as human beings with unawakened potentials.

The obsession in 'the labour metaphysic' with workers *as* workers has meant that many people on the left now fumble at the very time when they might seem to have opportunities. With the disintegration of the 'affluent' era with its promise of salvation through economic growth and full employment, capitalism has actually presented a contradiction. But they see this contradiction not as an opportunity, but as a problem – a problem that could be solved if only they could control industrialism by controlling the state. They would then be able to 'create jobs', and everything would be all right. But when they do gain political office in a country that reflects the capitalist image of society, they fail.

It is difficult for many people on the left to see that possibilities for new autonomy, with time for creative, liberating production, may now arise in two areas traditionally seen as the least likely for such a change: among the unemployed themselves, and in the opportunities for autonomy provided in 'spare time'. If for most people the workplace may be the area where creative autonomy is least likely, one can see how in Communist societies, liberation movements might also seek not only self-management in the workplace but also greater freedom *outside the workplace*. To put it mildly, such a policy is not on the agenda in any of those societies: a change in ownership of workplaces was supposed, in itself, to generate other liberations.

Perhaps one shock needed to change the 'realities' of the left might be to speak less of 'the working class' (who, in traditionally imagined terms, are in any case becoming a minority of the population) and to revive the phrase 'the people', or perhaps 'the mass of the people' (not in the sense of 'the people' being the same as 'the nation', but in the sense of the powerless).

It is for 'the people', above all, that we need a declaration that just as we have learned to speak of political, social and economic rights we must now learn to speak of cultural rights. It may be only by such means that 'myths' can be created that confront the 'realities' of a jobs-and-growth ethos (that is now failing in its function of legitimating systems of industrialism). Since it is through art and through intellectual life generally that we become human, it may be only by a re-ordering of 'reality' through art that we can discover new ways of imagining what it might mean to be human. Although art may have the power of subjection, it is also a principal opening out to liberation, in the sense of opening out new hypothetical 'realities', new ways in which we can imagine things, many of them beyond words, or at least beyond the modes of rational discourse. Yet it is a feature of modern industrial societies that, unlike members of folk and tribal societies, so far as participation is concerned, most of their citizens can be seen as, in varying degrees, culturally deprived. 'Art', if it happens at all, is something that for many citizens is done *for* them and *to* them. The idea of actually going so far as to *make* art could seem impertinent. Indeed a great deal of art is presented in such a way that it is done *against* the citizens.

Under these circumstances, if we were to make a declaration of cultural rights, what rights would we declare?

It is possible to imagine them in three interconnected groups: rights of access to the human cultural heritage; rights to new art; rights to community art participation.

Relics of the human heritage are what have survived of the old tribal cultures, ruling-class cultures and folk cultures, along with what has already been preserved from modern 'high culture' and mass-entertainment culture. It is all of it constantly reinterpreted in new terms – in theatres and concert halls, or in universities, in conserved monuments, or in museums and libraries. Frequently – perhaps usually – in the name of 'high culture' it can be interpreted in ways that can make it seem alien, even threatening, to the mass of people. There can be enormous mounds of rubbish within the storehouses of cultural heritages, some of which provide some of the prime anti-intellectuality of the age. There can also be much that is corrupting in the practices of their custodians: brutal snobberies, arrogant mystifications, obsessive suppressions, inane time-servings, moribund talmudisms, manic avant-gardisms. Some of its products and its practitioners can be turned to the advantage of prevailing social classes and prevailing social repression. But merely because the Bolshoi in Moscow and the Metropolitan Opera Company in New York become, some-times, display areas for the privileged does not make ballet or opera themselves ineradicable ruling-class art forms. Art is reinterpretable: the 'greatness' of 'great' works of art or the intellect may lie, partly, in the varied richness of their reinterpretability. Both art forms and intellectual forms – the artefacts of 'high culture' – are there for us to use for our own ends in making up our own views of existence and, if we care to use this facility, no one can prevent us. If one imagines the intellectual mode as a special, and self-conscious, concern with being a serious critic of existence, seeking meanings, then it is usually within the 'high culture' that this activity is pursued at any length. 'High culture' might be thought of as a battleground for the interpretation of the human heritage. Human liberation is not won simply by fleeing from this battleground.

As to new art: the 'experimentalism' of modernism has, throughout the century, alienated great masses of people, rulers as well as ruled. There has been a great deal of 'meta-art', art about how to make art, with effects that have puzzled or infuriated many people. But the style of this 'experimentalism' has been about a great human predicament: the crisis in 'reality' construction that became characteristic of societies as they modernized and industrialized.

There are signs that as the twentieth century nears its end

there is some wider understanding of this style crisis. To take one example: experimentalism in what has become known as 'movement' or inter-arts' theatre can now draw large audiences in some countries. Nevertheless it must be admitted that much of the 'experimentalism' of modernism would probably have remained alienating even if it had been presented to people in less mystifying ways. But one can also say that there *has* been a crisis in 'reality' construction and that, in this sense, 'experimental' modernism has been an example of art doing its job. New art should be thought of as a social right as well as an individual right. New art is an organizer, as it were, of new experience, of new perspectives, of new perceptions of the world and of human vision. Without new art, even the reinterpretability of old art would cease. And even if some of it can, at first, be seen as simply for the few, one might regard support for even arcane new art as the 'research programme', as it were, of the whole arts and entertainment industry and, for that matter, of the whole 'information' industry. Such a 'research programme' is developing new perspectives and styles that even if they do not reach the mass of people directly can reach them indirectly, by influencing artworks they are in touch with.

And community art participation is a restoration of art to life. If you are talking about a fully participatory art-performing society – which is the aim of community art-participation policies – you are talking about the end of 'industrial man'. For that matter, you are also speaking of the end of 'art', since if all the people became, in one way or the other, 'artists', you no longer need the word 'art'. I understood this when I visited the Neighborhood Cultural Center in San Francisco's Western .Addition. When I arrived there, a black American with a high reputation for mural paintings was at work on a mural on a side wall of the Center. The surface of the wall had been treated; the scaffolding was up; the outline had been sketched in for a mural on black entertainers. His apprentices were with him, learning their craft. Members of the community were around him, saying what they thought. That night I wrote down in my journal that the scene was medieval: but that was understating it. What one was experiencing again was the very beginning of art.

Who are the 'myth'-makers?

There are two qualifications to what I have been saying. One can be stated briefly. It is that there is more to change than a recognition of cultural rights, yet, without new cultural definitions, what changes can succeed?

The second qualification needs more argument. It is that if new 'myths' are to arise giving more realizable shape to desires for greater liberation, there is one sense in which they must come from 'the people', since a 'myth' of such force must be a complex act of folk creation. The 'myths' both of working-class solidarity and of working-class respectability ('independence') would not have acquired their force unless they had already been related to the way things were seen by millions of individuals. And it is clear that if one speaks of a change as momentous as the disintegration of the 'myth' of the work ethic, one is speaking of a social revolution – of a kind that might begin to seem realizable if, with greater unemployment and continuing disintegration of concepts of the value of 'work', frustrated cynicism becomes more widespread. At least in some countries such a cynicism, especially amongst the young, has already shown itself in the margins of the entertainment world, in music and the personal styles of 'self-as-art'. Here the 'guardians' of the public culture are weakest, as Stuart Hall points out in his essay, 'The State of Socialism's Old Caretaker'.

It may be true that apart from some resilient strains the traditional folk cultures have been attenuated into a few last souvenirs, many of them now part of museum cultures, and that the very word 'ethnic' can suggest a culture whose survival is threatened. But one should remember that it was from 'the folk' that all art forms derived – painting, sculpture, dance, chant, song, instrumental music, drama, verse, narrative. In art, unlike technology, there is not necessarily progress. A Picasso bull is not necessarily 'better' than a Lascaux bison. In nineteenth-century Europe folk culture was one of the invigorators of the arts, and indeed part of the cultural foundation of some of the 'new nations' of Europe. The liberations of so-called 'primitive' art from Africa and Oceania (even if misinterpreted) were one of the bases of twentieth-century modernism in painting and sculpture. Black American song, instrumental music and dance are key twentieth-century art forms. The Latin folk imagination enlivened art in murals, design, dance and song. Every year, to encourage the survival of old folk arts in the USA, the National Endowment for the Arts bestows National Heritage Fellowships to folk artists. The 17 artists honoured in 1984 included a Cape Breton dance fiddler, a Harlem tap-dancer, a practitioner of North Carolina stoneware pottery alkaline-glazing, a Nebraskan hammered-dulcimer player, a Lebanese lace-maker, a player of European Jewish klezmer dance music and a New Mexican Spanish religious chanter.

The process accelerates. In so far as there are still folk creations (the development of new art forms among the people, in a collective creation), they may be appropriated by the 'high culture'. Not long after the graffiti cult had taken over the New York subways, whole new graffiti art industries developed in the East Village. People now make careers out of graffiti art. When a movie popularized the break-dancing of street gangs in New York's South Bronx, the gyrations, jerks, headspins and backspins with which these gangs had danced 'battles' in defence of their turf became 'art': the San Francisco Ballet opened the première night of its new building with a break-dance prologue. And great art-creations of language style often come from 'the people'. 'The people' may be thought of as, very largely, art-deprived, but we must nevertheless recognize that while conversation can become as repetitive as a bus timetable, it can also, at its most vigorous, remain one of the liveliest forms of participatory art.

'Working-class culture' as such can, however, be seen as

something of a dead end, if by 'working-class culture' one means specific art forms emerging from class consciousness in a way in which specific art forms not only emerge from ethnic consciousness but *are* ethnic consciousness, or *demonstrations* of it. There is a significant qualification to this statement: perhaps it is in the very nature of 'work' in modern industrial societies that such forms as do emerge are likely to be those of protest or despair (which may then become collectors' items in the 'high culture'). But art is usually made *about* the proletariat, and, apart from protest and despair, not much in the way of new art forms comes *from* the proletariat *as a proletariat*. This is not to say that people of proletarian origin do not make art; it is simply to say that the art they make is not *proletarian art*.

One of the puzzles of a modern industrial society is the relation between the perceptions of 'the people' and the products of the mass-culture industries, particularly the entertainment industries. In his essay 'Television Screens: Hegemony in Transition', Todd Gitlin suggests that the mass-culture industries can register some of the alternatives existing in a modern industrial society, 'lived in fragments of everyday existence'. 'Popular culture is one of the cultural institutions where vital claims of ideology are sometimes pressed forward, sometimes reconciled.' But it is usually from the professionals of the entertainment and news industries that changes are negotiated. And in many matters they may be somewhat ahead of their audience. They have their eyes on the market, and they also have their own traditions and practices – and these are very largely those of what I called 'the critics' culture'. 'Myths' may be a folk creation, but it is in the critics' culture that they are most likely to be articulated, and in some cases the 'myths' may have a stronger currency, at least to begin with, among 'the critics' themselves.

What is the class basis (in the very general sense in which I have used 'class') in 'the critics' culture'? Some of the 'critics' may be 'workers' (in terms of the nature of their jobs or the jobs of their household money-providers), but if that is so then they are likely to be workers who have joined the 'critics' and speak in their language. At the beginning of the industrial age this used not to be so. As Richard Johnson has pointed out in 'Really Useful Knowledge', an essay on the intellectual base of early working-class radicalism, nineteenth-century radicalism was able to produce an indigenous working-class leadership because working-class intellectual leaders had scarcely anywhere else to go. As he puts it:

> Working people with an inclination towards mental labour *had* to stay within their own class, or occupy positions of great social ambiguity like elementary or private schoolmastering or journalism or lecturing. There were few open roads to co-option. At the same time an education and a sort of career were available within radical movements themselves.

As to the critics' culture, apart from those it co-opts, it has tended, right from its beginnings, to emerge from classes of people whose lives are associated with 'decision-making' or who pass through institutions (universities would now be the main example). When I was writing *The Great Museum* I suggested these people might be thought of as 'the deciding classes'. What I wanted was to find some word for people who participated in the famous 'bourgeois revolutions' of Europe – most of whom were not capitalists, although it may be true that their individualism and liberalism were something that capitalists were to do well out of – and people who now engage in 'protest'. In the late eighteenth and nineteenth centuries some of them were enlightened nobility, but most were (speaking rather vaguely) 'middle class,' as they are now. On the whole, they were not owner-entrepreneurs but lawyers, journalists, administrators, educators, intellectuals and students who, along with owner-entrepreneurs, lived in a world in which there could seem some possibility of *making decisions*. Such people could experience themselves as *effective*, or potentially so.

With the slow disintegration of the old ruling class over

several hundred years – in some countries earlier than others – strata had been developing of people who, in increasingly complex societies, engaged in, or were directly related to, the 'rituals' of decision-making. And they were doing that in a context in which the growth of modernity could suggest increasingly wider ranges for decision-making and in which, in some of the wilder dreams, humans might seem capable of almost anything. It is principally in a split among these kinds of people that there generates the critics' culture.

On the one hand, there are those who appear to run things. Nowadays they include officials of the great bureaucracies of business or political parties or governments, professionals, technicians and other 'experts': teachers, journalists, artists, intellectuals, performers, promoters and students (and in the capitalist societies, owners and, in general, the rich). Unlike wage earners in the industrial proletariat, they can have greater opportunities to discuss policies, ideas, ways of doing things, with the knowledge that what happens can have some relation to what they think and what they 'decide'. These 'decisions' are the main support for things as they are, perhaps providing the principal reason why it is so difficult to imagine revolutions in industrial societies. But on the other hand, some of them, in the sheer *élan* of imagining better decisions, can become bold and guileful enemies of many things as they stand because, in various ways – from revolt to reform, but usually reform – they have their own ideas about how things should be run. Sometimes they will speak mainly to each other, seeking action in political or administrative *coups*, but they are also specialists in intellectual articulation and also, sometimes, in developing programmes that depend on mobilizing 'the people'. Some of them are specialists in public articulation – in particular the artists and writers, the orators, organizers, publicists and 'news'-providers, who can become, as it were, professionals in criticism and who, if they work in organizations, are likely to find their institutionalized conscience in the ideals of criticism. Whether as professionals or, at times of public theatre, as protestors, they tend to be not only agenda-changers –

suggesting new items that politics should seem to be about – but 'reality'-changers as well, and, with the collaboration of sections of 'the people' in acts of folk participation, they can also be significant in the making of new 'myths'. Even where they are not originators of change – and this is especially significant in the case of movements that seem to begin with or gain their critical mass from the people – it is likely to be the critics who are the mediators of change. They translate change by turning it into their own language.

But here there arises an enormous difficulty: this language often becomes the language of modern scholarship, and it is in the debilitating concern with style in scholarly life – not artistic life – that high culture has done its greatest damage, because here the concern with style has been part of the disease, not part of its diagnosis. Many of the commanding heights of intellectual discourse have been occupied by professional academicians; knowledge has been subdivided into smaller and smaller 'subjects' of specialization and each 'subject' has developed its own language, so that there is no longer a general intellectual discourse using the common literary language. In the sense that it has abandoned the common literary language, much modern scholarship is non-literate. It has not been the mass-culture industries that have threatened 'high culture'; the threat has come from within 'high culture' itself, from its academic variant. It became industrialized, with extreme, and alienating, divisions of labour. Style ('methodology') goes far beyond the nature of the problems themselves. In fact some of the problems are fictitious. They are simply a product of a particular style.

If one believes in the possibility of a common intellectual (non-art) discourse, what is essential is that there should be a common literary language. With a common literary language, even the problem of specialist divisions of knowledge can be overcome: certain types of writing strategies can bridge these divisions. It is modern scholarship that has been the principal destroyer of a common literary language, and therefore of the possibility of common intellectual discourse. Yet there is nothing basic to scholarship that needs to have caused this act of destruction. The basic idea of a scholarly way of going about things is not of obscurity but of 'Learning', of expert knowledge obtained by study. The scholarly style may not necessarily *parade* learning. In fact it may conceal it. But it is based on knowledge and care. This does not mean that scholars must write cautiously and timidly – they may write boldly – but that what they write has come out of study and reflection. Yet use by scholars of the common literary language, of their use of literary strategies, can now appear 'unscholarly'.

Scholarship is not seen as based simply on study and knowledge. In fact, to sit down and read and think is not seen as carrying out 'research' at all. Scholarship becomes based on conventions of what makes a research programme and on the maintenance of certain technical language systems and the maintenance of certain apparatuses of knowledge. To say this is not to suggest that everything every scholar writes must be immediately communicable. A kind of 'half-culture' of scholars may be necessary in some fields – it is certainly necessary to the physical sciences – and their findings may necessarily be uninteresting or even unintelligible to non-specialists. But even with the physical sciences it is possible for someone with literary skill to introduce the principal findings of some field of science into a common literary language.

The obscurities of modern art and modern scholarships are both related to the industrialization of modern societies. But while the obscurities of the arts are, through their crises in style, *about* industrialization as a crisis in 'reality' construction, the obscurities of scholarship are part of the process of industrialization itself.

If new 'myths' are constructed to provide some sense of leverage on the future, they will inevitably be in the language of 'the critics', as was the language of the Declaration of Independence, the Declaration of Human Rights and the Communist Manifesto. And they will inevitably be an extension of the 'myths' of modernity with their the basic belief in the possibility of change and of human improvement.

I have left the 'myths' of modernity until last in order to end optimistically. It is true that they have been entwined with the 'myths' of industrialism. The very belief in engineering and in the factory style, in new product development and in economic growth have been thoroughly 'modern'. So has the belief that human happiness will be guaranteed by increasing product development. But the 'myth' of modernity is, as it were, a neutral vessel. It is a belief that by human effort things can be made better. Such a belief may be necessary for seeing 'employment policies' as essential to progress. But the same kind of belief is also necessary for developing a 'full employment policy' for the self.

Of existing 'myths' there are two others that have some of this element of neutrality. One is to be found in 'myths' of national identity. So long as nation-states are a principal form of organization, how 'the nation' or 'national life' is perceived will remain significant in the shaping of the public culture. Even if one is an internationalist, it is not sufficient to seek merely international forms. Since it is nations that internationalists wish to see changed, if internationalists take their struggle seriously, part of the struggle must be to inject into the perceptions of 'the nation' an image of the nation as multicultural, and thereby help disintegrate the public culture as a pretence at representing national life. A 'nation' can be seen as a staging camp to something better. But not chauvinistically, except in the sense that 'the nation' might be praised for its sense of humanity and equality. It is within the public cultures of nations that an important part of the definition of humanity proceeds: the struggles for equality of sex, race and ethnicity take place within the public culture of nations and so do more general struggles for human equality and for prospects of human fulfilment. Not to accept this is to be apocalyptical and millennialist, as if one day all the nations will suddenly crumble and at last humankind will be free. To be internationalist, one must first be national. But one can still hope for an end to 'the public culture'.

The other 'myths' that have an element of neutrality are to be found in those parts of the liberal 'myth' and 'myths' of secularism and humanism that are not concerned with property but with human relationships and not with freedom of the market but with human freedom. In this sense, even Marx was 'liberal'. It is also the sense in which 'liberal' became, in the 1980s, a threat word in the United States, used to curse those citizens who sought life, liberty and the pursuit of happiness, not through market competition and competitive individualism but through co-operation, greater equality and human freedom. In the land of the Bill of Rights, the word 'liberal' was assaulted with a ferocity matched only by fascists and Stalinists. That, in itself, recommends it.

Select Bibliography

Francesco Alberoni, 'The Powerless "Elite": Theory and Sociological Research on the Phenomenon of the Stars', in Denis McQuail (ed.), *Sociology of Mass Communications*, Harmondsworth, Middlesex: Penguin 1976.

Perry Anderson, 'The Antinomies of Antonio Gramsci', *New Left Review*, no. 100 (November 1976–January 1977), pp. 5–78.

Andrew Arato and Eike Gebhardt, *The Essential Frankfurt School Reader*, New York: Urizen 1978.

Thurman Arnold, *The Folk Lore of Capitalism*, Clinton, Massachusetts: Yale University Press 1937.

Paul Barker (ed.), *Arts in Society*, Glasgow: William Collins 1977.

Roland Barthes, *The Eiffel Tower*, New York: Farrar, Straus & Giroux 1979.

Roland Barthes, *Image–Music–Text*, Glasgow: William Collins 1977.

Roland Barthes, *Mythologies*, London: Granada 1973.

Daniel Bell, *The Cultural Contradictions of Capitalism*, New York: Basic Books 1976.

Robert N. Bellah, *Beyond Belief*, New York: Harper & Row 1970.

Robert N. Bellah, *The Broken Covenant*, New York: Seabury 1975.

Walter Benjamin, *Illuminations*, London: Fontana 1973.

T. Bennet, *The Media as Definers of Reality*, London: Open University Press 1977.

T. Bennet, *The Study of Culture*, London: Open University Press 1977.

John Berger, *Art and Revolution*, London: Writers and Readers 1969.

John Berger, *Ways of Seeing*, London and Harmondsworth, Middlesex: BBC and Penguin 1972.

Peter L. Berger, *Pyramids of Sacrifice*, Harmondsworth, Middlesex: Penguin 1974.

Peter Berger, *Invitation to Sociology*, Harmondsworth, Middlesex: Penguin 1963.

Peter Berger, *The Sacred Canopy*, Garden City: Doubleday 1967.

Peter Berger and Thomas Luckman, *The Social Construction of Reality*, Garden City: Doubleday 1966.

C.W.E. Bigsby (ed.), *Approaches to Popular Culture*, London: Edward Arnold 1976.

Burton J. Bledstein, *The Culture of Professionalism*, New York: W.W. Norton 1976.

Carl Boggs, *Gramsci's Marxism*, London: Pluto Press 1976.

David Borstin, *The Image: Or What Happened to the American Dream?* New York: Atheneum 1962.

Su Braden, *Committing Photography*, London: Pluto Press 1983.

Richard W. Budd and Brent D. Ruben, *Beyond Media*, New Jersey: Hayden 1979.

Francis G. Castles, *The Social Democratic Image of Society*, London: Routledge & Kegan Paul 1978.

Alan Casty, *Mass Media and Mass Man*, New York: Holt, Rinehart & Winston 1968.

John Clarke, Chas Critcher and Richard Johnson (eds.), *Working Class Culture*, London: Hutchinson 1979.

Stanley Cohen, *Folk Devils and Moral Panics*, London: MacGibbon & Kee 1972.

Stanley Cohen and Jock Young (eds.), *The Manufacture of News*, London: Constable 1973.

James E. Combs and Michael W. Mansfield (eds.), *Drama in Life: The Uses of Communication in Society*, New York: Hastings House 1976.

Paul E. Corcoran, *Political Language and Rhetoric*, St Lucia,

Queensland: Queensland University Press 1979.

James Curran, Michael Gurevitch and Janet Woollacott (eds.), *Mass Communication and Society*, London: Edward Arnold in association with the Open University Press 1977.

Jane Leftwich Curry, *Dissent in Eastern Europe*, New York: Praeger 1983.

Melvin L. De Fleur and Sandra Ball-Rokeach, *Theories of Mass Communication*, New York: Longman 1966.

John P. Diggins, *The American Left in the Twentieth Century*, New York: Harcourt Brace Jovanovich 1973.

Ariel Dorfman, *The Empire's Old Clothes*, London: Pluto Press 1983.

John Downing, *The Media Machine*, London: Pluto Press 1980.

H.D. Duncan, *Communication and Social Order*, New York: Bedminster Press 1962.

H.D. Duncan, *Symbols in Society*, New York: Oxford University Press 1968.

Umberto Eco, *The Role of the Reader*, Bloomington: Indiana University Press 1979.

Umberto Eco, *Semiotics and the Philosophy of Language*, London: Macmillan 1984.

Murray Edelman, *The Symbolic Uses of Politics*, Chicago: University of Illinois Press 1964.

Murray Edelman, *Politics as Symbolic Action*, New York: Academic Press 1971.

Jacques Ellul, *Propaganda: The Formation of Men's Attitudes*, New York: Vintage Books 1965.

H.M. Enzensberger, *The Consciousness Industry*, New York: Seabury Press 1974.

Edward J. Epstein, *News from Nowhere: Television and the News*, New York: Random House 1973.

Stewart Ewen, *Captains of Consciousness*, New York: McGraw-Hill 1976.

John Fiske, *Introduction to Communication Studies*, London: Methuen 1982.

John Fiske and John Hartley, *Reading Television*, London: Methuen 1978.

Michel Foucault, *Discipline and Punish: The Birth of the Prison*, Harmondsworth, Middlesex: Penguin 1977.

Michel Foucault, *The History of Sexuality*, New York: Random House 1978.

Jo Freeman, *The Politics of Women's Liberation*, New York: Longman 1975.

F.G. Gamst and E. Norbeck, *Ideas of Culture*, New York: Holt, Rinehart & Winston 1976.

Herbert J. Gans, *Popular Culture and High Culture*, New York: Basic Books 1974.

Herbert J. Gans, *Deciding What's News*, New York: Vintage Books 1980.

Carl Gardner (ed.), *Media, Politics and Culture: A Socialist View*, London: Macmillan 1979.

John A. Garraty, *Unemployment in History*, New York: Harper & Row 1979.

Alan D. Gilbert, *The Making of Post-Christian Britain*, London: Longman 1980.

Todd Gitlin, *The Whole World Is Watching: Mass Media in the Making and Unmaking of the New Left*, Berkeley: University of California Press 1980.

Todd Gitlin, 'Prime Time Ideology: The Hegemonic Process in Television Entertainment', *Social Problems*, vol. 26, no. 3, 1979, pp. 251–66.

Todd Gitlin, *Inside Prime Time*, New York: Pantheon Books 1983.

Todd Gitlin, 'Television's Screens: Hegemony in Transition', in Michael W. Apple (ed.), *Cultural and Economic Reproduction in Education*, London: Routledge & Kegan Paul 1982.

Glasgow University Media Group, *Bad News*, London: Routledge & Kegan Paul 1976.

Erving Goffman, *Gender Advertisements*, London: Macmillan 1979.

Erving Goffman, *Frame Analysis: An Essay on the Organization of Experience*, New York: Harper & Row 1974.

André Gorz, *Paths to Paradise: On the Liberation from Work*, London: Pluto Press 1985.

André Gorz, *Farewell to the Working Class: An Essay on Post-Industrial Socialism*, London: Pluto Press 1982.

Alvin W. Gouldner, *The Dialectic of Ideology and Technology*, London: Macmillan 1978.

Alvin. W. Gouldner, *The Coming Crisis of Western Sociology*, New York: Basic Books 1970.

Alvin W. Gouldner, *The Future of Intellectuals and the Rise of the New Class*, New York: Seabury Press 1979.

Antonio Gramsci, *Selections from Political Writings 1910–1920*, London: Lawrence & Wishart 1977.

Clement Greenberg, *Art and Culture*, Boston: Beacon Press 1961.

Michael Gurevitch *et al* (eds.), *Culture, Society and the Media*, London: Methuen 1982.

Jurgen Habermas, *Legitimation Crisis*, London: Heinemann 1976.

Nicos Hadjinicolaou, *Art History and Class Struggle*, London: Pluto Press 1978.

Stuart Hall, 'The State–Socialism's Old Caretaker', in *Marxism Today*, November 1984.

John Hartley, *Understanding News*, London: Methuen 1982.

Louis Hartz, *The Founding of New Societies*, New York: Harcourt, Brace & World 1964.

Kevin Harris, 'The Secondary School: Administration Wonder and Educational Absurdity', *Social Alterations*, vol. 2, no. 4, 1984.

Terence Hawkes, *Structuralism and Semiotics*, London: Methuen 1977.

Andräs Hegedüs, *The Structure of Socialist Society*, New York: St Martin's Press 1977.

David Held, *Introduction to Critical Theory: Horkheimer to Habermas*, Berkeley: University of California Press 1980.

Richard Hoggart, *The Uses of Literacy*, Harmondsworth, Middlesex: Penguin 1957.

Max Horkheimer and Theodore Adorno, *Dialectic of Enlightenment*, New York: Herder & Herder 1972.

Donald Horne, *The Great Museum*, London: Pluto Press 1984.

Norman Jacobs (ed.), *Culture for the Millions?*, Boston: Beacon Press 1964.

Orrin Edgar Klapp, *Symbolic Leaders*, Chicago: Aldine 1964.

Orrin Edgar Klapp, *Symbolic Leaders*, Chicago: Aldine 1964.

Orrin Edgar Klapp, *Heroes, Villains and Fools*, Englewood Cliffs, New Jersey: Prentice-Hall 1962.
York: Free Press 1960.

Christopher Lasch, *The Culture of Narcissism*, New York: W.W. Norton 1979.

Paul Lazarsfeld, Bernard Berelson and Hazel Gaudet, *The People's Choice: How the Voter Makes Up His Mind in a Presidential Campaign* (3rd edn), New York: Columbia University Press 1968.

F.R. Leavis and Denys Thompson, *Culture and the Environment*, London: Chatto & Windus.

Walter Lippman, *Public Opinion*, New York: Free Press 1965.

Michael Lipsky, 'Protest as a Political Resource', *American Political Science Review*, vol. 62, 1968, pp. 1145–58.

Alan Lomax, 'An Appeal for Cultural Equity', *Journal of Communication*, vol. 27, Spring 1977.

Georg Lukács, *History and Class Consciousness*, London: Merlin Press 1971.

André Malraux, *Antimemoirs*, London: Hamish Hamilton 1968.

Karl Marx and Friedrich Engels, *The German Ideology*, Moscow: Progress 1974.

Maxwell E. McCombs and Donald E. Shaw, 'The Agenda-Setting Function of the Mass Media', *Public Opinion Quarterly*, vol. 36, Summer 1972, pp. 176–87.

Denis McQuail (ed.), *Sociology of Mass Communications*, Harmondsworth, Middlesex: Penguin 1972.

Karl E. Meyer, *The Art Museum: Power, Money, Ethics*, New York: William Morrow 1979.

Alice Miller, *For Your Own Good*, London: Faber & Faber 1983.

C. Wright Mills, *The Power Elite*, New York: Oxford University Press 1957.

James Monaco, *Media Culture*, New York: Delta 1978.

Barrington Moore Jr, *Injustice: The Social Bases of Obedience and Revolt*, London: Macmillan 1978.

Meaghan Morris and Paul Patton, *Michel Foucault: Power, Truth, Strategy*, Sydney: Feral 1979.

Dan Nimmo, *The Political Persuaders: The Techniques of Modern Electoral Campaigns*, New Jersey: Spectrum 1970.

Frances Fox Piven and Richard A. Cloward, *Poor People's Movements: Why They Succeed, How They Fail*, New York: Vintage Books 1979.

Sidney Pollard, *The Idea of Progress*, Harmondsworth, Middlesex: Penguin 1971.

Michael R. Real, *Mass-Mediated Culture*, Englewood Cliffs, New Jersey: Prentice-Hall 1977.

Bernard Rosenberg and David Manning White (eds.), *Mass Culture: The Popular Arts in America*, New York: Free Press 1957.

Bernard Rosenberg and David Manning White, *Mass Culture Revisited*, New York: Van Nostrand Reinhold 1971.

William Ryan, *Blaming the Victim*, New York: Vintage Books 1976.

Anne Showstack Sassoon, *Gramsci's Politics*, London: Croom Helm 1980.

Anne Showstack Sassoon, *Approaches to Gramsci*, London: Writers and Readers 1982.

E.E. Schattschneider, *The Semi-Sovereign People: A Realist's View of Democracy in America*, New York: Holt, Rinehart & Winston 1960.

Wilbur Schramm, *Men, Messages and Media*, New York: Harper & Row 1973.

Michael Schudson, *Discovering the News: A Social History of American Newspapers*, New York: Basic Books 1977.

J.A. Schumpeter, *Capitalism, Socialism and Democracy*, London: Unwin University 1954.

R. Sennet and J. Cobb, *The Hidden Injuries of Class*, New York: Vintage Books 1973.

Colin Seymour-Ure, *The Political Impact of Mass Media*, London: Constable 1974.

Colin Seymore-Ure, 'Rumour and Politics', *Politics*, vol. 17, no. 2, 1972.

Tamotsu Shibutani, *Improvised News: A Sociological Study of Rumour*, Indianapolis: Bobbs-Merrill 1966.

Edward Shils, 'Mass Society and Its Culture', in Norman Jacobs (ed.), *Culture for the Millions*, Boston: Beacon Press 1964.

Jerome Skolnick, *The Politics of Protest*, New York: Ballantine 1969.

Hedrick Smith, *The Russians*, London: Times Books 1976.

Susan Sontag, *On Photography*, Harmondsworth, Middlesex: Penguin 1979.

Susan Sontag (ed.), *Barthes: Selected Writings*, London: Fontana 1983.

Hugh Stretton, 'Social Policy: Has the Welfare State All Been a Terrible Mistake?', in *Labor Essays 1980*, Richmond, Victoria: Drummond 1980.

Alan Swingewood, *The Myth of Mass Culture*, London: Macmillan 1977.

Gaye Tuchman, *Making News: A Study in the Construction of Reality*, New York: Free Press 1978.

Gaye Tuchman, *Hearth and Home: Images of the Women in the Media*, New York: Oxford University Press 1978.

Jeremy Tunstall (ed.), *The Media Are American: Anglo-American Media in the World*, London: Constable 1977.

Jeremy Tunstall (ed.), *Media Sociology*, London: Constable 1970.

Raymond Williams, *Culture and Society 1780–1950*, Harmondsworth, Middlesex: Penguin 1961.

Raymond Williams, *Keywords: A Vocabulary of Culture and Society*, Glasgow: William Collins 1976.

Raymond Williams, *Culture*, Glasgow: William Collins 1981.

Judith Williamson, *Decoding Advertisements: Ideology and Meaning in Advertising*, London: Marion Boyars 1978.

Robert Wuthnow *et al*, *Cultural Analysis*, London: Routledge & Kegan Paul 1984.

Jean Ziegler, *Switzerland Exposed*, London: Allison & Busby 1978.

Index

aborigines 97, 166, 199, 202, 206, 223-5; *see also* Australian aborigines
accents 66, 203
advertising 30, 31-32, 68-9, 124, 231
 'language' of culture 43-4
Africa 137, 205; *see also* Third World
age 44, 203-4, 232-3
Albania 136
Aman, Theodor 10
anecdotes 16-17, 62
animals: as icons 68
apartheid 97, 160-1
architecture, buildings 68, 131-3, 147
 'language' 42, 44-5, 46, 48
 nation-creating 10, 12, 13, 15
 White House 155
Armenian Republic 163, 164
arts 2, 6, 11, 21, 25, 29, 37, 48, 155, 239
 capitalists' 185, 192
 dissident 176, 179-80, 182, 193-4, 198
 avant garde 185, 235
 dissidents painted 175
 fascist 157
 gender myth 44, 93, 99, 102-8
 nation-creating 9-16 *passim*, 137, 138, 151, 163-4
 pop trash 29, 40, 47
 post-industrialism and cultural rights 210, 234-7
 religious 141, 147
 see also architecture; music
Asia, Asians 90, 137, 205-6
associational 'legitimations' 123-4
atheism 143, 145, 147
Australia 77, 112, 165, 166-7, 171
 architecture 44-5, 68
 conservation of environment 230-1
 icons 68
 legends 61, 63, 65
 monarchy 157
 working women 98-9

Australian aborigines 166, 206
 chauvinism: class 207-8, 209; race 95, 97, 199
 culture 5-6, 17-18, 183, 199, 201-2
Austria 132, 151, 161
automation 219
avant garde 185, 235

Balzac, Honoré de 177
Barthes, Roland 44, 47
Basques 116-8, 162
beauty 2-3, 6
 gender myth 44, 102-8, 203-4
Belgium 78, 117, 162-3
Berger, John 44, 108
Berger, Peter 58-9, 137, 227-8
big bang theory of change 196-7
biological determinism 95, 159
Bismarck, Prince Otto 129, 152, 213
black market (Soviet) 119, 192-3
Bledstein, Burton 89
body language 48, 227
books, publishing 29, 117, 192, 231
 critics' culture 181
 dissident 179, 180, 193
 printing press 26-7
 see also libraries; literature
Botticelli, Sandro: *Birth of Venus* 103
Braden, Su 33
brand names 30, 68, 124
Britain 31, 114, 142-3, 152-3, 165
 labour culture 171, 174
 monarchy 128, 156, 214
 myths 61, 62, 67, 112, 131-2; icons 68; pubs 46
building societies 168
buildings *see* architecture, buildings
Bulgaria 45-6, 60, 61-2, 77, 136, 147
bureaucracy, bureaucrats (Capitalist and Communist) 32, 35-6, 39-40, 121-2, 191-2, 197, 220-1

anonymity 35–6, 39–40, 191–2, 217
  careers 121, 210
  class 209–12
  protestors 241–2
  Singapore 90–1
  state (only) 77, 133, 222–3
business 20, 26, 152
business, big 119–21, 124–5, 191–2, 210–12
  monopoly as goal 34, 123
  transnational corporations 77, 112, 120–1, 125; Swiss banks 195
businesses, small 119–20, 125, 211–12
  Communist societies 35, 119, 125, 192–3

Canada 114, 143, 153, 157, 161–2
  aborigines 97, 166, 199
  bilingualism 161–2
capitalism 40, 88, 100, 119, 172–3
  Christianity 144, 148, 215
  control 128–9, 200, 202; managed 119–22, 189–90
  greed 39, 46, 152
  'myths' 65, 66–7, 76–81, 171–2;
    pervasiveness 215–6; unemployment 64, 83–4
  see also business; ownership
capitalism, concessionaire 158, 214
capitalism, crony 158
capitalist societies 31–2, 88, 148–9, 214
  compared with Communist 20, 29–30, 70, 100, 119–23, 204–5
  mixed economy 174, 193
  opposition within 216
  see also liberal democratic societies, capitalist societies, undemocratic 169, 179, 210–11
  legitimation 133–4, 157–8
  see also fascism
Castles, Francis 172, 174, 212–3
censorship 179, 180, 193, 197
ceremonies 1–3, 5–6, 11, 62, 70–1, 157, 169
  Communist 147, 191–2
  ethnic 164–5
  as 'news' 18, 191–2, 213–4
  religious 30, 141, 144–8 *passim*
Chamberlain, Arthur Neville 59
champagne advertisement 43–4
Chaplin, Charles *Modern Times* 39–40
Chauvin, Nicholas, and Chauvinism 93, 94
  anti-chauvinism 113
  critics' culture 113, 173, 181
  national 67, 113–6, 150–2
  race and sex 75, 76, 92–108, 114, 142, 173, 181
China 90, 137, 149

chivalry (neo-traditional) 151, 152, 156, 157
Christianity and the Church *see* Religion
cinema 18, 28, 37, 138
  Chaplin 39–40
  sex 102, 103, 191, 203–4
civil rights 50, 146, 148, 215, 220–2
class structure 20–1, 25, 39, 140, 152
  chauvinism 114, 118, 207–13
  critics 177–8, 239–41
  dividing concepts 54, 64, 66, 84, 183, 185–6; labour, working class 167, 238–9; ownership 36, 207–12
  middle 31, 84–5, 92, 213, 240
  peasantry and proletariat 85, 151, 167, 193, 212
  privileged, former ruling class 25, 54–5, 131–2, 150–2, 153, 155; today 183, 202, 235–6, 240–1
  welfare state 213
  see also workers
'the classics' 184
clothing, dress 66, 69, 85
  uniforms 150–1, 152, 155, 156, 157
clubs (leisure) 29, 45
coercion 25, 50–2, 52–3, 71–2, 82, 133
collectivism 64, 86–7, 122–3, 134–9
  Japan 128, 146, 215
  see also individualism
colonies *see* imperialism
colour 58, 203, 205–7, 224–5
  blacks in U.S. 144–5, 146, 160, 165, 206, 225–6
common sense 64, 71, 93, 133, 142
  dominant not necessarily pervasive 198, 199, 207, 215–6
  obedience 52–3, 82–3, 101
communality 45–6, 86–7, 144–5, 169
Communism, Communist societies 40, 79, 149
  change is possible 222–3
  class 153, 208–9, 210
  collectivism 134–9
  'contra-systems' 192–3
  critics' culture 179–80, 181, 185
  economics 119–23, 200–1; free enterprise 35, 119, 125, 192–3; ownership 32–8
  labour movement 169, 232
  leaders 192
  the 'news' 17, 20, 30, 191–2
  political power 70, 135, 155, 179
  publishing 26
  religion 143, 193
  revolution(s) 136–9
  shopping 29–30
  socialism and the worker 66–7, 83, 191;

women 99–101, 204–5
  see also Soviet Union, *etc.*
competition and monopoly 34, 123
conformity *see* obedience
conservatism 39, 143, 150–3, 213
consumer ethic 31–2, 34, 123–4, 133–4, 220
  consumer goods 70, 89, 138–9, 148
conversation 16, 238
Cranach, Lucas, father and son 103–5
'creative people' 36–7
creativity, hobbies 29, 85, 86–7, 200, 202,
  232–7
crime 126–7, 192–3, 195
criticism of 'realities' 22–4, 36–7, 113–4, 173
critics' culture 76, 174–86, 239–41
Cuba: revolution 137
cultural rights 218, 232–7
  failed by industrialism 218–20
'culture' 4–5, 183
  imposition 117–8
Curry, Jane Leftwich 192–3
Czechoslovakia 63, 65–6, 114, 136, 162–3
  dissidence 193, 216, 222–3

dance 29, 48, 237–8
Darwin, Darwinism 198, 199
death 3
  afterlife 87, 141, 143, 144
debate 174–5, 179, 180
Declaration of the Rights of Man 92
democracy 58, 63, 130–1, 150
  liberal 69, 216–7
  see also liberal democratic societies
Denmark: monarchy 157
denotation and connotation 43–4, 48
destiny and free will 87–8, 89–90, 143
determinism 95, 138, 159
dictators 31, 214–5
  see also fascism
Diggins, John P. 177
discipline and habit 53–4, 81–7 *passim*
'discovery' by explorers 60, 61, 89, 97
discrimination *see* equality
Disneyland 44, 60, 97, 205–6
Disraeli, Benjamin 152
dissidence 72, 76, 154, 175–6, 178–9, 181,
  185–6
  not in public culture 190, 190–3
divine right 58, 122, 142, 145, 159
dominance 198, 199
  see also chauvinism

eating and food 29, 42
Eco, Umberto 43, 46–7, 47
economic 'aid' 206

economy 21, 25, 50–1, 72, 75–81 *passim*, 88
  122, 190, 215–7
  economic growth 58, 80–1, 89, 119, 137–9
    passim; statistics 79, 80–1, 112, 189–90
  equality 202
  government intervention 173–4, 190
  mixed 174, 193
  religious, secular 141, 142–3
  see also collectivism; free enterprise
Edelman, Murray 18, 57, 69
education 11, 26, 61, 78, 120, 121
  cultural rights 234–5
  dissident opinions 181
  language 9, 15, 164
  literacy 112, 151
  multi-ethnicity 164, 165, 192
  research 184–5
  Scandinavia 174
  specialization 28–9
  for work 82, 83, 121, 218
  worker education; 29, 45, 46, 168
elections 31, 40–1, 146–7, 217, 230–1
  Soviet Union 41–2, 134
  U.S. 69, 115–6
  voting 69–70, 86–7, 134, 150, 194–5
electrification 79
Ellul, Jacques 21, 31, 71–2
Engelbrekt: legend 61
engineers 89–90
enlightenment 220–1
entertainment 49, 94, 192, 217, 237
  creative people 36–7
  critics' culture 180–1
  industry 180, 239
  multi-cultural 163–4, 165
  past 55, 77, 141, 144–5
environment 6, 24, 221–2, 227, 230–1
equality 58, 78, 111, 129, 131, 202, 244
  legislation 230
  selectivity 190–5, 195–9
  see also chauvinism
Estonian Republic 164
étatiste societies 179, 210–11
'ethnic compromise' 76, 114, 158–66, 181
ethnicity
  chauvinism 93, 114–5, 142, 151
  equality 205–7, 215–6, 221–2, 230
  minority groups 25, 31, 64, 66, 191, 193,
    206, 223–6
  monopoly 117–8
  nation-creating 14–16, 147
events 6, 17, 19
existence 4–6, 189
  criticism 22–4, 175–6
  perceptions are 'realities' 48

experience (self-conscious) 23–4
expertness 88–9
  cultural specialization 25, 28–9, 183
expoloration and 'discovery' 60, 61, 89, 97

faith, secular 30, 197, 245
Falklands 11–12, 112, 148
family 1–3, 70, 100, 101–2, 164, 191, 194
  see also home
farmers, farming 79, 119–20, 125, 134
  stereotypes 65, 66
fascism, fascist societies 37, 41, 179
  economy 123, 127, 133
  leaders 135, 194, 210, 210–11
  pervasiveness 215–7
  power 'myth' 153, 157–8; rich benefit 214
  work 54, 98, 169, 170
FBI building, Washington 126–7
fear 50–2
fellowship 70–1, 84
fighting *see* revolution(s); war(s)
Finland 68, 111, 161, 166, 206
  see also Scandinavia
folk culture 54, 156, 164, 183–4, 202
  cultural heritage rights 234–5
  new myths 237–9
Foucault, Michel 52, 53–4, 76–7, 81–3
France 68, 77, 88, 112, 131, 161–2, 165
  revolution(s) 60, 63, 65, 137, 142–3
  Basques 116–8
  Third Republic 150, 151, 154–5
Franco, General 133, 162, 214
free choice (of political parties) 129, 130–2,
  133, 135
free enterprise 46, 58, 63–4, 65, 123–33, 172,
  215–6
  in Communist states 192–3
free market 119, 121
free press 62–3, 129, 130
free speech 129, 130
freedom 175, 179–80
'freedom' for 'capitalism' 172
freedom of organization 129, 130
free will and destiny 87–8, 89–90, 143
Freeman, Jo 229–30
Friedan, Betty 95–6
fundamentalism 145, 146, 198

Gans, Herbert 20–1, 54, 165, 183–4
gardening 29
GDP statistics 79, 80–1
gender myth 25, 31, 58, 64–5, 93, 149, 215–
  6, 221–33 *passim*
  art 44, 93, 99, 102–8
  chauvinism 75, 76, 92–108, 114, 115;

'man the hunter' 85, 94–5, 98, 101–2,
  142, 149
  equality concept 202–5, 206–7; male
    attitudes cf male conduct 204
  selectivity 190–1, 193, 194–5
geographical regions 25, 65, 191, 199
Georgian Republic 164
Germany 46, 78, 151, 155, 169
  German Democratic Republic 147, 166
  German Federal Republic 153, 168
  Hitler and Nazism 59, 101, 136, 157–8,
    159, 170; class 210–11; conformity 50,
    51; economy and politics 97, 133–4,
    216–7; master race 93–4, 159–60, 205;
    (concentration camps) 85, 167;
    pervasiveness 216–7; propaganda 28,
    31; virtues 'myths' 76, 85, 89
Gilbert, Allan 142–4
gipsies: extermination 160, 205
Gitlin, Todd 180, 196, 239
God *see* religion
Goebels, Dr Joseph 28, 31
good and evil 55, 60–2, 64, 148
  morality plays 45, 62, 64, 65, 115
  original sin 152
Gorz, André 200, 201, 231
gossip 17
Gouldner, Alvin 92–3, 122
government 32, 33, 88
  collectivism 134–9
  economic intervention 65, 88, 119–20,
    123, 128–9, 173–4, 189–90, 213; welfare
    policies 83, 128–9, 213
  gender chauvinism 64–5, 93
  'the news' 20, 21
  representative government 129–32, 133,
    173
graffiti 103, 238
Gramsci, Antonio 4, 52–3, 71, 169, 216
Greece 61, 68, 133
Grigorescu, Nicolae *The Peasant Girl of
  Musecel* 11
groups not represented 190–3, 193–5, 198
  see also ethnicity
groups v. individualism, *see* collectivism

habit and discipline 52, 53–4, 81–3, 87
  self-restraint 84–5
happiness 31–2, 87, 144, 168, 175
  industralization 'myth' 79–80, 245
Harris, Kevin 82
Hart, Gary 20
Hawaii 158–9, 166
Hawkes, Terence 45
Hegedus, Andras 36

'hegemony' (Gramsci) 52–3, 216
heroes 17–18, 60–2, 66, 67–8, 131
  revolutionaries, martyrs 10, 13, 136, 137, 138
high culture 54, 183–6, 242
  cultural heritage 234–5
  new myth 238
history, historiography 93, 176–7, 206
  multi-ethnicity 163–4, 165–6
  nation-creating 11–17 *passim*, 137
Hitler *see* Germany
hobbies, creativity 29, 85, 86–7, 200, 202, 232–7
holiday, annual 30, 70–1
home ethic 29, 84–7, 202, 233
  see also family; work ethic
home-owning myth 124–5, 209
homosexuality 190–1, 194
hope 50–2
human improvement, liberation *see* progress
human rights 50, 92, 146, 148, 175, 215, 220, 221–2
humanism 135–6, 157, 165–6, 221, 245
  religious backlash 214–5
Hungary 61, 63, 151, 163

icons 67–9, 71, 169
  religious 142, 147
ideas themselves, and change 222
illusion-making 18, 37, 98
imperialism 11–12, 31, 44, 77–8, 96–7, 115, 117–8, 143–9 *passim*
  chauvinism 205–6
  colonies, dominions 120–1, 144, 150, 153, 157; today 195
  fascism 158
improvement *see* progress
India 90, 205
individualism 64, 65
  economic 'myth' 24, 122, 123, 126–9, 135, 144, 157
industrial societies 3, 5–6, 20, 26, 108, 141
  changing 25, 36–7
industrialism, industralization 26–7, 120, 173, 202
  accumulation of capital 75, 76–81, 150
  accumulation of men 76, 81–4
  changing 'reality' (post-industralism) 218–42
  chauvinisms 96–108
  class 208
  failures 218–9
  pervasiveness 200, 216, 217
industralization of culture 25, 26–38, 40

  research 38–41
inflation 63–4, 80, 81, 22, 221
information and culture industries 32, 35
initiative: doing what you are told 83
intellect 25, 95, 183
intellectual betterment 28–9, 78, 87–8, 234–7
intellectual forms 176, 193, 194, 242
intellectuality 4–5, 178
internationalism 244
interviews 19, 40–1, 192, 203
investment 77–8, 189–90, 195
Iran: Khomeini 215
Ireland 109–11, 145
  IRA 62, 110
  Irish abroad 165, 191
Israel 63, 69; *see also* Jews
Italy 61, 65, 68, 165–6
  Catholics 145, 155
  politics and economics 77–8, 131, 153, 169, 216–7

Jackson, Jesse 146, 206, 207
Japan 68, 118, 206
  monarchy 151, 156–7
  politics and economics 71, 77, 91, 128, 133, 210
  religions 141, 146, 149–50, 151, 157, 215
Jefferson, Thomas 175
Jews 146–7, 199
  Israel 63, 69
  Nazism 92, 93–4, 205
jobs 50–1, 72
  job creation 219–20, 233, 234
  see also unemployment
John, (Bad) King 61
Johnson, Richard 240

Klapp, O. E. 228–9
Kossuth, Louis 61

labour 212–13
  forced 167
labour culture 76, 81–4, 119, 128–9, 166–74
labour movement 20, 84–5, 138, 170–4, 193, 232–4
laissez faire 213, 214–5
landscape 2, 6, 9–10, 114–5
language(s)
  accents 66, 203
  nation-creating 9, 15, 65, 117–8, 160, 161–4
  of scholarship 242–3
'language' of a culture 42–7, 49
Lapps 166, 206

Latin America 50, 137, 153–4
  Church today 148, 215
  politics and economics 90, 127–8, 158, 212
Latinos and Mexican Americans 14–16, 165
Latvian Republic 164
law, rule of 58, 62, 63, 129, 132–3, 173
leadership 158, 185–6, 212, 215–7, 228–9
  changing 195–9
  Communist 139, 169–70, 179–80
  fascist 135, 157, 170, 194, 210
  Gramsci's 'hegemony' 52–3, 216
  labour movement 169, 172, 173
'left' and 'right' 152
legends 114–5, 116, 151
  Latin America 127–8, 142
'legends' illustrating 'myths' 59–67, 71, 169
  'the news' 16, 17–21
legitimations of power 119–39
  chauvinisms 93, 202–17
  constitutions 88, 134–5
  role of 'myth' 57, 75, 76
legitimations . . . associational 123–4
leisure 29, 85, 170, 200, 202, 219
Lenin, V.I.Y., and Leninism 13, 30, 55, 164, 197
  collectivism 134, 135–6
  'Communism' q. 79
  critics culture 179
  labour 232
  legitimation of Soviet Union 139
  revolution(s) 60, 137–8, 168–70
  vanguard party 139, 179, 196–70, 210
  women's rights 99, 101
liberal-democratic societies 31, 32, 68, 196–7
  class 66, 153, 210–11, 212–13
  critics' freedom 'myth' 180–2
  economy 50–1, 119–20, 122–3, 126–9
  gender 'myth' 98, 102–3, 193
  labour force 169–71, 212–13, 232–3
  'the news' 18, 21, 72
  protest movements 229–31
  republics 154–5, 216–7
  selectivity 191, 193–4
liberalism 129–30, 143, 144, 152
liberation movements 62, 215, 225
  see also revolution; war
libraries, stores of knowledge 26, 29, 71, 110–11, 141–2
  chauvinism 93, 95
  cultural heritage 234–5
  high culture 184
life after death 87, 141, 143, 144
literature 9, 11, 45–6

'the classics' 27, 29, 184
drama 9, 15, 17–18, 29, 93; theatricality 227–8
novels 15, 26, 93; realism 177–8, 191
Lomax, Alan 192

McCarthy, Senator Joseph and McCarthyism 41, 50, 72
magazines 26, 27
Malraux, André 26, 184
Malvinas 11–12, 112, 148
'man the hunter' 85, 94–5, 98, 101–2, 142, 149
market
  free 119–21
  rationality 88
marriage: women's names 102
martyrs 148, 169, 175–6, 178, 229
  nation-creating 13, 110–11
Marx, and Marxism 13, 30, 52, 147, 164, 215, 245
  class 36, 135–6
  collectivity 135–6
  revolution 136–7, 138, 168–9
  workers 39, 167, 232
'mass' 38
'mass culture' 26, 38–42
materialism, and material comforts 45, 144, 167–8, 218–9
  see also consumer ethic
media (news) see 'news media'
media, personally accessible 33, 231
Mexico 137
  Mexican Americans 14–16, 165
militarist societies 16, 37, 127, 214–5
military 112, 120, 133, 150–9 passim
  conscription 150, 151, 177–8
  soldiers 66, 150, 151, 167
Mills, C. Wright 232
missions, Spanish (in California) 15
modern art 176, 235, 243
modern culture 23, 25
'modern industrial societies' 90–1
  born modern 153
modernity 'myths' 87–91, 150, 173, 200, 236, 244
  nation, race, sex 92–118
  new myth extended 243–5
monarchy 128, 131–2, 150–7 passim, 212, 213–4, 217
monopolization of culture 71–2
monopoly and competition 34, 123
monuments, memorials 12–13, 45, 68, 164, 234–5
moral leadership (Gramsci) 52–3, 216

morality plays (modern legends) 45, 62, 64, 65, 115
Morris, Meaghan 44–5
Mother Theresa syndrome 148
multiculturalism 161–4
  multi-culture (Lomax) 192
museums 14–15, 29, 94, 205–6
  art 16, 44, 102–8, 126, 154–5, 163–4, 182, 184
  cultural heritage 234–5
  ethnic minorities in U.S. 223–6
  national 8–11, 110, 116–7, 136, 138
  of revolution 138–9, 147, 168
music 27, 29, 157, 169
  Christian 144–5, 146, 147, 165
  cultural heritage 234–5
  high culture 184
  nation-creating 9, 11–12, 42, 48, 137
  nation-states 115–6
  new myth 237–8
  protest songs 69, 231
'myths' 57–72
  diversionary 122

names, words and their significance
  America 115–6
  brand names 30, 68, 124
  capitalism, free enterprise 171–2
  denotation and connotation 43–4, 48
  married women 102
  movements 227
  unemployed, employed 55, 84
nation-creating 8–16, 117–8, 137, 147, 205
nation-states 30, 32, 108–9, 212
  authoritarian: concessionaire capitalism 158
national identity 9–10, 25, 42, 64–5, 108–18, 182, 247
  chauvinism 67, 113–6, 150, 157, 244
  multiculturalism 161–4
  religion 143, 146, 147, 149–50
  strategic imagination 75, 76, 112, 173, 217
Nazis *see* Germany
neo-traditional culture
  meaning 154
  'myths' 76, 150–8, 212, 213–4
Netherlands 66, 69
  politics and government 111, 112, 131, 209; monarchy 156
  religion and secularization 142, 143, 145, 148, 165–6
New Zealand 97, 153, 157, 166
  'the news' 3–4, 42, 189, 191–2, 195–6, 239
  critics' culture 176, 180–1

labour 171, 174
  legend-creating 62–7, 148
  nation-creating 16–22
  see also television
newspapers
  freedom of the press 62–3, 129, 130, 174, 179
  industralization of culture 26–7
  nation-creating 9, 17, 138 160–1
'the night of the chicken' legend 63
Northern Ireland 110, 165
Norway 65, 68, 111, 112, 132, 151
novelty itself 'myth' 176–7, 184–5
nuclear weapons 23, 90
nudity, female (in art) 44, 102–8
obedience 25, 50–3, 69
Olympic Games 67, 68, 115–6, 164
organizations, freedom of 129, 130
organizations: labour culture 169, 171, 172
ownership 32–8, 66, 138
  class not confined to ownership 208–12
  private 35, 36, 119, 123, 124–6, 158
  state 35, 134, 197, 201–2, 208; in capitalist societies 193–4

participation in culture 5–6, 25, 72, 183
  cultural right 234–7
  surrogate 18, 22, 29
patriarchy 85, 97–8, 100–101
patriotism
  exaggerated *see* chauvinism
  revolutionary 136, 137
patronalist societies 127–8, 133–4, 158
peace 115, 120, 148
'the people'
  as powerless 233–4
  myth makers 237–9, 241–2
  pop culture 239
The People's Choice 40–1
permissiveness and restraint 84–5, 144, 148–9, 203–4, 221–2, 227
personality cults 135, 148
pervasiveness 199
photography 1–8 *passim*, 27, 33
  'lanaguage' of a culture 42, 43–4
phrenology 95
Poland 61, 68
  Catholics 145, 147
  politics 155, 193, 216, 222–3
police 33, 50, 86–7, 121, 133, 167, 176
political freedom 61
political organization 12, 20, 88
political parties: freedom of choice 129, 130–2, 133, 135
  Communist 139, 179, 196–7, 210; top

class 210
labour 168–72 *passim*, 206
religious 143, 153, 215
political power 75, 76, 215–7
politics 5, 21, 23, 40–2, 48, 68–9, 111, 112
gender myth 64–5, 203
religion, secularization 13–14, 141, 142–3
sport 66, 67, 115
see also elections
pop trash 29, 40, 47
population control 206
popularization of the classics 27, 29
pornography 102–3, 197–8
Portugal 50, 61, 133
posters 16, 27, 33, 68, 197–8, 231
poverty and powerlessnes 144, 148, 190, 207, 221–2
power
justification of winning 34, 51–2
rulers 52–3, 54–5, 185, 191–2, 198, 210, 209
pragmatism and rationality 59
prayer *see* religion
printing press 26–7
private life 29, 54–5, 122, 123, 129–30
privilege 25, 54–5, 122, 123, 129–30
profit motive 123, 126
progress (improvement; prosperity) 138, 196–7
art 237–8
cultural rights 218–37; end of Industrial Man 236; new myths 237–45
humanism 135–6, 221
modern myth 87–91, 101, 136, 137, 200
socialists 168, 201–202
propaganda 27, 28, 30–2, 71–2
the news 21
protest 69, 227–31, 241–2
critics' culture 176, 180–1
demonstrations 69, 99, 138, 165, 176
public culture 55–7, 70
guardians 195–9
selectivity 189–202, 207; alternate, oppositional 195–9, 201
see also 'reality', public funds for arts 29, 33
public houses 46
public opinion 71–2, 129, 130
public transport 29
publicity-seekers 19–20
punishment 53–4, 81–3, 178, 179
puritanism 85, 149

race 25, 64, 221–2
chauvinism 75, 76, 92–108, 215–6;

imperalism 31, 60, 157; master race: (Apartheid) 97, 160–1; (Aryanism) 159–60
equality 202, 205–7
see also ethnicity
radicalism 39, 143
radio 27–8, 181; *see also* 'the news'
rationality 87–90
Reagan, President 13–14, 18, 69, 115–6, 128, 193
Real, Michael 42, 44
'reality' 189, 192, 198
changing 25, 36–7, 102, 181; big bang 196–7
constructing 1–22, 57
criticism of 'reality' 22–4
for the future 221–45; social not economic 221
fundamentally economic 78–81, 190
maintaining 25–34
records industry 27, 29
reform 222, 241–2
Reformation 141, 142
religion 20, 76, 78, 87, 193, 202
atheism 143, 145, 147
backlash: rich are winners 214–5
civil religion 12, 30, 148, 158
fundamentalism 145, 146, 198
God(s), supernatural 78, 95, 142–3, 146, 149–50; divine right 58, 122, 142, 145, 159; free will 87–8, 89–90, 143; prayer 5, 22, 23, 69, 87, 142, 143, 196; salvation 141, 143, 144
religious denominations (Christianity, Church) 37, 78, 141–50
alternate culture 198
art 104–5, 107
chauvinism 151, 206
Christ himself 148, 215
Christmas shopping 70
Communist societies 143, 147, 165, 193, 206
diversity 165–6
folk culture 54
good and evil 55, 60–2, 64, 148, 152
multi-ethnic societies 164, 165
neo-traditional 144, 150, 151, 155
political parties 143, 153
restraint and permissiveness 144, 148–9
separate community 169
specific denominations: Anglican 144, 148; Calvinist 30, 143; Catholic 15, 30, 63, 117, 144, 148–9, 150, 153, 165, 215; Dutch Reformed 160, 161; Lutheranism

143, 144, 147, 153; revivalist 144–5, 146, 215
religious dominations, other than Christian
  Buddhism 22
  Islam 147, 206, 215
  in Japan 149–50, 166
repertoires of submerged cultures 198–9
repertoires of the public culture 140–86
representative principle (Communist) 134–5
research 38–42
  into research 184–5
  scholarship 143
  statistics 189, 190
respectability 167–8, 185–6
revolt
  by bureaucrats 241–2
  within the Church 141, 142–3
revolution(s) 9, 10, 16, 220–1
  nation-creating myths 59–63, 109-11, 205;
    anti-chauvinist 113; collectivism 136–9
  suppression 43–4, 109, 115
  world 58, 222
rhetoric 11, 143, 241–2
  Communist 138, 191, 192
'right' and 'left' 152
'ritual' 67, 69–71
rituals 11, 16–21, 142, 169, 183; *see also*
  ceremonial
Romania 8–11, 136, 163
rules: obedience 64, 88–9
rumour 17

salvation (after death) 87, 141, 143, 144
Scandinavia 152, 174, 214, 232–3; *see also*
  Denmark, *etc.*
scholarship 174–5, 242–3
science and techology 32–3, 146, 198, 202
  improvers 89–90
  martyrs 175–6
  research 40–1, 184–5, 243
Scotland 165
secularism 30, 142–4, 145, 147, 197, 245
self-as-art 237
self-criticism, national 113–4, 179, 181
self-management of workers 210
self-restraint and permissiveness 84–5, 144,
  148–9, 203–4, 221–2, 227
semiotics 42–7, 47–9
Serra, Father 15
service industries 219–20
sexuality 'myths' 105–6, 149, 191, 227, 230
  abortion 149
  deviants 93, 190–1
  legitimation of gender myth 202, 203, 205
shops and shopping 29–30, 45, 71, 78–9,

119–20, 124, 125
gender myth 98, 101, 102–3
signs: cultural 'language' 42–9
Singapore 90–1, 141, 161, 210
slavery 96, 97, 166, 205–6, 226
  Nazis *Untermenschen* 160
Slavs 147, 160
Smith, Adam 88, 123
Smith, Hedrick 115, 205
social change *see* progress
social conflict 42, 80, 148, 167, 197
  liberation theology 148, 215
  national identity 109, 112–3
social-democrats 122, 174, 214
social order 21, 25, 31–2, 33, 51, 185–6
  changing 25, 34–8, 85–6, 168
  'mass society' 38–9
  see also class structure
socialism 66–7, 77, 129, 143, 169, 215–6
  labour movement 169–74, 232–4
  19th c. 152–3, 196–7, 220–1
socialist parties 135, 152–3, 194
socialist societies 88, 135
Solidarity 193, 216, 222–3
Sorel, Georges 59
South Africa 68, 85, 90, 1280, 195
  apartheid 97, 160–1, 205
Soviet Union 12, 13, 14, 83, 86, 114
  before Communism 60, 117–8, 161;
    Revolution 136, 169–70
  dissidence 193
  economics 77, 119; collectivism 134–9
    passim,
  private ownership 119
  labour force 89, 169–70
  legends 60, 61, 67, 68
  modern art 176, 179–80, 182, 198
  Moscow 13
  multiethnicity 163–4, 206; Russification 164
  nation-state 111
  news media, entertainment 17, 28, 33, 37
  patriotism 67, 115
  police 50, 86–7
  potential for change 223
  religion 143, 147, 165, 206
  Stalin, Stalinism 28, 37, 50, 79, 85, 99
  women's rights 64–5, 99–101
Spain 61, 116–7, 133, 162–3, 225
  Californian missions 14–16
  monarchy 156, 214
specialization, cultural 25, 28–9, 39, 88–9,
  183, 242
Spinoza 142
sport 18, 29, 64–71 *passim*, 88, 115–6, 215,
  217

statistics 111–12, 189–91
  GDP 79, 80–1
Steichen, Edward 178
stereotypes 64–7, 191, 203
  race 93–4, 114, 165, 191
story-telling 16–21, 62; *see also* legends
strategic imagination 75, 76, 112
structuralism 47
submerged cultures 198–9
superiority myth 93, 94
supernatural *see* religion
Sweden 45, 46, 61, 148, 161, 168, 174
  politics and economics 111, 112, 132,
    216; labour 168, 169, 212–3; monarchy
    156–7
Switzerland 111, 112, 132, 161, 166, 194–5

taxation 219
Taylor, F.W. and Taylorism 82
teams 29
technology *see* science and technology
telephones 33
television 69, 138, 145, 203
  realism 178
  'reality' 18, 29, 180, 213, 231
temperance 148, 168; *see also* self-restraint
terror 50, 53–4, 72
terrorism 62
Thatcher, Margaret 62, q12, 205
  Thatcherism 80, 193–4
theatre 180–1, 227–8, 234–5
Third World 79–80, 158, 200, 205, 206
  see also Africa, *etc.*
Thoreau, Henry David 17, 176
Tito, Marshal 61, 136
totalitarianism 39, 46 *see also* dictators;
  fascism
tourism 30, 70–1, 155, 156, 165, 206
trade unions 98, 119–20, 138
  freedom 129, 130
  labour culture 167–72, 212–3, 232–3;
  weak 170, 195, 208
  strikes 130, 138, 171
tradition 111, 128; *see also* ceremonial
Transylvania 163
trash, cultural 29, 40, 47
tribal culture 70–2, 234–4

Ukrainian Republic 164
unemployment 55, 63–4, 80–4 *passim*, 208–
  9, 219–21 *passim*
  unemployed not considered in labour
    movement 232–3
unemployment of human potential 218, 245
United States 12–13, 13–16, 20, 60–70

  passim, 77, 120, 205
advertising 31
architecture; buildings 45
born moderns 153
California 14–16
Chicago 45, 46
chauvinism 67, 97, 113–4, 115–6, 206
civil rights 50
class 167, 208–9
critics' culture 180, 182, 184–5
Disneyland 44, 60, 97, 205–6
ethnic groups 14–16, 164–5
  aborigines 97, 166, 199, 223–5
  blacks 144–5, 146, 160, 165, 206, 225–5
family 101–2
folk arts 238
icons 68, 69
individualism 126–9, 216
industrialism 80, 83–4, 245
Los Angeles 14–15, 45, 46
music; record industry 27
nation-state 151
neo-tradtional culture 150, 151, 154, 155
newspapers 26
politics 40–2
  change potential 229–30
  constitution 88, 132, 175
  governor buildings 132
  'hegemony' 54–5, 216
  poor whites 207
  religion 144–5, 146–7, 198, 215
  revolution 143
  trade unions 170, 208
transnational bus companies 120–1
'war on poverty' figures 190
Washington 12–13
women's rights 99
usefulness
  as justification for capitalism 122, 123,
    126

Vietnam 137, 205
virtues 76, 82–5, 149, 150–1
  moral order not 'news' 21

wages, salaries 84, 123, 124, 167
  basic wage 98–9
  'work ethic' 29, 54–5, 83, 86, 96, 98, 119
  working women 94–5, 98–102
Wales 61, 165
war(s) 31, 50, 60–2, 77, 115, 116, 136, 138,
  141–55 *passim*, 164, 224
  Falklands 11–12, 112, 148
Watergate 54–5, 62–3, 113–4
wealthy 211–12, 213–5

inherited wealth 25, 54–5, 123, 213–4
Weber, Max 34, 39, 50, 51, 88–9, 229
welfare, social 83, 128–9, 152, 173–4, 209, 213
winners in public culture 189–217
words *see* names, words
work 39–40, 63–4, 212–3
    Australian aborigines 199
work ethic (waged, salaried work) 29, 54–5, 83–4, 96, 119, 144, 200–2, 237
    consumer ethic 34, 123–4, 133–4, 220
    paid labour a form of unemployment 218
workers 167
    alienation 38–9
    class 209, 210
    Communist 134–5, 138–9, 191

free enterprise 125
guest, migrant 166, 191, 194–5
industralization 81–4, 150
labour movement 232–4
self-management 201
stereotypes 66
worker not people 138–9
working-class culture future, 238–9

Yugoslavia 61, 134–5, 136, 147
    multiculturalism 162, 163

Ziegler, Jean 195
Zola 177–8, 191